GARDEN LIBRARY
PLANTING FIELDS ARBORETUM

The Gardener's Computer Companion

D1529816

FISCHER LIBRARY
DE WADSWORTH

THE
GARDENER'S
COMPUTER
COMPANION

BOB BOUFFORD

no starch press
SAN FRANCISCO

#6845 12/23/98 GBC $35.11

THE GARDENER'S COMPUTER COMPANION. Copyright ©1998 by Bob Boufford.
All rights reserved. No part of this work may be reproduced or transmitted in any form or
by any means, electronic or mechanical, including photocopying, recording, or by any
information storage or retrieval system, without the prior written permission of the copyright owner and the publisher.
Printed in the United States of America
1 2 3 4 5 6 7 8 9 10—00 99 98

Trademarked names are used throughout this book. Rather than use a trademark symbol
with every occurrence of a trademarked name, we are using the names only in an editorial
fashion and to the benefit of the trademark owner, with no intention of infringement of
the trademark.

Publisher: William Pollock
Project Editor: Karol Jurado
Cover Design: Big Fish
Interior Design: Margery Cantor
Compositor: Magnolia Studio
Technical Editor: Ron LaFon
Copyeditor: Elinor Lindheimer
Proofreader: Katherine Kaiser
Indexer: Frances Bowles

Distributed to the book trade in the United States and Canada by
Publishers Group West, 1700 Fourth Street, Berkeley, California 94710
phone: 800-788-3123 or 510-528-1444, fax: 510-528-3444.
For information on translations or book distributors outside the United States,
please contact No Starch Press directly:

No Starch Press
401 China Basin Street, Suite 108, San Francisco, CA 94107-2192
phone: 415-284-9900; fax: 415-284-9955; info@nostarch.com; www.nostarch.com

The information in this book is distributed on an "As Is" basis, without warranty. While
every precaution has been taken in the preparation of this work, neither the author nor No
Starch Press shall have any liability to any person or entity with respect to any loss or damage caused or alleged to be caused directly or indirectly by the information contained in it.

Library of Congress Cataloging-in-Publication Data
Boufford, Bob.
    The gardener's computer companion / Bob Boufford.
        p.   cm.
    Includes index.
    ISBN 1–886411–18–2 (pbk.)
        1. Gardening--Data processing. 2. Computer-aided design.
3. Internet (Computer network)   I. Title.
SB453.B6825   1998
635'.0285--dc21   97-41637

Brief Contents

Contents in Detail

Chapter 2
Software: The Computer's Recipes

Chapter 3
Hardware: The Computer Toolshed

Chapter 4
Gardening by Wire

Chapter 5
Gardening Around the World

Chapter 8
Gardening References

Chapter 9
Plan(t) a Computer Garden

Chapter 10
Creating Your Electronic Garden

Acknowledgments

I would like to acknowledge the assistance and input of everyone on the CompuServe Gardening Forum. There are too many to list on this page.

Everyone should thank the publisher, Bill Pollock. He spent two years chasing me around the state of Ohio until I finally finished writing textbooks and agreed to write this book.

Behind any book author is the project editor, who is very much like a gardener, nurturing the author to "grow" the book, weeding out extraneous material, pruning the text, and managing other activities to produce the book. Thanks to Karol Jurado, my project editor. As a trade association newsletter editor, I know what Karol encounters with often slow-growing authors.

To my wife, Amy, for her patience while I worked on this latest book. And of course, our Baker Street Irregulars, for waiting patiently for me to let them outside to water and fertilize the lawn.

Preface

A former boss once said, "Computers can never be used for gardening, they are just too black and white." True, a garden is often all the colors between black and white. However, a computer can still be very useful for many of our gardening activities. Members of the CompuServe Gardening Forum are constantly describing ways they use a computer for their gardening activities. Every day someone new comes into the forum and asks how to use the computer for a particular garden activity, such as landscape and garden planning with *computer-aided design* (CAD) software. Just logging onto the Internet or a commercial network such as CompuServe and America Online is now one of the more popular uses of computers in gardening.

This book is a compilation of the ways in which you can use a computer in planning and tracking the myriad of things we like to do in the garden. While professional landscapers already use computers on an advanced level, the approach in this book is more basic, to fit the needs of the gardening enthusiast. Some of the chapters are derived from presentations given to the landscape industry, talks delivered at gardening conferences, and countless messages on the CompuServe Gardening Forum, with appropriate pruning and weeding to fit in a comfortable book.

For those not familiar with computers, there are chapters on their anatomy, along with some direction on buying a computer system. Since gardeners always want to select the right tool for the job, we approach the computer as a gardening tool like any of our other gardening tools. "A shovel always makes for a poor pry bar," so you will find information to help you select the best computer for your needs.

The chapters are in a semisequential order. However, you do not need to read the book from cover to cover. If you are already familiar with computers and want to learn how to use a computer for a particular activity, feel free to jump to the chapters that interest you. Each chapter has been developed so that you can read it with minimal reference to other parts of the book.

Even though the Windows-based computer is the most predominant computer platform right now, I have tried to provide activities that can be done on a wide variety of computer systems including older DOS-based computers and the Macintosh family of computers. Although gardening software titles may be limited for these other systems, there are many gardening-related activities that can be done using general purpose software.

The companion CD-ROM in the back of the book contains a variety of software that you can use for gardening activities. Some programs, such as *personal information managers* (PIMs), are not specifically gardening software. Yet you will see in this book how many gardeners use such generic software to perform a wide range of activities in their gardening. If you use any of the shareware software on the disk, we encourage you to honor the shareware agreement and make a contribution to its author. If you decide not to use the CD-ROM, I understand old CDs make good "scarecrows" when hung in a tree or on a pole.

1

What? A Computer in the Garden?

The original definition of a computer was "one who computes or determines an amount or number." Back in the early 1900s, a computer was a real live person, not a machine, and the basic functions of those human computers were similar to the basic functions of today's computers. They were responsible for calculating the results of large columns or tables of numbers such as a government census or corporate profit-loss statement. Now, instead of a human, a computer is an electronic device for storing and processing data, making calculations, or controlling machinery. Once installed and programmed, the computer can follow instructions without any additional intervention; it can even make logical choices. (Sometimes we wish teenagers could be programmed!)

So a computer in simple terms is an electronic machine capable of following a list of instructions to perform calculations at a very rapid rate. For a gardener, just as for a businessperson or student, a computer is a multipurpose tool that stores and processes information in ways not easily done with paper and pencil. In addition, always remember: A computer is basically dumb; it will do whatever you tell it to.

How Can I Use a Computer for Gardening?

A computer may seem like an odd garden tool, but there are many ways to use one for gardening tasks. The computer can help you to plan your garden's layout and choose the plants you will grow, manage information, communicate with other gardeners, and monitor environmental conditions within your garden.

Visually plan the garden

Industries use *computer-aided design* or CAD software to draw and design anything from automobiles to space shuttles to large landscape areas like parks and golf courses. You can use many of the same techniques for planning small gardens.

Visual imaging software allows the gardener to "plant" the garden around a digital photo image of the home, using plants from a library of digital photo images. Some of the visual imaging software programs will even "grow" the plants for you. Now you can see how those little yews will hide your living room window in ten years.

Find plants and other garden items

We want to put the right plant in the right place. This usually means paging through countless catalogs, consulting plant reference books, and dashing through garden centers in search of the perfect plant. Isn't there an easier way to find what we need without losing our breath? Well, we can let our fingers do the walking!

Many plant reference books, catalogs, and encyclopedias are now available in electronic form as CD-ROMs or through the Internet. Most of these references include full-color pictures along with the ability to order plants "online" from nurseries thousands of miles away.

Record garden activities

We all keep (or strive to keep) some sort of journal or other record of the plants in our garden, weather conditions, even shopping lists. Often this information is scattered on bits of paper or in different notebooks. For some of us, information becomes a virtual compost heap on our desks. Wouldn't it be nice to have a way to

organize all this information in a nice compact form without all the paper?

With certain software, we can record much of the bits and pieces of information about our gardens and garden activities. Recording information with a computer is like writing in a notebook, but computers make it easy to find specific information later or to change what we have written.

For example, how often have we tried to remember a gardening event from last year, such as "When did the Japanese beetles start feeding on my roses?" With paper records, finding out may require paging through notebooks or sifting through bits of paper to find the right information. A computer-based record could be searched fairly quickly.

Communicate with other gardeners and tap into worldwide information resources

One of the most rapidly growing uses of computers is to communicate with others around the world. By connecting a computer to the Internet—the worldwide network of computer networks— one can post messages to a worldwide gardening community. Messages range from simple "how do I" questions and answers to long discussions on the esoterics of gardening. The discussions can even take place live through electronic conferences and chat rooms. With a low-cost video camera and audio connection, even face-to-face communications with other gardeners is now possible.

Computer networks give us access to vast storehouses of information. The old card catalog at the local library is now an online catalog that is part of a much larger statewide catalog; you can even order books from other libraries online for delivery at your local library. Some library systems even provide access to materials such as periodical articles or abstracts through the network.

Monitor the garden

Computers are great tools for finding out what's going on in the garden, and for predicting problems. On a large scale, many landscape nurseries, greenhouses, and golf courses use computers to

monitor the growing environments. The computer continually samples many conditions and alerts the grower to possible pest attacks or weather-related damage.

Many advanced home weather stations can track the weather through a computer. When combined with record-keeping software, the computer can automatically maintain weather records. A digital video camera can be set up to keep an eye on the garden. With the computer and a tethered video camera, we have the tools to create that time-lapse view of how our garden is growing— complete with "silver bells and cockleshells."

Control irrigation and environmental systems

Most electronic automatic irrigation systems are controlled by computer. True, the irrigation controller does not look like a typical computer system, but the basic components of a computer are at its heart. With some parts from an electronics store, the gardener can use a computer to control watering and lighting in the garden. Several devices are now available that use existing household electrical wiring as the transmission lines. Combined with the above-mentioned monitoring devices, the system can be set up for automatic operation based on changing weather conditions.

What Is a Gardening Computer System?

A computer consists of *hardware,* the actual machine and accessories, and *software,* programs that control the computer. The combination of hardware and software makes a *computer system.* A personal computer or "PC" is small enough to fit on a desk. Many can now fit in the space of a notebook.

Computer software

The real key to a computer system is the software. Computer hardware is useless without programs.

Software is typically classified into major groups based on the purpose or function of the software. The five major functions are word processing, spreadsheets, database management, telecommunications, and graphics. Of course, we cannot forget entertainment software, like garden simulators, perfect for relaxing on a cold wintry night. (See The Garden with Insight garden simulator on the CD.) In addition, software utilities help manage the computer system, and development software is used for creating more software.

SEE CD-ROM

Although there are many types of software, most are based on one or more of the five major groups. For example, *personal information managers* (PIMs), combining datebook, notebook, and address book functions, include a mix of features from word processing, database, and communications software. Garden design software is often a combination of graphics software and plant databases.

Word processors

The word processor is a ubiquitous tool for any computer user including the gardener. Word processors are writing tools, like pencils and typewriters. But unlike pencils and typewriters, a word processing program stores your documents until you want to print them, making it easy to correct mistakes or make revisions, and to make them look just the way you want.

Word processors allow you to reuse previously written material without retyping the original. So you can personalize a "form letter" to request seed catalogs with very little additional typing.

Spreadsheets

Electronic spreadsheet software comes in handy for a wide range of calculations, from determining the number of annual bedding plants needed for each area of the garden to calculating fertilizer rates for the home lawn, to monitoring your gardening budget.

Spreadsheet software will allow you to answer "what if" questions like "What happens to my bedding plant count if I change from petite marigolds with a 6-inch spacing to petunias with a 9-inch spacing?" A spreadsheet-based plant list containing 50 garden areas can recalculate a new "total plant count" in a matter of seconds, based on changes you make in a couple of items.

Databases

In the simplest form, database software is the electronic equivalent of an index card or Rolodex file. A record in the database is the same as one index card on which information is placed in predefined fields. You can sort, arrange, and search records in a database in a variety of ways, based on the information in one or more fields. Database software lets you create an organized information management system—perfect for efficient record keeping around the garden.

Databases are great for research too. For example, you can search a commercial plant database to quickly find all the trees with a pyramidal shape that do not grow over 20 feet tall. To do the equivalent search with paper records might take a few hours of paging through reference books and nursery catalogs.

Graphics software

Computer graphics are pictures or drawings created on a computer. Graphics software lets you view and manipulate these images. You can use graphics programs to plan a garden and keep visual records of it—a lot easier than planting it all first!

When the core components of graphics software are combined with information from spreadsheets and databases, you can create charts and graphs. Pictures really are worth a thousand words—or numbers!

Communications

Communications software helps you connect your computer, using the modem, with other computers both locally and around the world. A modem is a device used to connect the computer to the telephone line to send and receive data. Communications software is the key to traveling the Internet. E-mail programs let you send mail faster than the post office can pick up your paper mail, and browsers let you travel the World Wide Web to garden places around the world.

Computer hardware and operating systems

Computer hardware is a combination of various integrated components, which together allow you to give the computer commands or input data, and which allow the computer to process that information and do something with it. The four major hardware components are the processor, memory, storage, and input/output or I/O devices.

Processor

The processor, also known as the *central processor unit* or CPU, is the computer's brain, the place where the computer processes data.

Memory

During processing, the processor needs space to work with data and programs, very much like a workbench or desktop that provide the space to work on equipment or do paperwork. The term for this workspace is random access memory or RAM, which is often called simply "memory."

Storage

If memory is like the potting bench in the greenhouse, you will need someplace to store the tools, seeds, soil, and pots when you are not using them. With a computer, you store programs and information on magnetic or optical disks.

Input/Output

In the garden, we plant seeds (input) and harvest vegetables (output). With computers, you use input devices for "planting" information in the computer and output devices for "harvesting" information from the computer.

The most common input device is the keyboard, which is like an old-style typewriter keyboard with additional keys. A mouse or similar pointer device (trackball, pen, touch screen, tablet, voice) is another input device for controlling the computer.

The two common means of output are video displays and printers. Video monitors are like televisions, but without the channel selectors. Some computer systems manufacturers have put the TV channel selector back into the monitor so you can watch your favorite garden show while designing your new garden.

When you type something into the computer and want to see it on paper, you send it to the printer. There are several different types of printers, including dot-matrix, inkjet, and laser. Each has its advantages and disadvantages. Laser printers and inkjet printers are very popular due to the high quality of their printed output. Some of these printers are also capable of printing in color.

Do I Need to Buy a New Computer?

If you already own a computer, you can probably do a lot with your current computer system. Or if your budget is limited, a used computer may meet your needs.

The key to deciding whether to buy a new computer or keep the old one is to ask yourself what you want to do with it. Once you decide what software you'll want to install on it, you can use the requirements of the software to guide you in selecting the right computer.

Do I Need to Use Gardening Software?

Most gardening programs are adaptations of general-purpose software. Plant reference libraries and plant encyclopedias are types of database management software. Garden planning software has a CAD engine at its core, with an attached database of plants. The big advantage of garden software is that someone else went through the effort of reprogramming the software and filling the files with data to meet the needs of the gardener.

As an alternative, a gardener can use general-purpose software to accomplish most of the tasks and features offered by the commercial gardening software. The downside is the drudgery of entering all the data or creating the various plant symbols for use in the CAD program. The benefit is total control over the software and data files, without having to sift through the extraneous information that sometimes comes with commercial software.

Where Can I Find Gardening Software?

Computer stores and mail-order catalogs are the prime sources for commercial gardening software. However, buying a full-fledged gardening program can be like buying a garden tractor with tiller when all you need is a shovel and wheelbarrow. For less elaborate software, we can turn to a variety of other sources.

Gardening software also comes as shareware, freeware, and public domain or free software. Shareware is a "try before you buy" type of software. The developer distributes the software at little or no initial cost; after using it for a period of time, you send the author a registration fee if you like the software and intend to keep using it. Freeware is software distributed for free, but the author retains all copyrights. Public domain software is totally free to anyone, including the right to change the program. This book comes with a CD-ROM containing a selection of shareware and freeware that I think you'll enjoy.

If you already own a fairly new computer system, you can probably skip the rest of this chapter, which discusses buying a computer system, and the next two chapters, which take a more in-depth look at computer software and hardware. But if you're new to computers or need a new computer, keep on reading.

DASSSHing Out for a Garden Computer

No, the spell checker did not miss a word in the heading. DASSSH is an acronym I use to describe my approach to buying a computer system. Even though DASSSH appears to mean "dashing" or running quickly to the store to buy a computer, it actually is a slow, thoughtful process of buying a computer system. I often use this concept in presentations to professional landscapers. While the DASSSH process has a business slant, the concepts behind it apply equally well to both business and personal computer use in our gardening activities.

People often buy their computer hardware before they know how they want to use the computer. Schools are notorious for buying hardware first, having fallen into the trap of "We have to get

computers for the students." Unfortunately, they often spend all the budgeted money for hardware, with no funds left for software or training. Many people still get caught in the myth that the teachers can develop their own educational software.

Families often get caught in the same trap. "Because the schools have computers, we need to get one for the kids." So the family goes to the local department store or discount chain and buys a computer. Unfortunately, buying a computer isn't quite like buying a microwave (which isn't to say that buying the right microwave isn't a challenge in itself.) Buying a computer system is more like buying a car or a home, just not as expensive.

Another problem with buying the hardware before the software is that it may be difficult to find the right software to run on the computer, particularly gardening software. For instance, while Macintosh computers are great—the epitomé of ease-of-use—very little gardening software is published for the Macintosh. Microsoft Windows-based computers vastly outnumber Macintosh computers; so most software developers focus on Windows machines.

But don't write off a Macintosh or another used computer right away. If you follow the steps outlined in DASSSH, you might find software that meets your gardening needs that just happens to also run on a non-Windows computer. **DASSSH** is an acronym for:

- ✳ **Do an Analysis** (of current or desired activities)
- ✳ **Select Software** (to match your practices and desired tasks)
- ✳ **Select Hardware** (to match the software you select)

DASSSH is a step-by-step way to buy a computer system to meet your gardening needs. After DASSSHing, you should have a computer that will meet both your current and future needs.

Cost is also a factor in buying a computer. A good up-to-date computer for business or home use can be had for about $2,000. This amount has stayed pretty constant over the years, while computing power per dollar has increased dramatically. But $2,000 is still a pretty good chunk of money. By DASSSHing, you may find that your needs can be met with a used computer and some simple software, or by a dedicated World Wide Web surfing machine.

Do an analysis

"Do an analysis" means that you should think about what you really want to do with the computer. Take the nebulous idea of "I would like to use a computer with my gardening" and make it specific with a wish list of activities you would like to accomplish with the computer.

Consider what you do now.

Do you keep a gardening journal and other extensive records about your garden and gardening activities? Paper record-keeping converts very well into a computer-based record-keeping system. To figure out what software you'll need, determine how extensive a record-keeping system you want to create. Some of us need only a simple electronic notebook for jotting down notes. Others want to tie all their different lists, catalogs, inventories, weather records, and notebooks into a comprehensive system that lets them sort the information in different ways.

What if you want to correspond with other gardeners about the latest variety of roses?

Going online with the Internet and commercial online services opens your garden gate to gardeners around the world. But the way you go online and your plans once you get there will affect your choice of computer system too. If all you want to do is surf the World Wide Web, simple terminal-like systems like an Internet TV may suit you just fine. If, on the other hand, you want to surf, send files, chat online, and build your own Web pages, you may want to consider buying a fairly sophisticated multimedia system capable of playing CD-quality sound and full-motion video.

What if you want to plan your garden?

Many of us like to plan our gardens but we can't draw a straight line. How comprehensive is your planning? Are you a sketcher or are your drawings extensive and detailed, complete with plant lists? The way you approach your garden planning will have a direct impact on both the software and hardware you choose.

How do you keep a record or make a wish list?

How do you keep a garden record book? The layout of each record can serve as a starting point for other types of the forms you might want in a garden database.

If friends use a computer for gardening, ask them how they use it.

Have them show you how they use their computer for some of their gardening activities. You may not do exactly what they do with a computer, but you'll get some ideas. The chapters that follow present lots of ideas for computerizing your gardening activities, too.

While listing the activities you would like to do now with a computer, think about what you might like to do with the computer in the future.

You may not need to search plant encyclopedias or online plant databases now, but you may want to in the future. Making a wish list will help you decide what computer to buy. You may not need a modem or CD-ROM now, but you might later. It may be cheaper and easier to get a modem and CD-ROM with the computer now, since many manufacturers include them. If you choose to wait, be sure the computer you buy is expandable and will let you add components.

Once you have your wish list, start looking for software. Even if you have only a basic wish list, it's better than walking into a store without any ideas.

Selecting software

The cost of your software can easily exceed the cost of your hardware. Try to match the type of software you need to buy to what you hope to do with a computer. Any type of record-keeping, for instance, requires some sort of database program. Which program you choose will depend on the complexity of the records you plan to keep. Simple plant lists, address books, and anything that fits on a standard index card can be kept with simple software known as a flat-file database; the Windows Cardfile is an example. However, if you want to keep a comprehensive set of records with several related lists and tables, you'll need a relational database manager, which may be more costly, and which will take some extra work to set up. Chapter 2 goes into more detail about the different types of software and how you can use them in gardening.

Match the software with the task or activity.

Just as you can use a spade for more than just digging soil, you'd do better with a pick and pry bar for removing a large rock. The same principle applies to software. Many word processors and most spreadsheet software can manage a database. However, for efficient garden information management, specialized database software is the best tool.

Similarly, you'll find different levels of painting and drawing capabilities in graphics software. You can use paint programs to sketch your garden plans, but for creating realistic landscape plans you need to look to computer-aided design (CAD) programs. Drawing and CAD programs are best for landscape planning when you need to change the design while maintaining precision, for later use in installation of the landscape.

What else does the software need?

When selecting software, take a close look at the operating system requirements for the program. Software that requires the Macintosh System 7 or OS 8 operating system will run only on Macintosh computers. Software that lists any three of the operating systems, DOS, Windows 3.1, or Windows 95, can run on any of the newer PC computers. You may find that a particular program you like will not run under the same operating system as your other program choices, in which case you will need to find an alternative.

It may not be important to you right now, but keep an eye out for software that will let you move your gardening information to another software program in the future. You may someday want to take the plant list in your garden database and move it into the

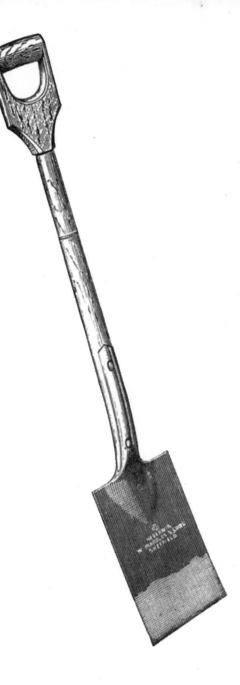

plant database of a more sophisticated landscape planning program. One of the major complaints about a popular landscape planning software package is its inability to add new plant lists or to export plant information to another program.

Selecting hardware

Following DASSSH, the software you choose will direct you to the hardware you need. This will help to avoid surprises when buying new software, such as discovering that you will need to add a larger hard disk and additional memory to your computer before you can run the software.

For example, a new release of a popular garden planning program now requires four times the memory, a better video display, and a faster CD-ROM drive than its predecessor. If your computer is a bit old and you haven't upgraded it recently, you may need to add close to $500 in hardware in order to run this $50 program.

Shop Computers Till You Drop!

One of the most important parts of getting a computer is deciding where to buy it. Finding a good retailer is important. Take time to shop around and ask the questions that will get you the best system for *you,* at the right price.

Like landscape plants, you can buy a computer from many different retailers, each with varying levels of prices and support.

Mail order

Mail-order computer dealers are like mail-order nurseries. You are responsible for selecting, purchasing, setting up, and supporting your computer.

Of course, like mail-order nurseries, some mail-order computer companies are a little shady and you take a real risk in buying from them. Many computer magazines recognize Dell Computer, Gateway 2000, and Micron Electronics as some of the mail-order firms offering quality products and service. Still, even with these firms, you may find it difficult to solve the inevitable problems on the telephone with your support person 2,000 miles away.

Department stores

Many department stores now sell computers alongside televisions and refrigerators. Of course, as with superstore garden centers, good luck finding a sales clerk with much computer knowledge! Service and support are likely to be limited too.

Also, while many of the computers sold in these stores are low cost, they may also be cheaply made with poor quality components. These stores may be okay for buying small items like cables or software, but for computer systems, it's buyer beware.

Electronics superstores

Electronics superstores are like the electronics departments in department stores—only bigger. The computers they sell tend to be a mix of low- to mid-range systems from the better manufacturers. The helpfulness and knowledgability of the sales staff varies from store to store and among chains. Support after the sale may be limited, with most support deferred back to the original manufacturer. The best buy from the "Perfect Purchase Superstore" may not be the best buy in the long run.

When shopping at these stores, find a savvy salesperson who knows the computer department, not a roving salesperson who sells toasters, TVs, and computers. If you know what you want, these stores can serve you well.

Computer superstores

Computer superstores, like CompUSA, are computer department stores. They are like full-service garden centers with a nursery, greenhouse, florist, and landscaping department. They usually offer competitive pricing, a wide selection of products (including a decent selection of gardening software), and a reasonably competent staff. I often find more gardening software at the nearby computer superstore than in some mail-order catalogs.

Computer systems can range from low-end systems to high-end brand name computer systems. Some stores will even assemble computer systems to your custom specifications, with their own label. They usually have a fully staffed service department along

with regularly scheduled training sessions or classes. Often these classes are included in the sale of a computer system.

Computer dealers

Computer dealers specialize in computer products and services, just like landscape equipment dealers or landscape contractors. They usually have knowledgeable salespeople and many offer training and support after the purchase. Most computer dealers are now focused on sales and support to businesses, with little or no walk-in customer service. They're best if you want to outfit a landscaping or gardening business.

VARs and custom service

Value Added Resellers (VARs) are dealers who target a specific vertical market, such as lawn care or nursery management. Using available hardware and customizable software, they develop a computer system tailored to particular needs. They also provide a fair amount of support and service after the sale. Some VARs will provide software only, while others sell both software and hardware.

A custom service or consultant develops a specialized system based on an analysis of your business needs. For example, if your business performs a unique management practice not accounted for in more generalized landscape packages, the service can add specific custom features to a software system to perform those tasks.

VARs and custom services are well beyond the needs or budget of most gardeners, but you may find them useful if you are in the landscaping business or thinking about starting one.

Which is best?

As you go from mail order to custom service, you'll need to do less work but the overall cost of your system will increase. Where you buy will depend on what you want to buy.

Avoid department stores and electronics superstores for system purchases, unless you are already comfortable with computers and can handle most problems.

Mail-order computer supply catalogs are good for purchasing software and accessories at a reasonable price, as long as you're willing to do your own installation and support. The more reputable companies even offer next-day delivery on most of their products. In many cases, mail order may be the only source for some products.

If you are buying your first computer and have no one—a friend, spouse, or teenager—to provide support and guidance, visit the computer superstores and computer dealers first. Concentrate on finding the software you want first, and then let the software dictate the hardware you buy. Any computer salesperson who attempts to sell you hardware first without finding out your software needs should be told "thanks, but no thanks" and bid goodbye.

For those of you on your second or third computer, a mail-order computer company such as Gateway, Micron, or Dell, along with a mail-order computer supply company like PC Connection, Micro-Warehouse, or PC Zone, may be good places to buy. The mail-order companies are also excellent sources for those of us who do not have a nearby computer superstore. I live over an hour from the three nearest computer superstores, and have found a mail-order computer company to be great for buying my sixth home computer.

Finding the best place to buy that will give you the most satisfaction (or least frustration) will depend on how well you do your homework. Ask your friends and relatives about their computer buying experiences. The computer buying experiences of your workplace may also help you decide. You may even qualify for an employee discount if you purchase through your employer.

The Smart Garden Computer Shopper Questions

Searching for a place to buy your computer is no different from searching for a good landscape equipment dealer or supplier. All of the rules you use for buying gardening equipment, supplies, and materials can also apply when buying computer systems, peripherals, software, and supplies.

Here are some questions to ask yourself and the salesperson as you search for the perfect garden computer system:

Is the dealer an "authorized dealer"?

Like new-car dealers, authorized computer dealers are usually required to have a trained sales, service, and support staff. However, "authorization" may not always have the same meaning. Department stores are "authorized" to sell some popular brands of computers, but they are not fully authorized service and support dealers.

Where is the dealer located?

As with garden tractors, buying from a local dealer may pay off when you need quick service or support, even though the equipment may cost more. Make this a top consideration if you live far from a big city.

What are the support policies and costs?

Support after the sale is wide and varied, ranging from none to almost unlimited support—for a price. The support you get will also depend on what you are buying. For example, while computer games are sold without support, high-end landscape design software will probably include some support. When buying hardware or software, ask about the support policies and any costs, including on-site costs as well as charges for travel time and phone support. Get everything in writing.

Do mail-order companies offer any local service and support?

Many local computer stores service and support only their own products and cannot help if your mail-ordered system goes down. Many of the top mail-order computer companies contract with a third-party service company to make local service calls.

Are the computers manufactured or assembled?

Because most of the pieces that make up a computer are standardized, it's easy for dealers to buy the different parts and assemble them. This is similar to putting together a home entertainment system with the TV, receiver, CD player, VCR, and speakers all coming from different manufacturers. With a little perseverance, *you* can assemble your own computer from standard components.

But assembled systems can have their problems. For instance, there may be just enough difference between components that a "gotcha" will appear later: a new modem may not work or your new gardening software will freeze up for no apparent reason. Many times, this is due to a hidden conflict between components.

In the case of manufactured systems, engineers design a complete computer system. The engineers' design ensures that all of the components will work together well.

What is the warranty on the computer?

Although warranty periods vary, most quality computers carry a three-year warranty. Beware of cases with seals that say "Warranty void if broken." Although uncommon in today's computer market, this is like a car dealer putting warranty seals on the hood of your car stating that the car warranty is void if you check the oil yourself instead of having one of the dealer's service technicians check the oil. Unless the seal is to protect you from high voltage injury, such as on a monitor, don't buy a computer with a warranty seal.

Do you continue to educate yourself?

The last but the most important aspect of buying a computer system is to continue to educate yourself. Many problems occur because people don't take the time to become educated consumers. Before and after you sign the check, continue to learn all you can about using computers for your gardening activities.

Once you finish this book, start reading other resources. The manuals that come with the computer hardware and software are a good start. Learn all you can. Too often people just do the basics and never bother to learn the additional features. (A classic word-processing example is continuing to hit the return key at the end of each line and using spaces to indent, when the word processor can do this all automatically.) Start reading computer magazines for new ideas on using the computer. Cruise the Internet and surf the World Wide Web for more ideas. Chat with some gardening friends online. Gardening is a lifelong learning activity, and computers can become part of that learning too.

Software: The Computer's Recipes

A computer without software is a useless box of plastic and metal. That's why you should find your software before you buy your hardware. Software is the tool that lets us perform a variety of activities with a computer. Just as a shovel or rototiller makes it easier to dig in the garden, software makes it easier to manage information about our gardens—and more fun to garden.

Software controls your hardware. Since we like to cook what we grow in the vegetable garden, think of a computer program as a recipe.

A recipe is a set of directions with a list of ingredients for making or preparing food. Software is the computer's recipe. With it, the computer knows, with our help, how to do tasks like produce a letter to a seed company requesting a catalog or find the perfect plant for our garden from a large list of plants. There are two major categories of software, operating systems and applications.

Operating Systems

Computers are so dumb, they need instructions for the simplest things, like drawing a character on the monitor, printing a character on a printer, or storing a character on a disk drive. Operating systems software is what shows the computer how to do things with its hardware.

In the old days, not that long ago, all commands to control a computer had to be typed in through a keyboard and only one computer program could be run at a time. Those were the days of DOS (disk operating system, but never mind). Today, with a Macintosh running OS 8.0 or a PC running the Microsoft Windows 95 operating system, we just point, click, and drag a mouse while running multiple programs simultaneously. That's what an operating system can do.

Applications

Applications software consists of the computer programs that allow us to use the computer as a tool to accomplish various tasks. Since applications are designed for specific tasks, we can group them by task. The main types of applications are:

* *word processors* for manipulating text and words
* *spreadsheets* for crunching numbers
* *database managers* for managing large amounts of data
* *graphics programs* for creating all sorts of pictures and images
* *communications programs* for talking to other computers
* *utility programs* for managing the computer and software
* *development software* for creating more computer programs
* *entertainment software* for a good time when you're not gardening
* *desktop publishing software* for preparing complex printed materials
* *presentation software* for creating and displaying sophisticated presentations

Where to Get Software

You can obtain software from several types of sources, including places where you can download software for free or almost free.

Commercial software

Most software we hear about is sold or licensed for use on a computer and purchased in a shrink-wrapped box. This is called *commercial software*. The cost of commercial software can range from a few dollars (for a dinky little program) to several thousand dollars for high-end software, such as computer-aided design programs.

Shareware

Back in the early 1980s some enterprising software developers started distributing software for free, on a "try before you buy" basis. The developers asked those who continued to use the program for payment in the form of a registration fee. This honor system of software distribution and payment became known as *shareware*.

Shareware abounds today, offering software developers a practical distribution method without the tremendous costs involved in retail marketing. To encourage payment, shareware doesn't come with extensive documentation or technical support—sometimes called hand-holding—until you pay. Once you pay, you usually get printed manuals, telephone or e-mail support, and sometimes even additional computer programs to support the main program. For example, many shareware gardening databases come with a small file of plants. When you pay, you get a much larger plant file.

Are shareware programs okay? Many are as good as (or better than) some commercial products. And shareware is often the only source for some specialty software, including specific gardening software. While shareware often does not have the extensive features found in commercial software, this can be a plus if you don't need the features or don't have the time to learn them.

Freeware and public domain software

Some people like to develop computer programs for fun. They are as passionate about developing programs as many of us are passionate about gardening. These hobbyist programmers give away programs the way we give away a plant cutting or perennial division. This freely distributed software is known as *freeware* or *public domain software*.

Generally, freeware implies that the software is free, but the developer holds all copyrights on the software. Usually, developers put some restriction on commercial distribution of their programs. For example, the software may be free for personal home use, but may require a license fee if used at work or school.

Public domain software, however, like other works put into the public domain, is released without any copyrights or other restrictions. Often the programs are useful but small utilities, such as a simple fertilizer calculator created as part of a programming course for agriculture students.

The "Big Five"

No matter what kind of computer you own, you should install at least one example of each of the following basic types of programs. I call these the "Big Five" because they're all staples in the software world.

Word processors

Word processors let you compose documents at your computer. The type of word processor you will need depends on the kind of documents you plan to produce. If you write primarily letters, most basic word processors will suffice, including shareware ones. However, if you are writing gardening books, sending customized form letters to seed companies, doing the garden club newsletter, or producing any document involving desktop publishing activities, you will want a high-end word processor.

Simple word processors

Once you have a computer, you will want to take advantage of its word processing capabilities. Keeping DASSSH in mind, if your needs are simple and few, such as writing letters and letting the students in the family do homework, a simple word processor is a much better choice than a large, sophisticated workhorse word processor like Microsoft Word, Corel WordPerfect, or Lotus Word Pro.

A simple word processor allows you to set margins and tabs, change fonts, set character styles, align text, and perform searches to find or replace text. Some of the more advanced simple word processing programs include spell checkers and simple mail merge.

The best part is that if you have Microsoft Windows, you already have a simple word processor—Write with Windows 3.1, and WordPad with Windows 95.

If you need more features but you're on a limited budget, several shareware and freeware word processors may do the trick. PC-Write, the first popular shareware word processor for DOS-based computers, will also run on Windows-based PCs; it can still be found in many shareware libraries and on computer networks. Word Express has been a perennial favorite Windows 3.1 word processor. Yeah Write is among the word processors that run on Windows 95 computers. Word Edit for the Macintosh even provides a spell checker.

SEE CD-ROM

Besides stand-alone simple word processors, the word processors found in integrated "Works" programs will also meet most basic word processing needs. A separate section on integrated programs appears later in this chapter.

Workhorse word processors

Whether in the office or at home, when you need to create a large variety of different documents with different styles, layouts, formatting, and page lengths, you'll need a more powerful word processor with lots of features. The three major programs are Microsoft Word, Corel WordPerfect, and Lotus/IBM Word Pro.

All of them have extensive features that go beyond typical word processing and start to cross into the areas of desktop publishing and Internet Web publishing.

If you already use one of the major word processors at work, continue to use it at home for your gardening activities. Since there are many subtle differences between word processors, using a different word processor for garden writing may be confusing. Using a program you are familiar with will save you time at the computer, thereby allowing you more time in the garden.

Spreadsheets

The program that brought the desktop computer out of the hobbyist basement and squarely onto the business desk was not a word processor, but an electronic spreadsheet called VisiCalc. Based on the paper ledgers of accountants and bookkeepers, a spreadsheet program allows you to perform a variety of calculations and analyses at lightning speed and without an adding machine, calculator, or paper and pencil.

In gardening, we are constantly dealing with lists and tables of numbers and performing a variety of calculations. Besides the business-related number crunching of budgeting and cost estimates for the garden, there are many nonbusiness activities in gardening that require extensive calculations. For instance, anyone who has designed a garden or lawn irrigation system is acutely aware of the pipe-sizing calculations needed to ensure that water comes out of the sprinklers.

A spreadsheet, like its paper ledger counterpart, consists of rows and columns, with a "cell" being the intersection of each row and column. Each cell contains a value, either a number or text. A value may also be the result of calculating a formula hidden inside the cell.

In basic operations, doing spreadsheet calculations on the computer is not very different from doing calculations on paper with a hand calculator. Entering values into a spreadsheet takes about as long as writing down the values on a paper ledger. The real power behind the spreadsheet is its ability to recalculate quickly when making a change to any value in the cells referenced by the formulas. With the spreadsheet we can perform what are commonly called "what-if" scenarios.

Imagine that your local garden club would like to make money by arranging for a year's worth of fertilizer applications on the lawns of all 100 members, each with a different size lawn. Then, "what if" the president of the club comes in griping that the brand of fertilizer you have selected is too expensive and you need to compare five other fertilizers, each with a different nitrogen analysis. Does anyone have a spare afternoon?

By using a spreadsheet, it will be easy to duplicate the information, adjusting for the other five fertilizers. If we include cost information in the spreadsheet, we can quickly determine which fertilizer best meets all our needs. (See Figure 2-1.)

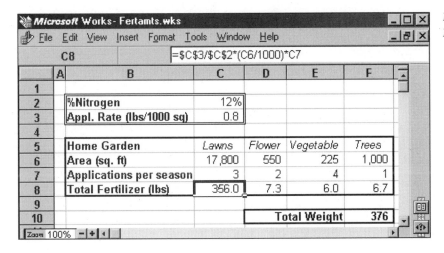

Figure 2-1
Fertilizer calculations in a spreadsheet

The values generated by a spreadsheet are only as accurate as the initial values and formulas entered in the spreadsheet. Entering an erroneous formula through misunderstanding of the problem (dividing feet by acres) or entering bad values (acres instead of the required square feet) will give a result just as wrong as doing it by calculator. Don't rely on the results of a spreadsheet until you're sure that it's been set up properly, especially when doing pesticide and fertilizer application calculations.

Keep DASSSH in mind when selecting a spreadsheet. Look at all the numerical calculation and analysis activities that you might want to perform. For many small one-time uses such as a fertilizer calculation, the spreadsheets found in integrated programs (Microsoft Works, Claris Works) are often sufficient. Several shareware spreadsheet programs also rival many entry-level commercial spreadsheets. These include VistaCalc for Windows and As-Easy-As for DOS. Macintosh owners still might be able to find Biplane in some shareware libraries. As with the workhorse word processors, the powerhouse spreadsheet software like Microsoft Excel, Lotus 1-2-3, and Corel Quattro are likely beyond the needs of most gardeners.

SEE CD-ROM

In addition to crunching numbers, many spreadsheets also have charting and graphing features. A chart or graph is a visual representation of related numbers. Mangling an old proverb, in many situations "a graph is worth a thousand numbers."

With charting capability, you can display a variety of numerical trends. A bar chart of monthly rainfall amounts, a pie chart of gardening expenditures (see Figure 2-2), and a horizontal bar chart of flower-blooming times are examples of such spreadsheet-generated output.

Databases

For most businesses, *database management systems* (DBMS) are essential. And if you use a home computer, you probably have several database programs already, although you may not recognize them as such. Checkbook programs, address books, home finance systems, and home inventory programs are all database programs

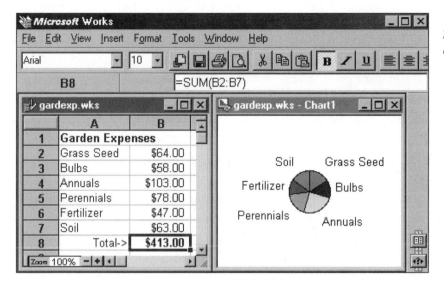

Figure 2-2
Pie chart of gardening
expenditures

in disguise. Garden encyclopedias and the plant lists inside landscape planning software have database management system technologies at their core.

A database system is the electronic equivalent of an index card filing system. Each "index card" is represented by one record in the database. Within a record, each line that contains a specific type of data is one field. With index cards, we can place any type of data—numbers, text, pictures—anywhere on the card. However, with computer records, we need to keep our data in a specific format. After all, we don't want our birth date appearing on the amount line of our paychecks!

Database management systems have a major advantage over traditional paper records. While data entry into an electronic database takes about the same amount of time as writing entries on paper, the electronic database allows much faster and flexible retrieval of the information at a later time. To find a particular plant in a catalog or index card file can take several minutes or more, depending on the number of catalogs or the size of the index card file. A search through an electronic database will probably take seconds.

When you need to group and summarize information, electronic databases are a true timesaver. For example, let's check the

SEE CD-ROM

rain gauge. How much rain did you get in your garden last month, last summer, and all last year? By keeping your garden weather records in a database, you can quickly create "on demand" rainfall summaries, grouped by month, season, and year. Weather Tracker on the CD-ROM (in the WthrTrak folder) is a good example of a simple database for keeping basic weather records.

Flat file database programs

The index card analogy describes a "flat file" database. The database component in most "Works" applications is a flat file database, as are the landscape plant databases found in landscape-planning CAD programs. Spreadsheets such as Lotus 1-2-3 and Microsoft Excel can be used as flat file databases. Although flat file database management programs can accomplish many simple record-keeping tasks, they are rather inefficient in larger applications. This is where relational database management programs shine.

Relational database programs

Do you keep an address book of all your seed suppliers, with a one-line reference to that address book in a separate seed list? If you do, you have the beginnings of a relational database.

Relational databases keep unique information in separate data files, usually called tables, with key fields that can be "related" to fields in another data file. The data file structures are kept separate from the forms for creating, displaying, and manipulating data in the database. In flat file databases, the "form defines the database." In a relational database system, you can display the data in many different ways without affecting the underlying structure.

Relational database management systems provide the power to manage large amounts of gardening information, but they require advance planning and organization to be effective. If your current paper information management practices tend to be haphazard, then implementing a relational database management system could be a major challenge, as computers abhor messy habits. You may need to develop a well-organized paper system before converting to a computer-based system.

Approach database management systems very carefully. Otherwise, you may find yourself drowning in a sea of data, tangled in a web of bad data relationships.

Graphics

Gardening is a very visual activity. One of the major reasons we grow gardens is to look at them. Many flower gardens exist only for their aesthetic value, which must be seen to be enjoyed. Plant lists in databases and price totals in spreadsheets are useful gardening tools, but you may want to take advantage of the graphic capabilities of your computer to visually plan and record the growth of your garden.

A new area of landscape planning goes beyond the traditional drawing of lines and pictures. Visual imaging allows the gardener to take digital photographs of a home and add an array of plants from an image library, to create a picture of the home with a new landscape or garden.

When using graphics for landscape or garden planning, be aware of the basic differences among various graphics programs. Each type has a specific function and you may need two or three different graphics programs to complete the landscape design.

Pencil sketches and finger paintings

Graphics programs fall into two broad categories, depending on how images are created, maintained, and displayed by the computer. The first category includes bitmap or paint programs; the second, drawing programs. Some graphics programs handle both painting and drawing images through a system very much like transparent layers of clear plastic, called layering. The paint-type images are kept on one transparent layer and the drawing-type images on another. You use different pieces of the program to modify your images.

Painting in memory

If you put a magnifying lens to a computer monitor, you will notice that the image consists of dots of light, just like the dots that make up a printed photograph. The more dots, or pixels, the greater the sharpness or resolution of the image. If you've seen Georges Seurat's paintings, such as *A Sunday Afternoon on the Island of La Grande Jatte* (see Figure 2-3), you'll recognize the underlying principle of computer displays. Even though computers were not around in Seurat's time, his inspiration for pointillism came from photographs, including those printed in newspapers.

Paint programs range from simple—the Paint program included with Microsoft Windows—to very sophisticated applications—such as Adobe Photoshop, which is capable of altering photographs. Usually, the tools in each program are adapted to the purpose of the program, that is, painting or photo editing, though there is often overlap.

With DASSSH in mind, ask yourself, "What type of images will I be working with?" Do you want to create artistic renditions of your garden, painting it like Monet at Giverny, but with an electronic instead of a camel's-hair brush? Or would you just like to play with existing images?

Figure 2-3
Georges Seurat's A Sunday Afternoon on the Island of La Grande Jatte, *bit-mapped graphics before computers*

Most gardeners are interested in visual imaging—manipulating photographs. Although almost any photo editor program will work for this purpose, a landscape visual imaging system, consisting of a specialized photo editor and a library of painted or photographic plant images, is a great resource.

The downside to paint programs and imaging systems is that like with real paint, once changes are made to an image it's not easy to correct it or return it to a previous "unpainted" state. However, newer imaging programs, both paint-type and visual imaging systems, are getting better at allowing for this "undoing."

Another problem with paint and visual imaging programs for landscape planning is that they are often "dimensionless." There is no easy way to determine the dimensions needed for constructing and installing a landscape based on a painted or photographic image. To create landscape plans to scale requires a drawing program.

Drawing the line

Drawing programs draw an image on the screen based on a formula that describes the image. All geometric shapes drawn on the screen (lines, circles and arcs, squares and rectangles, polygons and curves) are considered objects or entities.

One advantage of drawing programs is that they let you change one or more objects without affecting others. Of course, any change to an object requires the program to redraw the image on the display, and therefore drawing programs are slower than paint programs in displaying the image. While paint programs save your complete image, drawing programs save only the underlying object descriptions. For faster redrawing of images, you'll need a fast computer.

While painting programs are fairly dimensionless, drawing programs can associate real-world dimensions with the objects. If we want to "plant" flowers 6 inches apart, the flowers in the drawing program can be the equivalent of 6 inches apart. Drawing programs will allow you to create a precise design that will serve as an accurate guide for later garden construction and installation.

Drawing programs can be divided into two groups based on the types of drawings they produce. The drawing program you use will depend on the drawing's ultimate purpose.

Illustration programs are used to create stylized illustrations and artistic drawings primarily for print publications. Dimensions used in drawing programs are typically in pixels or inches, as they relate to standard paper dimensions. Adobe Illustrator and Corel DRAW are two of the more popular illustration programs (see Figure 2-4). While excellent programs for creating plant illustrations, they are not the best tools for garden planning, although some people use them as such. For garden planning, you should use a computer-aided design or CAD program.

CAD programs use real-world dimensions, thus allowing the gardener to draw precisely to scale. In addition to maintaining information about the geometric properties of an object, CAD programs can maintain other types of information as well. For example, a 20-foot-long thick brown line representing a garden fence may also contain information that the fence is made of dog-eared

Figure 2-4
An illustration program is best for illustrating the garden, but not for planning the garden

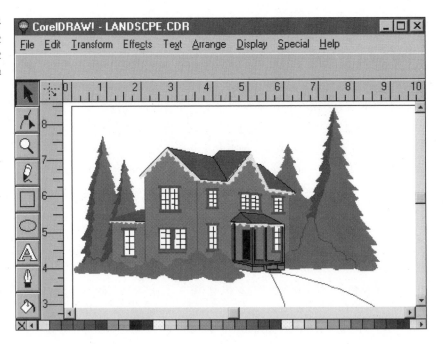

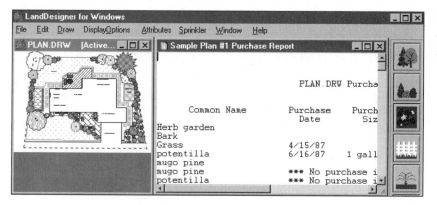

Figure 2-5
A CAD drawing of a landscape
plan with a list of materials report

wood, that it is 4 feet high, and that it costs $3.00 per linear foot. Since CAD programs can keep information on all the objects in a database, we can gather the dimensions, physical characteristics, and costs of the fencing to create a list of materials and a total cost estimate to accompany our drawing. (See Figure 2-5.)

CAD drawings represent most gardening information better than illustration-type drawings. When used in conjunction with visual imaging programs, the combined programs make for a comprehensive means of displaying and maintaining visual information about the garden.

Communications

In the past, when customers were buying computers the most important question was "What word processor does it come with?" Now, it is often "Does the computer come with software to access the Internet and send e-mail?" With the rapid growth of networks, the Internet, electronic mail, and the World Wide Web, communications software has moved into the limelight.

Most communications software fills a particular need for communicating over a network, like the Internet. Fortunately, much of it is cheap or free, like razor handles were in the days when only the blades were disposable. Razor blade manufacturers gave away the handles, recouping the costs through the sale of razor blades. Today, commercial online services give away communications software, recouping the costs through the sale of online services.

In upcoming chapters, we will cover communications, networking, online services, and the Internet on a more comprehensive level. So start flexing your fingers to do the talking.

Integrated Programs and Office Suites— Everything But the Kitchen Sink

In the earlier days of desktop computers, every application had a different interface or means of operating a program. The standard look of movable windows, menu bars at the top of the screen, and pull-down menus attached to the menu bar did not exist.

In the workplace, companies divided the major computer programs according to job responsibilities. The secretary used a word processor for typing, the boss used a spreadsheet for managing company finances, and the data processing department used a database manager for keeping client records. There was very little need for anyone to know more than one or two computer programs.

Today, there has been a major change in how computers are used on the job. Workers at many levels do some word processing, spreadsheet "what-ifs," and database managing (mangling?), along with surfing the Web and making presentations with overhead slides. With people having to learn five or six programs, developers created a group of programs with a common set of commands and interface (the way the program appears on the screen). Now users can easily shift among different programs, using the same data in various ways, remaining in a familiar screen environment. For the home, education, and small business market, integrated programs filled the need to provide a little of everything—a basic word processor, spreadsheet, database manager, and communications software. Like a hamburger with "the works," there are computer programs with "the works."

Works programs integrate basic word processor, simple spreadsheet, and flat-file database management modules (see Figure 2-6).

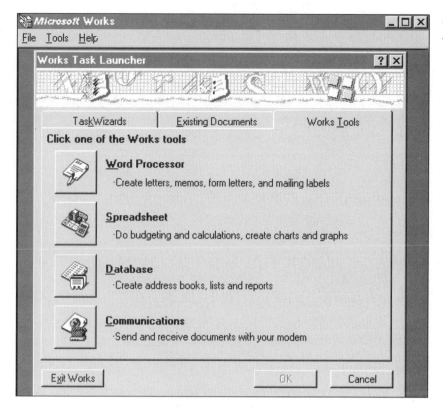

Figure 2-6

A program with "the works"

Many also have built-in communications capabilities, business graphics (bar graphs, pie charts), and basic drawing modules.

Works programs are great for general use by gardeners. Even though basic and limited compared to the major word processors, spreadsheets, and database managers, they can still meet the requirements of most computer gardening activities, with the exception of computer-aided landscape design.

Office suites

The office suite of software, like the living room suite of furniture, is a package of separate full-featured programs, all with similar menus and interfaces. Some office suites even let you automate a variety of tasks among programs.

Should you get an office suite? That depends. Did I mention backhoes and shovels? Getting an office suite for manipulating gardening information is like getting a backhoe for planting spring flowering bulbs when all you really need is a shovel to plant the bulbs. Office suites include a large list of powerful features, most of which you will probably never use. Unless you use one at work or it's included with the purchase of the computer, don't buy an office suite.

Stick with an integrated program instead, until you reach its limits—then you can shift to an office suite. In most cases, the information developed with an integrated program can be transferred into an office suite program.

In addition, if you're on a limited budget or using an older computer, you'll find that an integrated program costs less and takes up far less space on your hard disk than an office suite. Many basic computers and older systems can't store and run even one program from the latest office suite.

Utilities—Computer Garden Tools

We can grow ornamental and food gardens with just a shovel, a trowel, pruning shears, and a watering hose. Knee pads, garden carts, bulb augers, and weed poppers are additional tools that are not absolutely necessary, but that make gardening much easier and more enjoyable. Similarly, some claim they can cook anything with a pot, a pan, a knife, and a spoon. Yet for most of us, a greater variety of kitchen utensils make cooking a more efficient and enjoyable experience.

A wide range of tools, known as utilities, can make computer use much easier, more efficient, and less distressing if disaster strikes. Utilities are small programs or groups of small programs that do a variety of odd jobs on the computer. You can get by without many of these utilities, but some are as indispensable as pruning shears and watering cans.

There are thousands of utilities of all kinds. *PC Magazine,* a popular computer magazine, divides utilities into thirteen basic groups, as shown in Table 2-1. For now, we will briefly focus on only one utility used to control those pests known as computer viruses. In later chapters we will come back to some of the other ones.

Table 2-1 General utility groups

GENERAL COMPUTER	INTERNET/NETWORKING
Antivirus	Network Backup/Management
File Viewers	Internet Essentials
Diagnostics	Offline Browsers
Uninstallers	Offline Searching
Performance Enhancers	Filtering
Operating Systems	E-Mail Encryption/Management
Miscellaneous	

Controlling computer viruses

Computer viruses are tiny programs that, like biological viruses in a host organism, can take over a computer application or operating system. Once in a host computer, the virus replicates itself and attaches the replicas to other computer programs. If the newly infected program is transferred to another computer, the virus can infect all the programs on that computer. Some viruses are so virulent that merely accessing a floppy disk in an infected computer is enough to infect the floppy.

Many computer viruses are simply obnoxious, like gnats, flashing stupid or nasty slogans on the monitor. Some are outright malicious, damaging files or even erasing entire hard disk drives, and generally doing more damage than a horde of beetles in a rose garden.

Who writes viruses? Without going into a long discussion on the sociopathic disorders of misguided computer hackers, let's just say they are in the same group as those who sometimes trash the garden. At times, we need to put up fences around the garden to keep out dogs, deer, and troublemakers.

Antivirus utilities are designed to protect against computer viruses. One group of antivirus utilities checks for existing viruses and eliminates them from programs, like looking for grubs before they emerge as hungry beetles. The second group consists of small,

continually running programs that constantly watch for virus attacks, stopping a virus before it can infect the computer. Of course, like biological diseases and insects that become resistant to pesticides, the virus developers are always finding ways to bypass antivirus protection, while the antivirus program developers are constantly developing new controls.

If you plan to download programs from the Internet or an online service or you let the kids trade programs with their friends, borrow a shareware antivirus program from the local library or buy an antivirus utility. Their low cost, about $50 or less, could save you hours or days recovering from a malicious computer virus attack.

Selecting Software on the Road to Hardware

Once you have determined the type of software that meets your needs, you should ask several questions before making a purchase. When buying plants, we often have a mental checklist of items we need to consider while looking at various specimens. We might ask:

* What's the flower color?
* Is it disease resistant?
* Is it healthy?
* Does it come with planting instructions?
* Is there a warranty?

Similarly, one should also have a software checklist before going into a computer store or paging through the catalogs. Here are some common questions to ask about any software.

What operating system does it require?

Most current gardening programs require Microsoft Windows. Some new gardening programs will work only with Windows 95 or later versions, while older gardening programs and many freeware/shareware gardening programs are DOS-based, but may still run under Windows. A small number of gardening programs are available for the Macintosh operating system. A few commercial gardening software titles have versions available for both Windows and Macintosh operating systems.

As you consider different gardening software, look closely at the operating system requirements. This will be an important factor in your hardware selection.

What are the hardware requirements? Any unusual ones?

As a rule, if your hardware meets the operating system requirements, then any program that runs under that operating system will also run with the same hardware. However, some software, particularly the newer multimedia programs, require additional hardware, such as fast CD-ROM drives, a large amount of computer memory, or an audio output device. Read the requirements on the box to make sure your system can run a program before you buy it.

What kind of help systems, tutorials, and documentation come with the program?

Even with the development of easier-to-use operating systems and applications, many programs are still difficult to learn. Many now have built-in help systems. Some are very good, complete with built-in tutorials and cue cards to guide you through a process. Others are not worth the space they take up on the computer.

A recent paper- and cost-saving trend among software publishers is to place all the reference manuals and user guides on CD-ROMs. Since at times you may want to read a manual away from the computer, find out if printed manuals are available.

Is there a money-back guarantee?

One major problem faced by software publishers is that their programs can be copied easily without loss of quality. This results in software piracy or illegal copying. To avoid the problem of someone buying software, copying it, and returning it, many software companies have a no-returns policy. Thus, we may discover that software we have purchased doesn't meet our needs and yet be unable to obtain a refund.

As a way to maintain customers, some software companies—including some that produce gardening programs—now offer a money-back guarantee. Some allow returns only if the software will not work on your computer. Other companies offer full-satisfaction guarantees—if you don't like it, return it. When shopping for software, find out about the guarantee.

Depending on the software, you'll likely have some additional questions. For instance, you may want to find out if a word processor includes a spell checker, thesaurus, and grammar checker. Before purchasing a landscape planning program, you will want to know how extensive a plant symbol library it includes. As we cover the different garden computer activities, we'll discover additional questions that you will want to ask.

Hardware: The Computer Toolshed

With the software list in hand, we now know what kind of hardware we will require. Let's look at the meanings behind the hardware requirements listed on the software package to help us determine the software we need to buy to set up our computer system.

Experienced gardeners always notice neophytes in the garden centers during the spring season. New gardeners are attracted to all of the plants, wanting one of everything, it seems. But the new gardener has likely not given much thought to landscape design and how the plants will fit in. As with gardening, where every plant should have a purpose, think carefully about your computer's purpose and how you'll use it.

Now that you know what software you'll want, pay close attention to the software's recommended system requirements rather than its minimum system requirements. Though the software may run with only the minimum requirements, it will probably be painfully slow. Running software with only the minimum requirements is like cutting grass with a pair of grass clippers. The recommended hardware requirement is your power mower.

What's a Byte Besides Something to Eat?

Before getting into the different parts of a computer, you need to be familiar with some computer terms. In gardening we talk about loppers, bypass pruners, and sweetening the soil. These terms may be confusing to new gardeners, but once explained they're easy to understand. If you're new to computers, the terminology may seem similarly indecipherable. RAM is not a type of pickup truck and ROM is not the name of some little Ferengi helping his brother run a bar on *Deep Space Nine*. The Sunday newspaper commonly carries computer ads with computerspeak, just as the car ads talk about "MPG" and "horsepower." Understanding this terminology is very important when buying a computer. Let's look at what some terms mean.

A bit of nibbling on byte-size words

In gardening, we use gallons, cubic yards, and inches as units of measure. When we talk about computers, the basic unit of measure is the *byte*.

Your computer is based on a binary or two-number system, using just the numbers 0 and 1. Bytes are a way of representing larger binary numbers. For our purposes, think of one byte as the same as a number between 0 and 256 or a character in the alphabet. When we see terms such as "megabytes of storage," we can relate that to the quantity of numbers or characters that the computer can store or manage at one time. Sixteen megabytes of memory tells us how much data the computer can manipulate at one time. A 1.2 gigabyte hard drive gives an indication of how much information can be stored in the computer. Kilobytes (thousands), megabytes (millions), and gigabytes (billions) are the terms you'll most commonly see today when computer memory and storage are discussed. Gigabytes are bigger than megabytes, which are bigger than kilobytes, and the more your computer has of either, the more information it can store or work with at one time.

Here's an example that will make these terms a little more real: the average double-spaced typewritten page is approximately

2,000 characters or 2 kilobytes in size. So when we read an advertisement stating that a computer has "32 megabytes of memory and a 3.5 gigabyte hard drive," we realize that we are dealing with a lot of electronic paper.

Bits, which are smaller than bytes, are another unit of computer measurement. They represent the individual binary numbers 0 or 1. When bits are used to describe a monitor or an audio device, we're talking about a measure of the device's capacity to show colorful images or play high-quality sound or music. The higher the bit number for the device, the better the quality of its output. For example, an 8-bit color video display can show 16 colors out of a palette of 256, while a 24-bit color video display can show 256 or more colors out of a palette of a few million. An 8-bit audio device will play music that sounds like it comes from an old AM radio, while a 32-bit sound card will provide bass tones to shake your tummy.

Bits are also used to describe speed, particularly with regard to modems and computer networks. Most modems, devices for transmitting computer data over telephone lines, can reach average speeds of 33,600 *bits per second* (bps). The higher the bit number, the faster the modem.

What's in the Box?

Now that we understand some of the terminology, let's look at the key components that make up the hardware portion of a computer system.

The processor or CPU

No, the processor is not for chopping, slicing, and dicing vegetables. Rather, the processor, often referred to as the CPU or central processor unit, is at the heart of a computer. The CPU is where all of the number crunching takes place.

Operating systems are designed to run on specific processors, so Windows won't run on a Macintosh CPU and the Macintosh operating system won't run on a PC with an Intel

processor. Most new desktop computer systems sold today contain an Intel Pentium or compatible CPU. Older systems will have earlier generation CPUs, such as the 286, 386, or 486 processor. These systems are called PCs or IBM-PC compatibles. The speed increases with the processor number. The Pentium series would be equivalent to a 586 or 686.

Newer Macintosh computers use the Motorola PowerPC family of processors (602, 603, 604). Older ones used the Motorola 68000 family of processors (68000, 68020, 68030, 68040). Even though the PowerPC is a different family of processors from the 68000 family, Apple Computer did some engineering design work to allow older Macintosh software to run on PowerPC-based Macintoshes.

0 to 200 MHz in one second flat

In addition to knowing the type of processor in a computer, pay attention to the speed of the processor, sometimes listed as its clock speed. All computers work to the lockstep ticks of a clock. Every computer instruction, each byte of data moved around the computer, every pixel drawn on a screen is done to the beat of the clock, like a metronome ticking away on a piano. Each "tick of the clock" is considered a cycle. Computer processors usually run at millions of cycles per second. A million cycles per second is called a *megahertz* or MHz. Processors found in most of today's computers run at speeds of 166 MHz to 233 MHz. High-end computers are now sporting 300 MHz processors, and faster processors are always just around the corner. Is speed important? If you plan to work with complex graphics, such as computer-aided design with full 3D display, then processor speed is very important—the faster the processor, the quicker an image is drawn on the screen. The current crop of highly graphic landscape planning programs with walk-through features requires a fast processor, but for most software, a current middle-of-the-road processor speed will be sufficient. If you're buying a PC today, get a system with a processor *near* the upper end of available processor speeds. Usually, the fastest processor available on the market is also the newest and the most expensive.

Buy the fastest processor you can afford that is one to two speeds behind the fastest available. This will get you the most cost-effective and long-lived system.

Processor speed is not the only thing that will affect the overall speed of a computer; other components factor in as well. One of these is the amount of memory installed in your system.

Memory, like the shadows of the mind

When people talk about computer memory they're not talking about long-term storage—that would be your hard disk drive. The memory they're referring to is traditionally called RAM or random access memory. Another term is *working memory,* which the computer uses to hold programs and data for easy access by the processor. Fetching programs and data from a disk drive is slower than getting it from the working memory.

Working memory is volatile. No, it will not blow up when disturbed. Rather, working memory holds data only while the power is turned on. When the power is turned off or someone trips over the power cord, everything in memory disappears like dandelion seeds in the wind.

How much memory should you specify for your computer? The more working memory, the better off you will be now, and the more prepared you will be later when you get newer programs.

Buy twice the working memory that is considered a standard configuration. If the current standard configuration is 16 megabytes, you should add an additional 16 megabytes for a total of 32 megabytes. However, if you cannot afford additional memory now, try to buy a computer with enough additional memory slots that will not require you to throw out the existing memory module to add the new larger memory module.

Your computer's video subsystem can have its own working memory, usually one to four megabytes. The more video memory in your system, the more space your video system has to work in and the faster it's likely to get images onto the screen. Larger video memory can also display more colors at a greater resolution.

Most of today's processors run much faster than the computer's memory (RAM). To reduce the amount of time a processor has to wait until data is fetched from memory, the processor uses a special area of high-speed memory known as *cache,* pronounced *cash.*

Cache is like a pants pocket. Normally we keep all of our tools in the garden shed. As we work in the garden, we stuff our most-used hand tools into our pants pocket. We don't want to keep walking back to the garden shed to get the pruners.

Modem

With the continuing growth of the information superhighway, the *modem* has become a standard computer component. A modem is a device that converts computer data into a form that can be transmitted over standard telephone lines. We'll go into more detail about modems in the next chapter.

Stuffing filing cabinets

Since working memory is volatile and subject to going blank any time the plug is pulled on the computer, we need to put anything in working memory into a semipermanent or permanent form. Also, there is a limit, both physically and economically, to the amount of physical memory that can be contained in a computer system cabinet. It's the same as with a desk. We can't keep all of our papers and books on our desk (though others may swear that we try to!). So we keep computer programs and information we do not need at a particular moment as *files,* leaving room in our computer's memory, as on the desk, to work on current projects. Disk drives and related storage devices are our computer's filing cabinets, in which we store our electronic files.

The hard disk drive

The hard disk drive is the computer's primary storage area (see Figure 3-1). It consists of one or more rigid platters coated with a magnetic material similar to that found on video and audiocassette tapes. The platters spin quickly while a recording/reading head floats just above the surface of each platter. Unlike videotape, which moves linearly, a hard disk head moves across the platter like a tone arm on a turntable. This movement allows the computer to very quickly record or read any program or data on the hard drive.

An ad listing a computer with a 1.2 gigabyte hard drive tells us the drive can store about 1.2 billion bytes of computer programs and information—about 600,000 typewritten pages! That may sound like a lot, but today's operating systems and application software can take up space very quickly. Microsoft Windows or Macintosh OS 8, along with Microsoft Office (Windows or Macintosh version), can easily take up 250 megabytes or more of storage space. Get an even larger hard disk if you will be working with CAD or multimedia, such as digital photographs, movies, or sound.

The current rule-of-thumb is to buy a hard disk drive with three times the space that you'll need just to install your software. That is, if the software you plan to install along with files that you plan to create adds up to 300 megabytes, you should get at least a 1 gigabyte hard disk drive. If you cannot afford a large hard drive now, try to buy a computer with a case large enough to accept a second hard disk drive later.

Figure 3-1
A computer hard disk drive

Floppy disk, flexible storage

Floppy disk drives are similar in operation to hard disk drives. The prime difference is that the recording/read head sits right on the media, just like the play head of an audiocassette player.

The common removable disk used in all of today's computers is a hard-shell floppy disk or diskette. The term "floppy" actually describes the flexible material inside the shell. If you break open the shell and pull the disk out, it will flop around when you pick it up. Most standard floppy disk drives and diskettes have a capacity of 1.44 megabytes.

CD-ROM

CD-ROM drives (*Compact Disc-Read Only Memory*) are standard on most new computers; you shouldn't buy a new computer without one. Because they can store 630 megabytes, or about 440 floppy diskettes, worth of data, and because they're relatively cheap, CD-ROMs have become the standard means of distributing software. One CD-ROM disc can contain an entire office suite of software (word processor, spreadsheet, database manager, presentation program), along with complete electronic versions of the user manuals, plus some clip art to fill in any leftover space.

High capacity removable media devices

As hard disk drives have become larger, new types of removable storage media have been developed to enable users to back up their gigabytes of data. Since standard 3.5-inch floppy diskettes hold 1.44 megabytes of data, creating backup copies from the now-standard 1.2 to 4 gigabyte hard disk drive would require about 600 to 1,000 diskettes. The tape drive has been a traditional means of making a duplicate copy of an entire hard drive, but two new methods have become equally popular.

Floppy-based high-capacity drives

One device for transferring and backing up large files is the Iomega Zip drive. Zip disks hold 100 megabytes, making them a good choice for transferring large amounts of data, such as scanned pictures of your garden, quickly and easily. Another new device is the 120 megabyte Imation SuperDisk LS-120 drive, which can also read and write standard 1.44 megabyte 3.5-inch floppy diskettes. Both drives are relatively inexpensive. (Remember the razor handle and razor blade analogy mentioned earlier.)

CD recorders

CD-Recordable (or CD-R) drives use a special laser to "burn" the data into a recordable compact disc. The big advantage of CD-R drives is that a CD-R disc recorded in this device can then be used in a standard CD-ROM drive.

The cost of CD-R drives has dropped considerably in the past few years. With recordable compact discs now costing only a few dollars each, CD-R drives are starting to replace tape drives for regular hard drive backup. They are also great for the gardener who wants to create a multimedia picture book of all the plants in the garden.

How Do I Communicate with the Computer?

The basic parts of a computer—processor, memory, and storage—do us no good if we can't enter information into the computer and give it commands to control it. The devices we use to enter data and control the computer are known as *input devices*. The primary input devices are the keyboard and the mouse.

Keyboards

A keyboard usually comes with the computer, like a steering wheel comes with your car. If you have a choice, get a keyboard that fits your hands, matches your work habits, and is made of quality, dependable materials. If you plan to do extensive typing with your computer, try finding one that will make typing a pleasure and not a pain.

Mice and other input creatures

The *mouse* is a small device with one to three buttons that you move around on a flat surface to select icons or menus on your screen. You point to items on your screen with the mouse cursor (usually a little arrow moved by the mouse), and you select the items by clicking on them—a process called *point and click*.

Computer mice come in a variety of sizes, shapes, and colors. Like a good pair of pruners, you'll work more efficiently with a mouse that fits comfortably in your hand. As with a cheap pair of hand pruners, the wrong mouse in the wrong position on your desk can lead to a sore or numb hand and wrist.

Trackballs (you roll a ball that sits in a cradle to point and click) and touch-sensitive pads (you move your finger on the pad to point and click) are mouse alternatives. One big advantage they offer is that they take up less space on your desk.

Other input devices

There are many other types of input devices. Scanners, digital photo cameras, video frame grabbers, and environmental sensors are some input devices that may be useful in our computer gardening activities. We will look at some of these in later chapters.

See Me! Hear Me!

Once we process information with the computer, we need some way to get the results out of the computer. The devices that show the results generated by the computer are known as *output devices*. The *video display* or *monitor* and the *printer* are the computer's prime output devices.

Video displays

A video monitor is like a television. Like televisions, monitors come in a variety of sizes from 9-inch to 25-inch diagonally measured screens, and at a range of prices. When buying a monitor, note its *resolution* and *dot pitch*.

Resolution is a measure of the sharpness or clarity of an image. The greater the resolution, the sharper or less fuzzy the image. Monitor resolution signifies the total number of pixels or dots on the screen, in pixels per row by the number of rows. (Remember the earlier mention of Seurat's work in pointillism?) A standard monitor resolution is 800 x 600, or 800 pixels by 600 rows. Some professional monitors support resolutions up to 1800 x 1440.

When selecting a monitor based on resolution, match the monitor's resolution to the video output of a computer. If your computer will generate video resolution of only 1024 x 780, you'll be wasting your money if you buy a monitor that supports higher resolutions.

A monitor's dot pitch is a measure of the vertical distance between each pixel on the monitor screen. The closer the pixels, the clearer and sharper the image, and the less we have to strain our eyes to see. You should get a monitor with a dot pitch of at least .28mm or less.

Printers

To get any output on paper, you need a printer. It is much easier to send results to a printer than to copy the information from the screen with paper and pencil.

There are three basic types of printers: impact dot matrix, inkjet, and laser. Printer resolution is measured in *dots per inch* (dpi), with higher resolutions producing sharper text and less fuzzy images.

Once the printer of choice, dot matrix printers are no longer popular. The higher quality inkjets and laser printers are now affordable for general printing purposes. However, the dot matrix printer still has its place. For the gardener, the dot matrix printer is still the best way to print on plastic plant labels.

Over the past ten years, the laser printer has been the printer of choice for the office. Using a photocopier-like technology, a laser printer "draws" the characters with a laser instead of a strong light reflecting an image from a document.

An inkjet printer is a good alternative to a laser printer. Many inkjet printers also support color printing at a fraction of the cost of color laser printers. For most home computers and for many small offices, an inkjet is a fine choice. Along with lower purchase costs, inkjets are more "eco-friendly," requiring far less power than laser printers.

When choosing which type of printer to buy, look at sample printed output to compare resolutions, and find out the cost-per-page to run the printer. Inkjet cartridges are much less expensive than laser toner cartridges, but the real question is how long a cartridge lasts. And if you can shop for a printer in person, see how it feels to operate, and how much space it will require in your office. These intangibles may end up determining how happy you are with your purchase a few months later.

Sound

Along with a high-resolution monitor and a CD-ROM drive, the sound card is an important part of the multimedia computer system. With a sound card and speakers, we can not only see the plants, but also hear the pronunciation of their tongue-twisting Latin botanical names. Many gardening reference CD-ROMs have small video movies that are useless without a sound card with which to hear the audio portion.

Most home computer systems are now sold with pre-installed sound. Some systems even connect the sound card to the modem, creating a built-in speakerphone complete with a software-based digital answering machine.

Big and Little Computers

Computers come in a variety of sizes, ranging from small hand-held devices to notebook-size portables that will fit comfortably on your lap, to full-size desktop systems with room to grow.

Desktop systems

The desktop computer is the most popular size for most computer activities. Though we can't take it into the garden, a desktop computer, like a component stereo system, is easy to change or upgrade. Desktop computers are also the most cost-effective machines for the dollar.

Notebook computers

A notebook computer is a computer crammed into a case about the size of a typical three-ring binder. We can take this computer wherever we go, including out into the garden. But this portability comes at a relatively high price, and notebooks are not very weather resistant.

Palmtops and personal organizers

Palmtops or handheld computers are about the size of a checkbook or small paperback book. They are limited to maintaining an address book, notes, and expense records, or running custom programs. Some of the newer handheld computers use a slimmed-down version of Microsoft Windows to provide some compatibility with desktop systems.

A personal organizer is a much smaller dedicated computer, more like an overgrown calculator with memory. It is usually a combination electronic address book, calendar, datebook, expense sheet, and memo pad.

Both handheld computers and personal organizers allow you to transfer information to a desktop computer. In a later chapter, we'll see how you can use a personal organizer or handheld computer to extend computing activities into the garden.

Internet TVs and network computers

A new type of computer on the market is the *Internet TV*, the sole purpose of which is to let you connect to the Internet and the World Wide Web. This dedicated computer with modem uses your home television as a monitor. It has no hard or floppy disk drive for storage.

A computer related to the Internet TV is the Network Computer or NC. An NC is a compact computer system with a fast processor, extensive memory, a small hard disk drive, and a means of connecting into a computer network. One of the visions of the proponents of network computers is to keep all software in a central place, transferring the programs to the network computer on demand. Though network computers are targeted at large corporations, they may hold promise for home use, especially when cable television providers and phone carriers start offering expanded computer networking services.

If your aim is simply to access the Internet and the World Wide Web, an Internet TV may be a low-cost alternative to buying a full computer system. However, as with cable TV and the phone system, there will be a cost to connecting into the Internet that can quickly negate any savings.

So What Do I Buy and How Much Will It Cost?

For new computer users, a good mainstream multimedia computer system is the optimum choice. Any computer configured to meet the requirements of the Microsoft Windows operating system or the Macintosh operating system will meet the requirements of most gardening software. Of course, you must make sure there is adequate software available to meet your gardening computer needs. Remember to DASSSH!

As to cost, remember that processor speed and functionality of computers are constantly increasing, while prices remain fairly stable or even drop.

When I bought my first computer in 1981, an Apple II Plus with a 6502 processor, 64k of memory, and one floppy disk drive, it cost me about $2,000. Seven years later, my IBM PS/2 50 MHz with an 80286 processor, 1 megabyte of memory, and a 30 megabyte hard disk drive, cost about $2,000. I just bought my latest home computer, a Pentium computer with 32 megabytes of memory and a 3 gigabyte hard disk drive, for $1,800—and that included a color inkjet printer!

 As a rule-of-thumb, when buying what is considered the mainstream computer at a particular point in time, the cost of the computer will usually be around $2,000. You can buy a computer at a much lower price of around $1,000, but be aware that continuing advances in software will shorten the usefulness of the budget computer.

This chapter is just an overview of the types of hardware components that comprise a computer system. When shopping for a computer system, take the time to learn more about computer hardware by reading computer magazines and introductory computer books.

Gardening by Wire

Gathering new gardening information is like watering our plants one bucket at a time. You need an electronic faucet and hose for connecting to the reservoir of gardening information, to let the information flow into your computer like water to the plants. The modem is the faucet, and communications software is the hose; you can use them to connect your computer to a network for finding new information and meeting new gardening friends.

Going online and interacting with other computers is relatively simple with current equipment. With a computer and the right setup, we can access far more information than we could ever store on our home computer. By accessing a horticulture information service we can get the information we need in minutes, compared to searching for hours through traditional paper-based references.

Telecommuting, avoiding the drive to the office by linking the home computer to the office computer network, is a growing use of computer communications. Wouldn't it be nice to sit in our home garden while "at work"? Or how about reprogramming the garden irrigation system from work because a weather radar image downloaded from the Internet says there's a good chance it will rain?

Figure 4-1
Telegarden: A remote robot garden
you can control from your computer

You can even plant a distant garden with a robot! Engineering scientists with the University of Southern California have developed a garden area that anyone can plant and maintain by controlling a robotic arm from a computer anywhere in the world, as long as the computer is connected to the Internet as shown in Figure 4-1.

Going online offers lots of possibilities. For now, let's focus on how to connect our electronic faucet to the electronic pipelines known as networks and that monster reservoir, the Internet.

Connecting to the World with Modems

The device you need to tap into the phone system and connect to another computer or computer network is a *modem*. A modem converts (*mo*dulates) computer signals into a form that can be transmitted through the phone system. The modem also converts (*de*modulates) signals from the phone system back into a form understandable by the computer.

A bit of speed

Modems have different speeds. The standard measure for data transmission speed is *bits per second* or *bps*. All of today's modems transmit and receive at speeds in thousands of bits or kilobits (k). Currently, 33.6k bps modems have become standard, with 56k modems rapidly taking over that position. You should buy the fastest modem you can afford, because transmission speeds keep increasing and the phone lines keep getting better. The faster the transmission speed, the quicker you can grab files from the network, and the less time you'll need to spend online.

There is one caveat, though: You may run into speed bumps and rough roads along the way to the information highway. Old telephone lines, archaic switching systems, and too many phone customers trying to get online may prevent your modem from connecting at its fastest speed, or from connecting at all.

Just the fax!

Most modems sold today are fax modems—they let you send a document directly from your computer to a fax machine or another fax modem. The faxes sent by fax modems are often of better quality than the ones you can send with a fax machine.

Inside or outside?

Modems come as internal cards and external boxes. Most new home computers include an internal modem, but if your computer doesn't have a modem, you have a choice to make.

An internal modem plugs into a slot or connector inside the computer. When the modem is not in use, it can share the phone line with your telephone. An internal modem offers less clutter on your desk, with fewer cables and no blinking plastic boxes.

An external modem sits outside the computer and connects to one of its ports with a cable. If you have several computers or an older computer that cannot accept an internal modem, an external modem is a cost-effective means of connecting. Then, as you upgrade computers, you

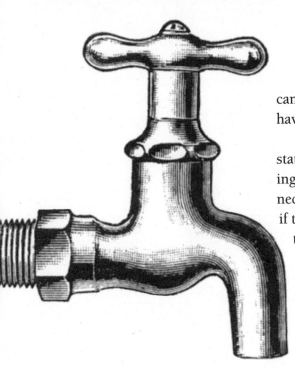

can just move the external modem to the new computer without having to open the CPU's case.

One advantage of most external modems is that they have status lights that indicate if the modem is transferring data or waiting for a response. Call waiting, for example, can quickly disconnect a modem from a phone line even though the computer acts as if there is still a connection—and you're left waiting for something to happen while the phone bill keeps getting bigger.

Coming soon!

Several new modem technologies and networks that promise faster speeds and intensive multimedia support will be in place in the near future.

ISDN

Short for *integrated services digital network*, ISDN is an international standard that supports voice, video, and data over telephone lines. You may have received advertisements in your phone bill for ISDN services. ISDN promises transmission speeds up to 1.5 megabits per second.

Currently, ISDN services are limited to major metropolitan areas. The connection is expensive, and requires a special modem; thus, standard modems are more cost effective for most gardeners.

ADSL

Short for *asymmetric digital subscriber line,* ADSL is an emerging technology that may supplant ISDN and cable modems. ADSL will permit downloading data, including video and voice, to your computer at speeds up to 9 megabits per second and upload from your computer at speeds of 800 kilobits per second. Since most Internet and World Wide Web use involves downloading data, this unbalanced, "asymmetric" method may be the most cost-effective.

Industry pundits predict the equipment costs for ADSL will be the same as today's standard modems that only transmit and receive as speeds of 56 kilobits per second. We should see this new technology emerging around the year 2000.

Cable modems

Like standard modems, cable modems convert computer signals into a form that can be sent over cable TV networks. Many cable television networks now support two-way transmissions, with more being upgraded to do so. However, access is still limited, so don't discard your standard modem yet.

Wireless modems

Wireless modems connect without wires or through cellular telephones. While expensive, the technology is in place for us to take a small handheld computer with a wireless modem into our gardens, while keeping in touch with the larger desktop computer in the house.

Communications Software

Communications software lets you send and receive data and files. With some communications programs, your computer acts only as the keyboard and video monitor for another computer system connected to yours via the modem. With other communications programs, the distant computer will send you data that your computer must finish processing.

Terminal programs

Almost all communications programs allow you to send (upload) data and receive (download or capture) data. Terminal programs are multipurpose communications programs that let you access many different computers and networks. You can use the same terminal program to access a computer at work, a bulletin board system on a computer across the country, or some commercial online services. (See Figure 4-2 on page 68.)

With terminal programs, all of the processing is done by the host computer. A terminal program displays only what is sent by the host computer and transmits only input from your computer. There is no real processing taking place on your computer when you are using a terminal program.

Figure 4-2
A terminal display of an online
library catalog. All of the formatting
on the screen was done by the
host computer, 6 miles away

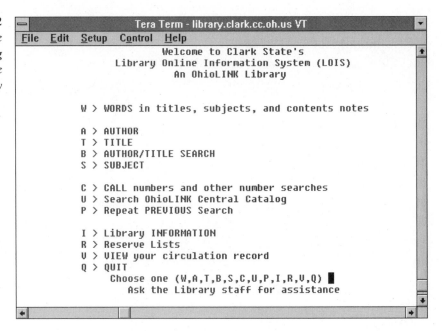

The major commercial online services and most *Internet service providers* (ISPs) require specialized communications software designed specifically to access them. You will need different software to access each commercial online service. The major ones give this software to you for free—then you pay to connect. Internet service providers usually include the cost of software in the startup fee you pay when you sign up.

Tapping into the Internet

To connect to the Internet, you will need a *dialer* or dial-up utility. In Windows 95, this is called dial-up networking.

The dialer is typically a small program that connects you to the Internet. Once you're connected, it sits in the background while you use other programs for accessing the different services available on the Internet (see Figure 4-3). Such programs might include an e-mail program, a Web browser, a newsgroup reader, or a special program that updates the weather forecast for you.

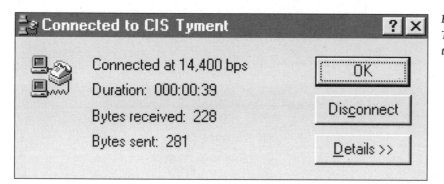

Where can you find communications software?

Most operating systems include a simple telecommunications program; Windows 95 and later versions, along with Macintosh OS 8, also include dial-up networking programs and other Internet-related software. Most modem manufacturers ship their products with general purpose communications software, as well as the software you'll need to connect to the major commercial online services or the Internet. "Works" programs have a simple communications module—sufficient to get you online to download more sophisticated programs.

In addition to the above, there are also numerous freeware and shareware communications programs and utilities that you can find online. Many of these are quite sophisticated, with features equaling or exceeding those of some commercial programs.

The Seeds of Online Gardening: The BBS

A *bulletin board system* (BBS) is like a cork bulletin board where you can post, read, and retrieve messages or files. Most BBSs also have areas where you can find files, such as shareware and freeware programs, that you can download for the price of a phone call. Some systems support multiple modem connections, which allows you to *chat* live with other people accessing the BBS—you type in messages and they type back to you.

Figure 4-4
A vendor bulletin board for
downloading software updates

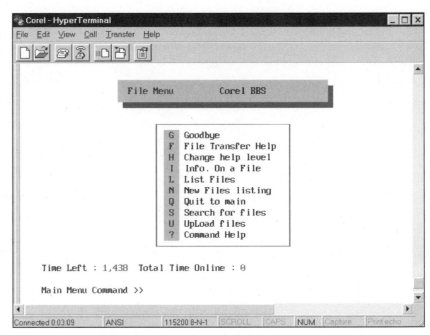

Most BBSs focus on a special interest or area. I often used to visit a BBS for golf course superintendents. Many computer software and hardware companies have bulletin board systems to provide technical support and software updates (see Figure 4-4). Although the Internet and the commercial online services have become the preferred source for technical support, many companies still support a BBS.

In the 1970s and 1980s, BBSs were very popular, numbering in the tens of thousands. Callers could access most BBSs for the cost of their phone call. There were several gardening BBSs around the country, including a few supported by government agencies. However, with the growth of online services and the Internet, many bulletin board systems, including most gardening BBSs, have disappeared or have been converted into Web sites.

Commercial Online Services

Commercial online services are networks of computers offering proprietary services and Internet access for a fee. All provide access to a large number of different information resources, such as news services, reference databases, airline travel guides, and weather and stock market information, as well as special interest areas for gardeners. Here's where gardeners have gathered and gardening activities have been discussed for the past several years.

CompuServe

CompuServe was one of the first commercial online services. While not the largest, it is still one of the most organized and flexible. One of its strengths is a well-organized group of special interest areas known as *forums*.

A forum is a combination of message board, bulletin board, file libraries, and chat areas called conferences. A forum administrator and one or more system operators or *sysops* manage each forum. Sysops offer assistance to forum members, moderate messages and conferences, manage messages and files, and perform other housekeeping (garden keeping?) chores.

In a forum, both the message board and the file libraries have several *sections*, each covering a more specialized topic or interest. In many of the forums, the section name in the message board also matches the section name of a file library. For example, in the Gardening Forum (Go GARDEN), Section 12: Lawns/Turf in the message board has a matching Library 12: Lawns/Turf, which contains additional files related to lawn care. (See Figure 4-5 on page 72.)

 In CompuServe, to access a forum or other special interest area, you use the GO command. In the older terminal mode, you would type a command go goodearth to reach the Good Earth forum. With the newer software, you click on a green stoplight or select GO from a menu and enter an abbreviated forum name in a dialog box.

CompuServe's highly organized forums and libraries let you focus on a particular area. If your main interest is vegetable gardens, you can quickly jump to the sections related to vegetable gardening. Since my work interest is turfgrass management and computers, I usually hang around the lawn care and garden soft-

Figure 4-5
The CompuServe Gardening
Forum showing some of the section
names along with other features

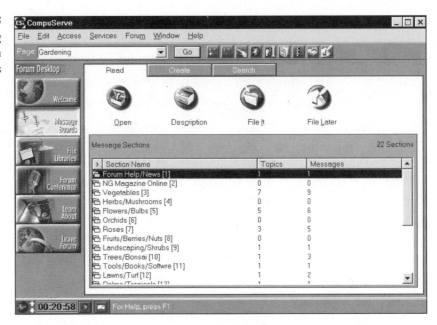

ware message sections. Other message boards, particularly those on the Internet, often lump all messages into one area.

CompuServe's main gardening forums are The Gardening Forum (Go GARDEN) and the UK Gardening Forum (Go UKGARDFOR). Several other forums have one or more sections devoted to gardening, including the California Forum (Go CALIFOR) and the Florida Forum (Go FLORIDA). These regional sections are very helpful if you need assistance on plants that grow in your particular area.

CompuServe supports offline readers—special programs that you can use to quickly do your business on CompuServe and log off. Two popular ones are OZCIS and OZWin (Go OZWIN) and TAPCIS (Go TAPCIS). You set up the offline reader to log on and download all your mail, forum messages, and files; it then disconnects you from the service. You can read and reply to messages at your leisure, without paying connect charges.

The software supplied by CompuServe will download forum messages for offline reading, but it won't do so automatically. While an offline reader might take one or two minutes to get all the messages and log off, it might take you 10 minutes to mark the messages you want to download using the general CompuServe software. If you read and reply to a lot of messages in the gardening forums, invest in a second-party offline reader. You will end up spending as much time in the CompuServe gardens with an offline reader as you will going online manually, but you will use your online time more effectively.

America Online

America Online (AOL) appeared in the late 1980s and has grown like zucchini ever since. AOL is now the largest commercial online service in the United States. Much of AOL's success is due to its easy-to-use graphical software and strong marketing.

AOL's strength is in providing a wide variety of content that may be of interest to anyone in your home. For example, as an avid bicyclist, I regularly visit *Bicycling Magazine Online* (Keyword: **bicycling**) for up-to-the-minute news and information on bicycling.

*At America Online, every place has a keyword assigned to it. To go to a place without clicking through several menu screens, select the menu item **Go To Keyword**, enter the keyword into a dialog box, and press the **GO** button.*

AOL does not have a highly organized forum structure for special interest areas. Rather, a special interest area can be a mix of references, message boards, file libraries, and chat areas. Some special interest areas may have only references pertaining to a topic, while other special interest areas will provide a wide range of services.

AOL's prime area of interest to gardeners is The Garden Spot (Keyword: **Garden**), with message boards, links to garden Web sites, and some online magazines (see Figure 4-6 on page 74). There is no file library in The Garden Spot; to download gardening-oriented software, go to AOL's main software library area and browse the Home and Garden software list for titles that interest you.

America Online's message boards store messages in folders. The Gardening Message Center folder shown in Figure 4-7 on page 74 contains a wide variety of topics (almost 100 at last count), although some of the topics are similar.

Figure 4-6
The gardening resource
area on America Online

Figure 4-7
One of two gardening message
centers on AOL's The Garden Spot

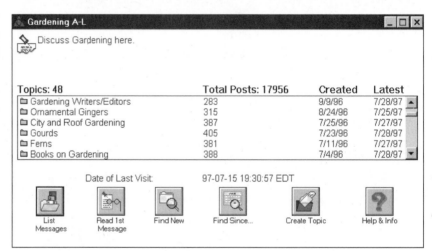

Several special interest areas also provide gardening resources. *Woman's Day* magazine's "Ideas for Better Living" contains a section on gardening, including additional references, message boards, a file library, and a chat area.

To access AOL, you must use AOL's software. Everything is done online (there are no offline readers), which poses a problem for anyone who has to make a long distance call to AOL or use a surcharged AOLnet 800 number. While AOL charges a monthly flat rate for unlimited access, you still have to bear the cost of connecting to AOL if you cannot make a local phone call.

Fortunately, you can access AOL through the Internet, though of course you will still have to pay to access the Internet through an Internet service provider. Still, if there's no local AOL number in your area, the flat monthly rate for most local ISPs will probably be much less than the long distance charges or surcharges you might incur otherwise. Also, a local ISP may connect to AOL faster than an AOL access number.

Microsoft Network

A relative newcomer to major online services, Microsoft Network (MSN) has grown very quickly thanks to the backing of Microsoft, one of the largest and most influential computer companies in the world. MSN appeared with the release of the Windows 95 operating system. At this writing, you can access MSN only with Windows 95.

MSN has several different gardening areas. In fact, it has the largest variety of gardening interest areas of the major online services, including forums, BBSs, chat areas, and file libraries. Classic MSN (an earlier version still included with Windows 95) offers about 100 topics in Gardening A-to-Z, while the newer MSN 2.5 (which integrates with the World Wide Web) offers many more. (See Figure 4-8 on page 76.)

Like America Online and CompuServe, you can access MSN through Microsoft's dial-up network or through an ISP. MSN also provides Internet services at a rate comparable to CompuServe and other Internet service providers although, as of this writing, the number of local access points is still limited. If you don't have local access to MSN, check to see if you can get to it through your ISP before signing up.

Though MSN offers many features of interest to the gardener, you won't be able to access it if you don't use Windows 95. Its lack of sufficient local access phone numbers limits its accessibility to gardeners even further.

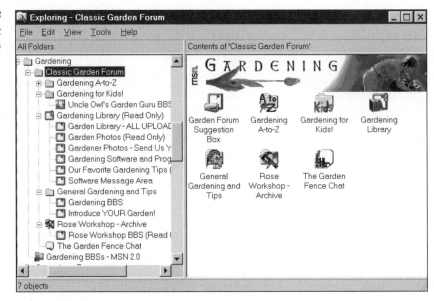

Figure 4-8
Gardening on the Microsoft
Network (MSN Classic)

To get a sampling of MSN's features, visit their Web site at
http://www.msn.com.

Prodigy

The Prodigy online service's offerings come in two forms: Prodigy
Classic and Prodigy Internet. Prodigy Classic is the online service
most comparable to AOL and CompuServe, and it offers similar
services. As with AOL, you can access Prodigy Classic only with
Prodigy's proprietary software.

Prodigy Classic's limited array of services, features, and content
coupled with outdated software places it way below the other online
services in usefulness. The Prodigy Classic software is not as easy to
use as that of either CompuServe or AOL. While Prodigy Classic
offers a gardening bulletin board, chat area, and some integrated
Web pages, compared with the other online services it looks like a
flower suffering from severe fertilizer deficiency. (See Figure 4-9.)

Prodigy Internet, on the other hand, is a full Web-based online
service. Unlike Prodigy Classic, which uses proprietary software,
Prodigy Internet uses a standard Web browser. Using a Web
browser, you can travel between Prodigy's proprietary Web-based

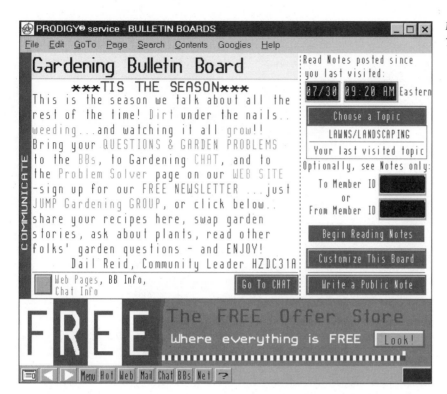

Figure 4-9
The Gardening BBS on Prodigy Classic

content and Web sites outside of the Prodigy service. The Green Thumb Web site (shown in Figure 4-10 on page 78) is Prodigy's proprietary Web-based gardening content area.

> *All of the commercial online services, not just Prodigy, are shifting to a Web browser instead of a proprietary program to access their service. To keep anyone from looking at their content, an extra module is added to the browser to identify you as a paying member. Without the module and some other security features, you cannot view their content even on the very public Internet.*

Consider Prodigy Internet if you plan to focus your online travels mostly on Internet-based gardening content. Also, for small to medium size cities, Prodigy may be your best choice for local access to the Internet.

You can find additional information and startup software at the Prodigy Internet Web site (**http://www.prodigy.com**). Prodigy

Figure 4-10
The Green Thumb gardening
forum Web site available
through Prodigy Internet

Classic client software is available direct from Prodigy. If you buy a new computer, you might find the Prodigy software included on the hard disk drive, along with software from the other online services.

Which Online Services to Till?

With all of the online services offering gardening forums and related information, it may be difficult to choose. If you are new to computers, consider America Online as a first step, although their gardening content is eclectic. CompuServe, with its strong forum structure complete with message boards, bulletin boards, file libraries, and chat areas, is great if you want to do your online gardening all in one place. MSN's garden content is strong and should continue to expand rapidly. Prodigy Internet is a renewed contender and may provide the best Internet access among the commercial online services for some of you in smaller communities.

To check out each service's gardening resources, request a free trial membership from the service. And remember, as you explore the various gardening forums and communities online, these electronic garden clubs share the same social and political dynamics found in any old-fashioned garden club. The ebb and flow of personalities occurs as much online as it does in person. Tread carefully and enjoy yourself.

The Internet: Access to the Global Garden

The *Internet* is a worldwide network of computer networks, connected in a way that enables individual networks to easily transfer information. The Internet is a lot like the telephone system that connects various telephone companies (Ameritech, United Telephone, Rural Telephone Service, Bell Atlantic) and carriers (Sprint, MCI, AT&T) to form a worldwide telephone network.

The Internet is not a place, but a means of getting to other computers, just as the interstate highway system is a way to travel between cities. Instead of traveling on pavement, we travel the network cabling of the information highway.

The Internet began as a small group of universities who wanted to share data and information on Department of Defense research projects. They did so by connecting their networks. With all of these university networks connected to form a larger network, the researchers could access information on computers across the country.

Gradually, more universities and some corporations connected their networks to this larger network and the network expanded. The early 1990s saw explosive growth in the Internet, as it grew to become an independent entity, supported, managed, and funded by a loosely knit consortium of universities, businesses, and government agencies.

Much of the Internet's growth came when the initial group of universities and corporations agreed on a set of rules (called *protocols*) for transmitting data between their networks. With consistent rules, even individuals (with the right equipment) could connect to the Internet.

The Internet grew because it was perceived as free. Countless students at universities connected to the Internet found that they could send messages and files to people at other universities at no cost (the university was paying), and they were hooked. As these students have graduated and moved into the workforce, they have encouraged their employers to "get on the Net."

The Internet can also provide access to bulletin boards and electronic mail without the long-distance phone charges or commercial online service access charges. In many communities, Internet access is just a local call away.

How the networks talk on the Internet

Before we can start cruising the information highway to all sorts of gardens and gardening sites, we need to spend some time in Internet driver's ed so we don't end up getting lost in our travels.

Internet protocols: How networks talk to each other

All networks on the Internet follow an *Internet Protocol* (IP), a set of rules that network operators follow to allow information to move across through the Internet. A companion protocol, TCP/IP or *Transfer Control Protocol/Internet Protocol,* is the way data moves from a single computer into a network on the Internet. All computers connected to the Internet must use software that supports TCP/IP.

What's the address?

All computers and networks connected to the Internet have an *IP address,* which is just like a "phone number" or "street address" on the Internet. When you dial into an Internet network, even your computer is assigned a temporary IP address. The Internet uses your IP address to find your computer and send information with your address on it, just like the post office uses your address on a letter to get it to your house.

Domains

Because IP Addresses are a series of numbers, computers connected to the Internet also have a *domain name.* While the IP address for No Starch Press is 205.162.14.83, its domain name is www.nostarch.com. Domain names are much easier to remember.

A *Domain Name Server* or DNS is what converts the numeric IP address to the domain name and vice versa. A domain name server is a computer that translates domain names into IP addresses, like an electronic phonebook. So when you get a weird message like *Site not found* or *DNS cannot resolve the host name,* you can start looking for the reason—usually you mistyped the name or the DNS was busy looking up IP addresses for someone else.

Hooking into the Internet

You can connect to the Internet through an existing network (at work or school), or through your modem. If your work or school computer is networked but you cannot access the Internet, speak with the network administrator about possible access.

 Remember when you are using the Internet from work or school that someone is paying for the connection. Be aware of all policies and procedures for connecting to the Internet, and follow them.

A more common way to connect to the Internet is by dialing into an ISP, using your modem. An ISP has one or more modems connected to a computer known as a *gateway,* which in turn has a direct connection into the Internet.

You should have little trouble finding an ISP. They are appearing everywhere, ranging from small operations run by a local computer store or computer club to the global telecommunications companies of AT&T, Sprint, and MCI. Just about any new computer you buy today will include trial software for the major ISPs.

The commercial online services have embraced the Internet in a big way. If you don't want to struggle with getting connected through an ISP, try one of the commercial online services. Besides providing a wide range of their own content, these services now offer seamless integration with the Internet. If you already have an account with a commercial online service, you also have access to the Internet.

With any ISP, there is going to be a cost to connect. Some offer a flat-rate monthly fee, while others have an initial flat rate for a set number of hours, followed by an additional charge for each extra hour. Try to find a local ISP so that you won't incur long-distance phone charges when you dial in. Consider, too, that it may be cheaper to access the commercial online services through the Internet.

When shopping for an ISP, be careful about choosing one just because it has the lowest price. Many small, local ISPs have a limited number of modems or a slow connection into the Internet. You may end up paying for busy signals or very slow file transfer rates, which could end up costing you more in the long run. As with landscaping services, it pays to shop around for the best, not necessarily the cheapest, service.

Doing the electronic plumbing

If you are new to connecting to the Internet, a commercial online service may be your best route. You will receive excellent software for getting online and, while the cost may be higher than going with a local ISP, connecting to the Internet may be much easier. In addition, you'll also get access to the service's own support and content. Then, once you are familiar with the Internet, you can consider going with a pure ISP. On the other hand, if you mostly want Internet access, a standard ISP may prove more cost effective. You may want to hang on to the online service as a backup in case your ISP goes down or if you travel—the commercial services will probably provide the most local access points wherever you land.

Now that the electronic plumbing is in place, let's travel the world for new gardens!

5

Gardening Around the World

Every day, it seems, we see or hear the statement, "Visit our Web site!" with an odd-looking address that starts with "http:// ." The Internet is a major new communications medium. Many prognosticators predict it will replace television as our society's central communications medium. From articles in the newspapers and newsmagazines, there are already indications that many people are spending more time on a computer than watching television.

The piece of the Internet that has attracted the most interest is the *World Wide Web*, commonly called "the Web." The Web is the Internet's prime resource for gardening information.

The Web offers gardeners tens of thousands of different resources, including extension bulletins, how-to gardening articles, plant references, online ordering of next year's seeds and bulbs, and much more. Several of the top seed companies and mail-order nurseries keep a presence on the Internet, including full-color catalogs and online ordering. Now we can really let "our fingers do the walking" when shopping for gardening products.

Before we delve too much into the Web and its gardening Web sites, we need to have a basic understanding of the Web so we don't get tangled up in it.

The World Wide Web

The genesis of the Web was in the mid-1980s when a computer scientist, Ted Nelson, predicted that all documents would one day be available in electronic form, with every document linked in some way to other related documents. The word "soil," for instance, would be linked to electronic soil science textbooks and scientific articles on soils. If you needed to expand your knowledge of soils, you could click on the word "soil" and another document would appear with more detailed information. Any text that had links to other text was called *hypertext*. At the time, the technology was not yet in place to bring Dr. Nelson's concept of hypertext to a network, but it began to be used in programs to link one section of data to another, especially in computer-assisted instruction software.

In 1989, Tim Berners-Lee, a scientist involved in high-energy physics projects, proposed a way to link research documents across the Internet. This was the beginning of the World Wide Web, a set of communications and system software that resides on the Internet. When you look at a graphical representation of all the hypertext linking of documents across the Internet, it indeed appears like a spider's web.

The real growth in the World Wide Web began with the development of Web applications that could display both graphics and text. Instead of having just hypertext, we now have *hypermedia* where not only text, but also pictures, sounds, and video can have links to other types of media. This means a Web document can display a map of your garden with links to other Web documents containing written descriptions of the plants in your garden.

A unique feature of the World Wide Web is this ability to link documents. Linked documents can be on the same computer, across several computers within a network, or across several networks within the Internet. The World Wide Web is truly a global phenomenon. You can just as easily visit the Royal Botanic Gardens at Kew, England (**http://www.rbgkew.org.uk/**), shown in Figure 5-1, as the Missouri Botanical Garden in St. Louis (**http://www.mobot.org/info.html**) and the Australian National Botanical Gardens (**http://155.187.10.12/anbg/**).

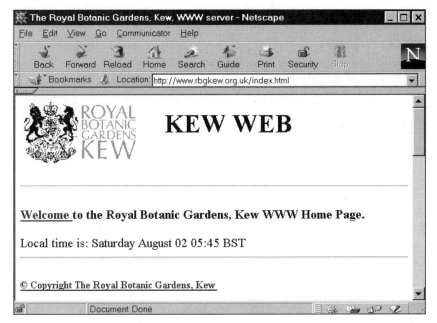

Figure 5-1
Gardens around the world right from home! Visiting The Royal Botanic Gardens at Kew, England, from the Midwest United States

All components of the Web follow rules for formatting, browsing, and transfer of Web documents, to allow access and viewing on a variety of computer systems. Regardless of whether you own a Windows PC or a Macintosh, you should be able to view basic Web documents, no matter what type of computer is sending out (serving) the Web pages.

Where's the Web?

The Web is a collection of *Web sites,* each of which is a collection of linked documents. Web sites are created using tools that work like word processors to insert graphics and embed links, and then they are posted to the Internet for anyone to read.

Usually, one viewable document on the Web is a *Web page* even though the document would be several pages long if it were printed. A *home page* is the first Web page, "title page," "magazine cover," or starting point to a Web site. To view Web pages and navigate to different linked Web pages requires a *Web browser.*

Web site addresses: The URL

To visit a Web site or a single Web page, you need to know its Web address or URL, the *Uniform Resource Locator* (pronounced "U-R-L," not "earl" or "ural").

The URL is composed of three parts. Once you know what the different parts mean, you will understand how to interpret and use a Web address. You'll know what to do when you get weird error messages like *Site is not in a DNS* or *Page not found.*

The URL for the Missouri Botanical Garden's Web site is **http://www.mobot.org/info.html**. Let's dissect it.

> *The first part,* http://, tells the server how to access the page. The letters *http* stand for *hypertext transfer protocol*, which tells the server how to transfer the hyperlinked Web page. Another protocol, ftp://, tells the server to use *file transfer protocol* to upload or download a file.
>
> *The second part of the URL,* www.mobot.org, is the name of the computer where the Web pages reside. In this case, it is found within the domain of mobot.org.
>
> *The last part,* /info.html, is the name of the file containing the Web page.

When you want to visit a specific Web page, it is very important to type in the correct address. Pay attention to the type of slash you use; you'll almost always use the forward slash (/), rather than the backward slash (\), commonly used on PC computers to change directories. Type the address incorrectly and you'll probably get an error message like *"Site not found."*

Crisscrossing the Web with a browser

Web browsers are document viewers. All have a similar look and set of controls for moving around the World Wide Web. Regardless of the type of computer you own, there is likely a Web browser for it. There are even text-based Web browsers for older computers that cannot display graphics.

While several different browsers exist, the two most popular are Netscape Navigator from the Netscape Corporation and Microsoft Internet Explorer from Microsoft. Any new computer or modem you buy these days will come with at least one of these browsers; you may well have one already. You can download other browsers from the Internet.

Quick Clicks on Using a Web Browser

The Web browsers in Figure 5-2 on page 90 show the typical controls found on all Web browsers:

Navigation

Your browser keeps a record of the Web sites you visit. If you're visiting one page and you click on a link to go to another page, the **Back** button brings you back to where you were. To return to the page that you just left, click the **Forward** button. If the page you're visiting didn't come through okay, click the **Reload** button to transfer it again. Click **Home** to go directly to your browser's starting page and **Stop** to stop the downloading of a page from the server.

URL: (also Address:, Location:, Go To:)

If someone tells you to visit their Web site at **http://www.mygarden. Web**, enter the address in this field (sometimes labeled Go To:) and press ENTER.

Page display

The center of the window displays the Web page. If the Web page is larger than the viewable screen area, you can use the scroll bar on the right side and bottom of the window to move around the page. Many Web sites use frames to split the window into two or more window panes, each pane with its own Web page.

Links

The underlined text shown in Figure 5-2, Location, Hours and Admission, Featured Pages, and Download Center, are links to

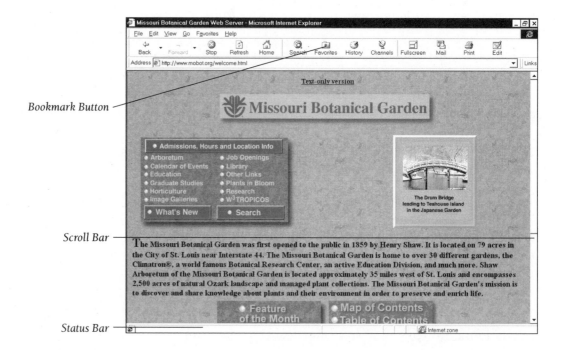

Figure 5-2
Two popular Web browsers with
similar controls but different layouts

Bookmark Button

Scroll Bar

Status Bar

Bookmark Button

Scroll Bar

Status Bar

other Web pages. Placing your mouse pointer over a link changes the cursor arrow () to a pointing finger ( ) to show that it is a link. Some buttons on Web pages are linked but not underlined, like the **Education**, **Horticulture**, and **Research** buttons to the right of the photograph showing the Climatron geodesic dome.

Status bar

The status bar at the bottom of the browser window displays assorted information, depending on the activity. In the figure, the status bar shows the underlying URL to the Featured Pages link. Other items displayed in the status bar include a timer and download status to show you how much longer it will take to download a page or images from the server and the size of the downloading page or image. If transferring the page or image is taking too long, you can use the **Stop** button to halt the current transfer, and display only what the browser has so far received from the Web server.

Other items

Depending on the browser, you will find a number of additional controls, button bars, and menus. The most useful one is the Bookmark button in Netscape and Favorites button in Internet Explorer. These are lists of Web sites you've visited and want to keep track of, hence their names. When you find a Web site you want to revisit, select the **Add bookmark** or **Add favorite** command to save the URL of the Web page you are viewing.

Finding Web Pages

The World Wide Web is a vast body of information that grows and changes daily. Web sites appear, grow, mature, and disappear as quickly as weeds. There are too many Web pages to visit them all, but you don't have to. To find what you want on the Web, you can use search sites, called search engines or Web guides (see Table 5-1 on page 92).

Once at these search sites, you enter a keyword or keywords to describe what you're looking for, like "garden pests," and start the search. The search site then goes to work, returning a list of links that may or may not be relevant. Each site searches the Web, indexes the links, and displays the results differently. Because of this, you will probably want to use different search engines at different times.

Table 5-1
Several popular Web search sites (search engines and Web guides)

SEARCH ENGINES

AltaVista	http://altavista.digital.com
Hot Bot	http://www.hotbot.com
AOL NetFind	http://www.aol.com/netfind
Electric Library	http://www.elibrary.com
WebCrawler	http://webcrawler.com

WEB GUIDES

Yahoo!	http://www.yahoo.com
Excite	http://www.excite.com
Infoseek	http://www.infoseek.com
Lycos	http://www.lycos.com
CNET Search.com	http://www.search.com
LookSmart	http://www.looksmart.com

SEARCH ENGINE OF WEB SEARCH SITES

Metacrawler	http://www.metacrawler.com

Search engines search the entire World Wide Web, creating a massive index of just about every word in every accessible Web page. Using a search engine is like going through a computer-generated and unedited index at the back of a book, in which every occurrence of the word you are looking for is cited, whether it is important or completely trivial. On the other hand, *Web guides,* a different sort of search tool, search the Web and organize the results by topic, keyword, or category—more like a professionally written index. Using a Web guide is also like going through the catalog in the library, where you start with a general topic and work your way to more specific subjects. *Topic-specific* Web search sites list Web sites that match a particular interest, such as gardening. These sites may also have an internal search engine to look for specific topics, such as water gardening.

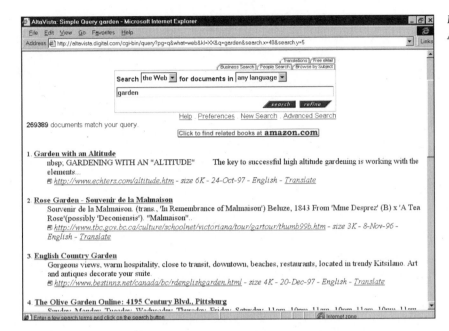

Figure 5-3
A search engine query of the word "garden"

Search engines like AltaVista and Hot Bot will list any Web page containing the search words. So a search using the term "garden" will return a list of actual gardening Web sites, along with the Web sites of the musical group Soundgarden; the town Garden City, Kansas; and the arena Madison Square Garden. General terms, like "garden," will generate thousands of results—over 300,000 if you type "garden" as a search query in AltaVista (see Figure 5-3).

When using search engines, think first and use thoughtful queries to refine your search. Use specific terms first. If you want to know more about water gardening, use the terms "water gardening" or "hydroponics," rather than the general term "gardening."

To look for Web pages containing both "community" and "garden," enclose your search words in quotes, as shown in Figure 5-4 on page 94. The more specific your terms, the narrower the results, with one caveat: if you use too many words or your search is too specific, you may get no results.

Unlike search engines, Web guides are less prone to erroneous hits. Like library catalogs, sites are reviewed and categorized. So, for example, to find information on community gardens, you might

Figure 5-4
A search engine query of the
phrase: "community gardens"

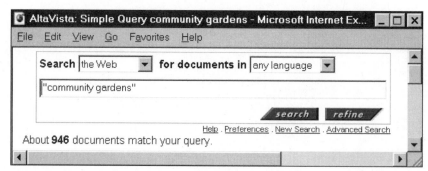

Figure 5-5
A Web guide hierarchy of
topics for community gardens

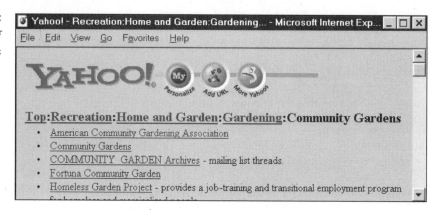

start at the highest topic level, *Recreation;* work down to the next topic level, *Home and Garden;* and then to *Gardening;* and finally *Community Gardens,* as shown in Figure 5-5.

You can search Web guides just like the search engines, but the results are usually limited to the Web guide's catalog of sites. Web guides may be a good place to start for your first search on a topic because they filter out the clutter, and they usually display the newest sites within a category.

Search engines are best if you want to "fish" for Web sites, casting out a keyword to see what shows up. I use search engines to explore new topics or to find out the breadth of coverage on a particular topic. Used wisely, search engines can be very effective investigative tools. But use them carefully, as they often find unrelated Web sites or out-of-date, dead links, where there will be no Web site at the end of the link when you click.

Popular Gardening Sites on the World Wide Web

You can visit several Web sites to start your gardening tour on the Web. The text that follows lists nine of the more popular ones; most have links to other gardening and horticulture-related sites. Because the Web is so dynamic, remember that these sites are just a few of the many sites available, and their look, content, and even addresses are all subject to change.

If there is a Web address change, the old address should link to the new one. If you do end up with a dead link, search one of the other garden Web sites for an updated address.

You'll find many more sites listed in The Gardener's Internet Yellow Pages. These are just some of the favorites among many who garden on the Web.

Figure 5-6
The Garden Gate

The Garden Gate

http://www.prairienet.org/garden-gate

The Garden Gate (Figure 5-6) was one of the first major Web sites devoted to gardening, and Web administrator Karen Fletcher constantly updates it with new resources. She also writes a regular gardening column on The GardenWeb Web site (**http://www.gardenweb.com**).

Entering The Garden Gate is like walking into a well-stocked gardening library. The site is arranged by area. Among the areas are The Gardener's Reading Room, where you can read online publications; The Sun Room, for indoor plant gardeners; Down the Garden Path, where you can visit garden sites around the world;

and Mailing Lists and Newsgroups, for gardeners who don't get enough to read from their e-mail.

I like The Garden Gate's minimal use of graphics in its first few pages—a blessing if you have a slow modem or when there is heavy traffic on the Internet.

Figure 5-7
GardenWeb

GardenWeb

http://www.gardenweb.com

The GardenWeb (Figure 5-7) is like a garden magazine with articles, tip sheets, calendars, contests, merchant directories, and meeting rooms. Like The Garden Gate, it uses few graphics in its first few pages, focusing instead on easy-to-read content and useful links.

Features include The GardenWeb Forums, where you can post messages and discuss gardening with other gardeners; The Garden Exchange, for requesting seeds or items to trade; and The Green-Leaves Bookstore. You'll also find links to Gardens of the World.

GardenWeb also has European forums in English, French, German, and Italian as well as a GardenWeb site in Australia if you want to go Down Under.

Figure 5-8
Joe & Mindy's Web Garden

Joe & Mindy's Web Garden
http://www.nhn.ou.edu/~howard/garden.html

Joe & Mindy's Web Garden (Figure 5-8) has been around for a
few years, and it's a good starting point for traveling to other garden Web sites. Run by two amateur gardeners who work at the
University of Oklahoma in astronomy and chemistry, it includes
links with small site descriptions. The site's graphics are colorful,
but small enough to keep Web page downloading time to a minimum. It's a fun site to visit.

Figure 5-9
WebGarden at Ohio State University

WebGarden
http://www.hcs.ohio-state.edu/hcs/webgarden.html

WebGarden (Figure 5-9) is managed by Dr. Tim Rhodus and students of the Horticulture and Crop Science Department at Ohio
State University. As a university Web site, it provides a useful collection of reference materials for both students and gardeners,
including most notably a comprehensive, searchable plant dictionary complete with photographs. While developed for primarily for
students in a plant materials course, it's a great tool for selecting
new plants.

Another of its useful features is a searchable database of nearly
10,000 fact sheets and bulletins from various extension services
around the United States and Canada. Some of the fact sheets are
text-based, which you can read through your Web browser; others
are portable documents that require a special reader, but which
provide an almost perfect copy of the original version, complete
with formatting and graphics.

For those in the Ohio or Midwest region surrounding Ohio, the
site also contains every issue of Buckeye Yard and Garden Line
(BYGL, which they tell me is pronounced "beagle"). The BYGL is a

weekly summary by OSU horticulture extension specialists of growing conditions, pests, and cultural problems that occur during the growing season.

SEE CD-ROM

Most portable documents found on the Web are Adobe Acrobat Portable Document Format (PDF) files. They overcome the limited formatting of Web pages. PDF files retain the same look as the original printed version but can be displayed on a variety of computers, including Windows, Macintosh, and UNIX systems. A Windows version of the Acrobat Reader is on the CD. You can download other versions from Adobe's Web site (http://www. adobe.com/acrobat).

Figure 5-10
Gardening-"Dot"-com

Gardening.com
http://www.gardening.com

Gardening.com (Figure 5-10) is the companion Web site to Books That Work, a home and garden software subsidiary of Sierra On-Line (**http://www.sierra.com**). Two flagship products for gardeners from BTW are a landscape-planning program, 3D Landscape, and a gardening reference, The Garden Encyclopedia. The site's three main features are a plant encyclopedia, a garden site directory, and the revived Ortho Problem Solver. The site also has links to yellow pages of garden suppliers and a magazine rack of gardening magazines on the Web.

The plant encyclopedia, a subset of BTW's The Garden Encyclopedia, allows you to find plants using the plant name or attributes. It lists over 1,500 plants and includes images. The Ortho Home Gardener's Problem Solver has been around for several years. The Web-based version helps you to diagnose and treat over 700 problems.

The garden site directory is one of the best-organized directories of garden and gardening Web sites on the Internet. The sites are not only organized by topic, but also by region. If you are interested in visiting gardens in your area, you can search by region to see which ones have Web sites.

Figure 5-11
Garden Escape

Garden Escape
http://www.garden.com

Garden Escape (Figure 5-11) is a commercial venture with advertising, gardening supplier Web pages, assorted resources, and message boards. The site is like an online garden center, where you can ask questions, buy gardening supplies, and read the Garden Escape magazine. One of the neat features of the site is a Web-based garden planner program that allows you to design a flower garden. Like some of the other sites, Garden Escape has a plant finder.

To take full advantage of Garden Escape you need to join, but membership is free. Membership brings with it the ability to save any gardens you design with the garden planner. It also includes an e-mail subscription service that sends weekly gardening information updates to your e-mail account.

Figure 5-12
Virtual Garden

Virtual Garden
http://www.pathfinder.com/vg/

The Virtual Garden (Figure 5-12) is a part of Pathfinder.com, an extensive Web site maintained by the media giant Time-Warner.

Many of the resources found in the Virtual Garden are online versions of Time-Warner's extensive gardening book and magazine collection.

A couple of features not found on other sites include the chance to check your local weather and locate your planting zone. The weather pages are okay, but not as good as The Weather Channel's Web site (**http://weather.com**) for your local area. When locating your planting zone, you might get a false reading if you live near the border of a zone. The site kept showing that I live in zone 6, which by a USDA map starts about 80 miles to the south.

Figure 5-13
GardenNet

GardenNet
http://trine.com/gardennet/
GardenNet (Figure 5-13) is an online garden center like Garden Escape. It includes an online gardening magazine, and links to other garden Web sites and associations. Its online garden shop is one of the best.

For catalog junkies, GardenNet is *the* place to request catalogs. A very convenient one-stop resource, many people tell me they receive catalogs more quickly by requesting them through GardenNet than by using the postcards found in gardening magazines. Along with ordering catalogs to be sent by mail, GardenNet also provides links to sites that allow you to order from their catalogs online.

Figure 5-14
The Gardening Launch Pad

The Gardening Launch Pad
http://www.tpoint.net/neighbor/

The Gardening Launch Pad (Figure 5-14) is a list of links to other gardening sites—over 2,000 in nearly 60 categories. All these categories are arranged in a table on a single Web page. Visiting a category displays a comprehensive list of links with a brief description of each. The depth of content is extensive and well worth a bookmark. You'll probably find some useful Web sites here that are not listed elsewhere.

Newsgroups and Web Boards

USENET is the Internet's bulletin board. Whereas the Web provides information resources, USENET is the place for active discussions on any topic under the sun. USENET newsgroups are like CompuServe's forum message boards and AOL's message centers. Each newsgroup contains *articles* that can be posted by anyone. An article is the same as a message on CompuServe or AOL.

USENET newsgroups are organized by subject into eight major categories, shown in Table 5-2 on the following page.

Many of the categories have more defined subgroups separated by periods. For example, the main newsgroup for gardening, a recreational activity, is *rec.gardens,* shown in Figure 5-15 on page 102. One of the more specific subgroups is *rec.gardens.roses.*

Table 5-2
The eight major newsgroup subjects

alt	**alt**ernative; anything is fair game, including adult content
comp	**comp**uter, computer topics
misc	**misc**ellaneous topics that do not fit anywhere else
news	**news** on USENET and the Internet
rec	**rec**reational activities and hobbies, including gardening
sci	**sci**entific research and related issues
soc	**soc**ial issues and discussions
talk	**talk**, discuss, and debate social issues

To subscribe, read, and respond to articles in newsgroups you need a news reader, incorporated into most Web browsers. To read the articles in a newsgroup, you *subscribe* to the newsgroup. Once you subscribe, the newsreader keeps track of all the articles in the newsgroup, downloading only the titles (*headers*) of articles you have not read. You read a particular article by selecting its header; the newsreader then displays the article. In Figure 5-15, the header "lilac bushes not blooming" is selected, with the article displayed just below it.

Figure 5-15
Articles on the newsgroup rec.gardens

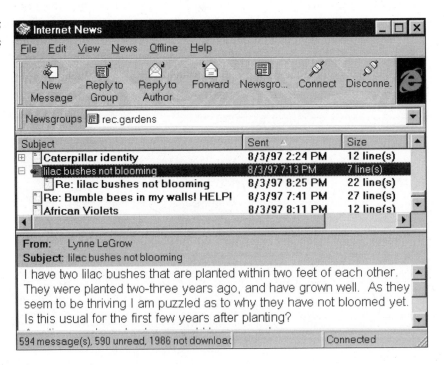

Anyone can reply to a newsgroup article by *posting* a response to the newsgroup, or by forwarding your response via e-mail. All replies begin with "Re:" which is shorthand for "in response to." When you reply to an article, your message becomes part of an article *thread*—a series of posts and replies. Notice also in the figure that the reply "Re: lilac bushes not blooming" is indented below the original message. This tells you that this is an article thread. On some newsgroups, threads can go for a hundred or more articles.

Newsgroups are either moderated or unmoderated. In a moderated newsgroup, a moderator or group of moderators controls the content, weeding out articles that are off-topic or against the rules. In unmoderated newsgroups (the majority of newsgroups on the Internet), anyone can post any type of article, even if the article is off-topic. Some newsgroups are flooded with adult-oriented messages by senders using automated message delivery programs in a process called *spamming*. So don't be surprised to find messages about adult phone services and adult Web sites among some newsgroups.

To avoid the problems with newsgroups, some Web sites offer *Web boards*. You can post, read, and reply to messages on these Web boards as you would a message board on a BBS or online service. Web boards are not subject to spamming. At the commercial garden Web sites, the Web board moderator is likely an employee who is a skilled horticulturalist.

Many of the gardening Web sites, including GardenWeb, Joe & Mindy's Web Garden, Garden Escape, and Virtual Garden, provide a Web board on which you can ask questions and interact with other gardeners. If you cannot access newsgroups or you would like a place that is a little more intimate and controlled, the Web-based forums are a good place to visit.

E-Mail: Faster Than Slugs and Snails
While discussion groups, forums, newsgroups, and Web boards are great for open discussions about gardening, you will some-

times like to communicate privately with another gardener, away from the crowds. This is where electronic mail, commonly known as *e-mail,* becomes your garden letter-writing tool, and it's much faster than the postal mail (*snail mail*), without the need for paper and a stamp.

To use e-mail, you need an *e-mail account,* which is an address where someone can send you the mail. If you are a member of an online service, you automatically have an e-mail account. Many Internet service providers also provide an e-mail account as part of the package. Each day, more and more of us get an e-mail account at work or at school. We will soon reach the day when not having an e-mail account will be like not having a phone number.

Besides an e-mail account, you will need *e-mail software* to send and receive e-mail. Again, the commercial online services provide e-mail capabilities inside their particular client software. Internet service providers will include a separate e-mail program in their setup package or recommend using the e-mail capabilities built into the major Web browsers. Your company or school e-mail system may use a particular version of e-mail software.

 If you have a company e-mail account, find out the company's policy on using it for your personal gardening mail. Some companies have very strict policies regarding private use, while others are fairly open. Also, be aware that current laws side with the company when it comes to e-mail privacy issues—there isn't any privacy.

E-mail systems and the messages they can handle range from simple text to highly formatted text with attached files. Files attached to an Internet e-mail message are converted to a special text format before the mail is sent out. When the mail is received, the attached files are converted back to their original format. When selecting an e-mail system, look for this automatic encoding and decoding capability. The most common encoding/decoding standard is MIME, Multi-purpose Internet Mail Extensions. All Web browser e-mail components and the commercial online services support MIME, so you can send pictures of your garden along with your letters to friends.

Several free e-mail or *freemail* systems have appeared in the past couple of years. All of these are supported by advertising. As you read and write your e-mail messages, you have to watch the advertisements go scrolling by. So like advertiser-supported commercial television, it's not really free—you pay for it in "hassle factors."

For e-mail only, Juno (**http://www.juno.com**) is currently the only stand-alone free e-mail system. All you need to use it is a Windows-based computer and a modem. Even though a call into the Juno e-mail system may involve a long-distance charge, it is strictly for sending and receiving mail. All of your composing and reading of your mail is done offline.

There are also several Web-based free e-mail systems. Hotmail (**http://www.hotmail.com**) and RocketMail (**http://www.rocketmail. com**) are two of the more popular ones (see Figure 5-16). As long as you can get to a Web browser, you can use a Web-based e-mail system. Nor do you need your own Internet connection. Many libraries and schools offer free or low-cost computers for you to use for browsing the Web or for sending and receiving Web-based free e-mail.

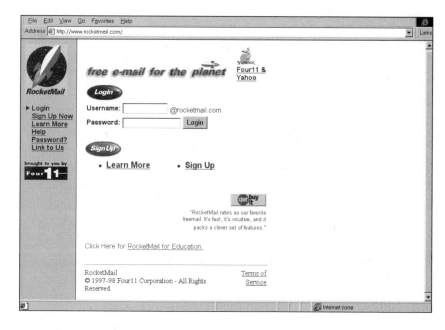

Figure 5-16
If you have a Web browser, you can enjoy free e-mail with RocketMail

Listserv Mailing Lists: Electronic Chain Letters

Electronic mailing lists, managed by *listserv* programs (mailing *list servers*) are another means of electronic discussions. Although eclipsed by newsgroups and the Web, listservs are still very popular. They are usually much more focused on a particular topic than newsgroups and Web boards. If you have limited or only e-mail access to the Internet, a listserv mailing list is an alternative to other methods of electronic discussion.

A listserv is an automated system that distributes e-mail to every member of a mailing list. You subscribe to the mailing list by e-mailing a request to the list administrator or the listserv computer itself. Once your e-mail address is on the mailing list, you start receiving all the discussions in the form of e-mail messages. If you want to participate in a discussion, you send your comments in an e-mail message to an administrative address. The listserv program then duplicates your message and sends it to all other members of the mailing list.

To subscribe to a mailing list, enter the e-mail address into the **TO:** field of your message. In the body of the message, you usually enter just one line at the very beginning,

subscribe *<list name> <your name>*

For example to subscribe to the Gardens and Gardening mailing list at the University of Kentucky, you would send e-mail to **LISTSERV@LSV.UKY.EDU** with **Subscribe GARDENS Joe Smith** in the very first line of the message.

If the messages from a mailing list get overwhelming, you can usually stop the mailing by sending a message to the listserve with

Unsubscribe *<list name> <your name>*

in the message. To quit getting mail from the Gardens and Gardening mailing list at the University of Kentucky, you would send a message to **LISTSERV@LSV.UKY.EDU** with **Unsubscribe GARDENS Joe Smith** in the very first line of the message.

Where do you find listserv mailing lists? In the past, listserv mailing lists were passed around by word of mouth or published in various journals. Many are often temporary, as part of a confer-

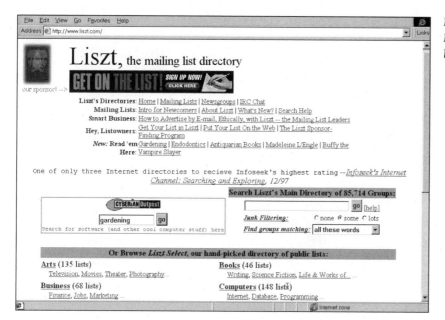

Figure 5-17
Liszt is an extensive directory of mailing
lists and other online resources

ence or project; once the conference is over, the mailing list disappears. For ongoing listserv mailing lists, you can find a comprehensive listing at **http://www.liszt.com** (Figure 5-17) or **http://www.tile.net/tile/listserv/index.html**. Also, use a Web search site and search with the keyword "listserv." Some listserv administrators will duplicate a mailing list discussion on a Web site where you can then pick up the listserv address.

6

Growing Your Gardening Knowledge

We have seen how online services and the Internet give us access to a global body of information that puts up-to-the-minute gardening information at our fingertips. Now let's see how we can tap into these resources to increase and organize our gardening knowledge.

Organize Your Information in a Garden Data Toolshed

Information systems managers in corporations talk about keeping all of the company information in data warehouses, with easy access by employees and in a unique, readable format. While we do not need a warehouse, a nice garden data toolshed would be useful.

Word processors can be used for storing information, and they are best at providing a unique, readable appearance for text, complete with formatting and layout. However, word processors do not work as well at handling discrete chunks of information that need to be searched, sifted, and sorted.

Spreadsheets can also be used for information storage and management. However, they are best at sifting, sorting, and crunching numerical information, such as calculating how much fertilizer to apply or determining the number of growing-degree days to see if crabgrass is ready to germinate. Spreadsheets tend to fall short at searching through large chunks of text-type information with a multitude of questions. Spreadsheets do have a place in managing garden information, but more in a supporting role to database managers. They are useful for creating tables or graphs based on sets of numbers, such as bloom charts with starting and ending dates.

When it comes to storing, organizing, and managing garden information, the database manager is the best computer tool for filling our garden information toolshed. Even the garden journal, which one might think should be written with a word processor, is easier to create and use in database format. Good database managers can handle searching, sifting, and sorting large bodies of text, while still maintaining them as discrete chunks of information. Some database managers can even handle pictures and drawings.

Most garden encyclopedias, references, and journals, including many of the plant finders on the World Wide Web, are database managers in disguise. When you search for a plant on a Web site, you are accessing a database.

As you've gathered your gardening information on paper, you've probably developed a system to meet your needs. You will probably want a computer-based system that mirrors the way you are already keeping your garden information toolshed. While you can find several programs to help you manage gardening information (including one of my own), many may not suit you.

So instead of reviewing existing commercial and shareware gardening information programs, let us spend some time on how to use various general-purpose tools to develop your own personal garden information toolshed. Even if you do not want to build your own plant reference files, an overview of how to "grow" a plant reference system will help you make better decisions when evaluating commercial plant references.

Track Your Activities in an Electronic Garden Journal

The garden journal is the gardener's most indispensable "tool." It should be the first tool you get and the last tool you use each day in your regular gardening activities.

By most dictionary definitions, a journal and a diary have similar meanings—they are both personal records of occurrences, events, and experiences. In practice, however, a journal also includes reflections, analysis, and insight about this information. A journal includes *reactions* to what you have recorded, not just a collection of recorded data.

A garden journal is a record of your garden: the plants you grow, the dates the bugs appeared for their annual garden feast, and the daily weather conditions. It's also a way of looking back at your garden to help you decide what you'll do differently next season.

While there is something organic about keeping a paper-based garden journal, a computer-based one will help you quickly find that specific bit of information you sorely need. How often have you paged through a journal looking for something like last year's final frost date—or the last frost date for the past five years? About the worst gardening journal you can keep is the one you keep in memory. Our memories tend to leak—we forget what we planted by the fence last spring. Here's an example: I have five hosta growing right now, but I can't remember their names, even though I buried the name tags next to the plants. The plants have grown around the tags and digging them up would destroy half the plants.

Gardeners' journals vary in style. Some are blank bound books or notebooks. Others, like mine, are loose-leaf notebooks that become veritable compressed compost piles of eclectic gardening bits and pieces. You may find a database system that can be tailored to your journalistic ways.

An article on garden diaries in *Fine Gardening* magazine a few years ago listed various approaches to garden journal keeping, including scientific, nostalgic, sentimental, statistical, romantic, and practical. Here's a look at some of these approaches and the software that best fits each.

The narrative garden journal

Nostalgic, sentimental, and romantic journals follow a traditional "Dear Diary" approach to writing about events. Most paper-bound garden journals found in bookstores, with their nice lined pages and pretty graphics, are best adapted to a narrative style of writing.

Using a word processor

You can use a word processor for a narrative journal, but you may want to use the word processor more for printing a clean copy of your journal than as a storage medium.

Organizing and searching in your journal with a word processor is not easy. Whether you create a new file for each day you make an entry or put all of your entries in one file, finding a particular bit of information will take some time.

If you choose to use a word processor, pick one with outline capabilities that will allow you to collapse or expand the document into various heading levels. In this way, you will be able to scan the headings for a particular entry. (See Figure 6-1.)

Use a word processor that lets you generate a table of contents or a simple index. By inserting special codes or applying special styles around the date and journal entry title, you can automatically gather these marked entries into a table of contents. Some word processors, such as Microsoft Word, have a feature allowing you to click on a table of contents entry to jump to a particular section of a document.

Using a journal program

There are several general-purpose journal programs available as shareware or freeware. These programs are usually simple custom databases. Most are organized by date of entry, like a typical paper-based journal. (See Figure 6-2.)

Figure 6-1
A word processor–based garden
journal displayed as an outline

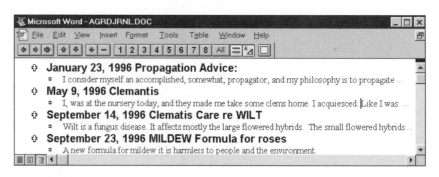

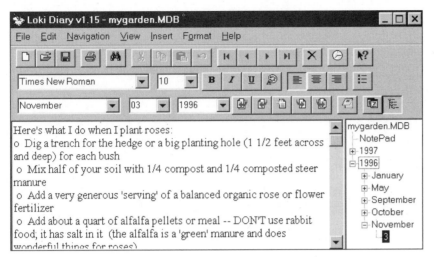

Figure 6-2
Loki Diary, a general purpose
journal program that you can
use as a narrative garden journal

Loki Diary is a very popular shareware/freeware diary or journal program for Microsoft Windows. Older versions are freeware, while the latest versions are distributed as low-cost shareware. A nice feature of both versions of Loki is a floating calendar that allows you to jump to a particular date. The Windows 95 version creates a tree display of all journal entries.

SEE CD-ROM

All Loki Diary entries are kept in a database file that is compatible with the Microsoft Access database management system. Should you decide to develop a more comprehensive garden information management system with MS-Access, you will be able to link your existing journal files into the bigger database. You can continue to use Loki as the "front end" for your garden journal, and MS-Access for heavy-duty garden data sifting.

If you ever watched the television show *Doogie Howser, M.D.*, you have seen the program OMNIDay. At the end of the show, the main character types his journal into a computer using the DOS version of OMNIDay. (See Figure 6-3 on page 114.)

SEE CD-ROM

To make an entry in OMNIDay, you enter the date, and then type your report of the events and reactions to them for that day. Clicking OK saves your entry. A Reminisce window displays a table of all dated entries along with the first line of each, which

SEE CD-ROM

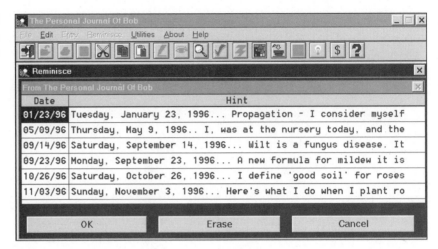

Figure 6-3
The OMNIDay reminisce display
to quickly scan journal entries

gives you a hint as to what they contain. To view an entry, you highlight a particular date and click OK. While reminiscing, you can navigate forward and backward through your journal.

One problem with Loki and OMNIDay is that they keep only text; so you can't keep any type of graphics—such as sketches, pictures, or clippings—with your entries. The journal program Scraps will let you do both. Scraps is a multimedia-based journal database that allows you to include images and audio clips in your journal.

Loki, OMNIDay, and Scraps are three journal programs that you can use for a narrative garden journal. Software programs are like new flower varieties; new ones are always appearing. You can find them at Web sites, at FTP download sites, and in the file libraries of online services. These three programs may not meet your needs or work on your computer system, so do not hesitate to go looking for another journal program that will work for you. A good place to start is by searching the CNET's SHAREWARE.COM (**http://www. shareware.com**) and DOWNLOAD.COM (**http://www.download. com**) Web sites. Both CompuServe's file libraries (GO filefinder) and America Online's Software Center (keyword: software) have several journal programs you can download.

Using a database management program

If none of the available programs work for you, you can create your own customized garden journal with a general-purpose database program. Should you go this route, choose a database that will handle large chunks of text in *memo fields,* and be sure that it will let you easily edit these fields. The database managers found in most "Works" applications will not have enough features for journal writing.

A big advantage to creating your own garden journal using a database program is flexibility. You can create a narrative garden journal similar to Loki Diary, and create another type of journal for organizing observational data.

The record book journal

Scientific, statistical, and practical journals are all variations on the record book journal. Instead of waxing eloquently about your garden, you approach your gardening like a researcher, with detailed and organized data based on observation and experimentation. You record daily observations and results, notes on plant growth, literature references, and project ideas. In a scientific garden journal, much of the information is recorded in a forms-based format.

This practical approach to journal keeping is like an accountant's ledger, recording activities, materials, expenses, purchases, and assets. You may even take the data one step further and use statistics to plot trends or chart progress. For example, you could use the starting and ending bloom dates of all your plants to plot a flower bloom chart. You might crunch your local weather recordings to determine an average seasonal temperature or rainfall, to see if this season was warmer and wetter or cooler and drier than previous seasons. Database programs are the best way to keep scientific or practical journals.

Using garden-specific record book software

Some gardening programs include record book journal features. With The Seed Program, you can record information about garden seeds (see Figure 6-4 on page 116). You enter the crop and number

Figure 6-4
*The Seed Program, a type of record
book journal for tracking garden seeds*

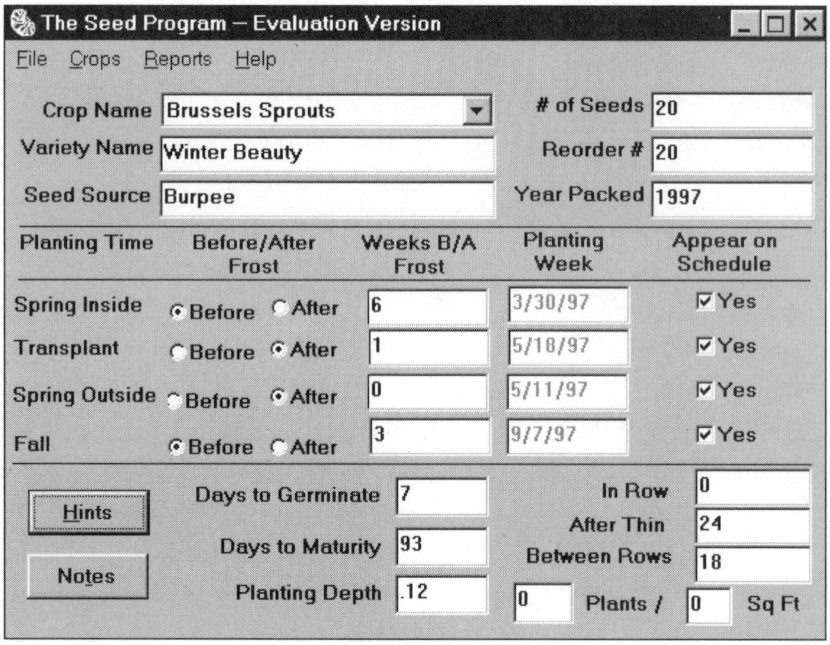

of seeds ordered from a seed source, as well as the optimum time before or after the first and last frost for sowing the seeds or transplanting seedlings. The program then generates a report detailing the dates when you need to sow or transplant. A notes section lets you enter your observations about the germination and growth of your seeds, with sufficient space for fairly extensive narrative.

You can use WinGarden to keep track of the performance of garden plants, particularly vegetables (see Figure 6-5). Like The Seed Program, WinGarden will calculate sowing, transplanting, and harvesting schedules based on the first and last frost dates for your area. It also lets you track where you purchased the seeds for each year and allows you to keep notes on a particular plant.

The Horticultural Manager is a DOS-based program for keeping information on plants in your garden (see Figure 6-6 on page 118). Unlike The Seed Program and WinGarden, it tracks existing plantings. As you enter plant names, you assign a hardiness zone and up to six categories for each plant. A reference section lets you keep notes on the plant, including a monthly task list in which you can enter the work that needs to be performed.

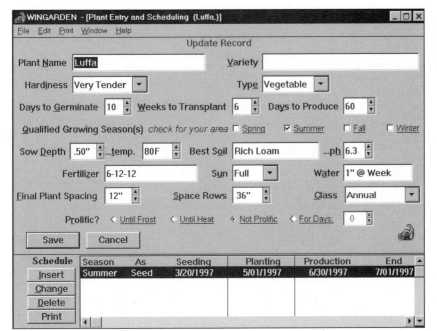

Figure 6-5
WinGarden, another garden database and record book for tracking garden plant seed performance

As you accumulate information on the plants in your garden or landscape, you can print out a monthly work list for all of your plants. In October, your work list might include such activities as planting tulip bulbs, raking the leaves of Norway maple trees, and fertilizing the lawn. The Horticulture Manager's greatest downside is that it's DOS-based—Windows and Macintosh programs are just more fun to use.

Using a database management program

With its flexibility and power, a general database program may be the best software for keeping a record book journal. You might want, for example, to enter additional data that you feel is important to your gardening. The record book journal programs we have just seen have no options for such additions.

Database management systems range from very simple *flat-file managers* to *multilinked data file* (pseudorelational) *managers* to full-featured *relational database managers*. Which type you choose will depend on how much and what type of information you would like to store in your record book journal.

Figure 6-6
The Horticulture Manager, a task-oriented garden record book journal

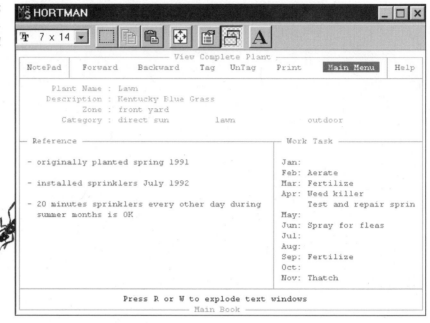

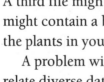

A flat-file database manager is similar to an index-card file, with each item of information kept in a separate field. The fields in most flat-file databases must be the same for all records: The amount of rainfall always goes in the *Rainfall* field and the date it rained always goes in the *Date of Rain* field. While it may take a bit longer to enter information into a flat-file database, you'll be able to easily manage your information once you're done.

In a flat-file database system, the journal is actually one or more separate data files, with each file organized to serve a particular purpose. One file might contain records of all the plants in your garden, with taxonomic and cultural information. Another file would contain records of cultural practices for various plants. A third file might be a narrative garden journal, while a fourth might contain a bibliography of books and magazine articles on the plants in your garden.

A problem with flat-file database systems is their inability to relate diverse database files. We should not have to re-enter a plant name and taxonomic information into a cultural record database when we've already entered it in a list of all the plants in our

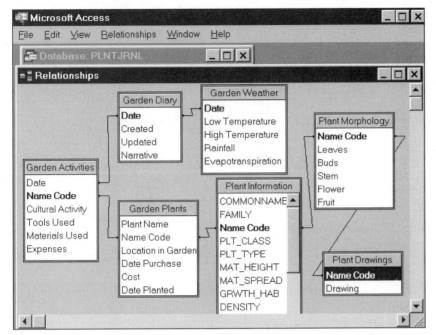

Figure 6-7
A record book garden journal setup in a relational database. The lines between the different fields are the links between the different tables

garden. We need a way to connect the cultural records in one database file with the plant information records in another database file. With a relational database manager, we can establish a link between the records in the two database files using a common *key*, such as the name of a plant (see Figure 6-7). A relational database manager uses multilinked database files stored in the database as *tables*. For assembling a comprehensive garden record book journal, a relational database manager is the best software tool.

Relational databases allow you to establish links among their different fields. Changes to one record will result in changes to linked related records. For example, imagine you made weather, garden activity, and garden diary entries on Saturday, August 17, 1997. If you look at an old calendar, you will see that the date was actually August 16. By correcting the date in the Garden Activities table, the dates in the related tables, Garden Diary and Garden Weather, are automatically corrected. And if you delete the plant information record on black-eyed Susan (*Rudbeckia hirta*), all of the related records containing a reference to black-eyed Susan would be automatically deleted.

Figure 6-8

With a relational database system for your journal, you can create a variety of different forms

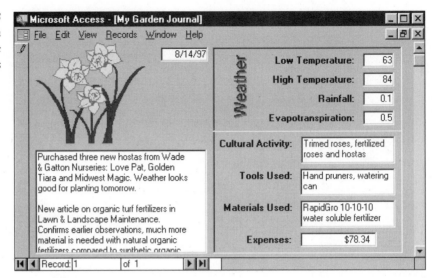

Figure 6-8

With a relational database system for your journal, you can create a variety of different forms

Another advantage of most relational databases is that they separate the tables that store the data from the forms used to display the data. This feature allows you to develop a large number of different forms to display and manage the data in the tables (see Figure 6-8). You might use one form to enter all of the information for one day, and another to enter just weather information.

Using a spreadsheet

Databases are great for managing text, but spreadsheet programs are the best for number crunching, particularly if you need to see continually updated results. With spreadsheets, such as that shown in Figure 6-9, calculated values are automatically updated every time you add or modify information.

For example, let's say you want to keep track of water use in your garden by recording various gains and losses of water. You plan to use this information to determine when to turn on the sprinkler system. With a spreadsheet, you can enter rainfall and irrigation values, along with water losses through evapotranspiration and percolation, and instantly see the current water conditions in the soil. If you start seeing negative numbers in the calculated results, you know it is time to turn on the sprinklers.

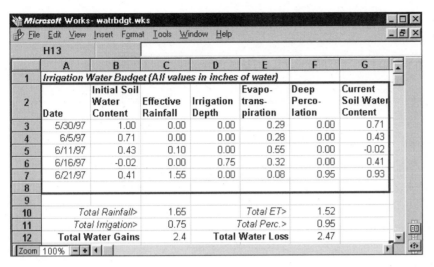

Figure 6-9

A spreadsheet used to keep track of irrigation water use

	A	B	C	D	E	F	G
1	Irrigation Water Budget (All values in inches of water)						
2	Date	Initial Soil Water Content	Effective Rainfall	Irrigation Depth	Evapo-trans-piration	Deep Perco-lation	Current Soil Water Content
3	5/30/97	1.00	0.00	0.00	0.29	0.00	0.71
4	6/5/97	0.71	0.00	0.00	0.28	0.00	0.43
5	6/11/97	0.43	0.10	0.00	0.55	0.00	-0.02
6	6/16/97	-0.02	0.00	0.75	0.32	0.00	0.41
7	6/21/97	0.41	1.55	0.00	0.08	0.95	0.93
8							
9							
10	Total Rainfall>		1.65		Total ET>	1.52	
11	Total Irrigation>		0.75		Total Perc.>	0.95	
12	Total Water Gains		2.4		Total Water Loss	2.47	

The water budget is one of the methods professional turfgrass or landscape managers use to track water usage that gardeners can adapt to their gardens and home landscapes. **Evapotranspiration** *(ET) is the loss of water from the soil by evaporation and the loss of water from the plant by a process known as transpiration.* **Deep percolation** *is water that has moved out of the reach of plant roots. A gardener can use several simple tools for determining ET. A search on the Web using the term "evaporimeter" will bring up helpful information, tools, and techniques.*

Spreadsheets also offer stronger charting and graphing capability than most databases. Most will also automatically update a chart or graph as you enter new values into the spreadsheet.

One unique way to use this charting feature is for tracking the growth and bloom duration of perennial flowers (see Figure 6-10 on page 122). Using the spreadsheet's line graph, you can chart when perennials begin growing, start and finish blooming, and die back. You might also use this chart to track the growth of vegetables and annuals.

You can also use spreadsheet charting features for graphically analyzing a variety of other garden information, including rainfall, temperature, numeric evaluation of plants, plant pest severity, and vegetable garden yields.

Figure 6-10
Using a spreadsheet to chart
perennial growth and bloom

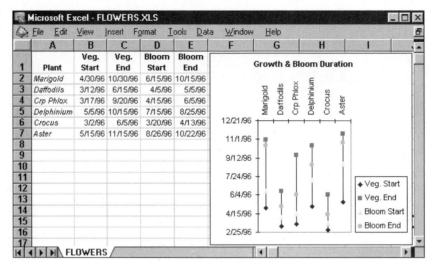

Figure 6-11
A database (watrbdgt.wdb) is used
for managing information, while a
spreadsheet (watrbdgt.wks) is used
for calculations and analysis

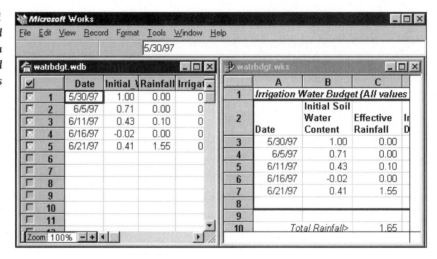

Databases and spreadsheets as companion tools

Spreadsheets don't make the best databases, and databases don't make the best spreadsheets, but fortunately they can often be used together. The database serves as the main information storage and management system; the spreadsheet is the analysis tool (see Figure 6-11). Many databases can even transfer their information to a compatible spreadsheet.

A variety of journals

As you can see, there are many ways to keep a garden journal. Depending on your situation, you may find that one program meets all of your journal-writing needs, or that you need two or more programs to manage your diverse record-keeping activities.

If the off-the-shelf software doesn't meet your needs, consider developing your own journal system. While the learning curve is steep, your efforts will be rewarded with greater flexibility, just as your own home-grown vegetables reward you with better taste.

7

The Garden Information Manager

As you develop a garden journal, you may find yourself tracking expenses, planting dates, garden club meetings, and the names and addresses of suppliers and nurseries. To track all these gardening activities just as you might plan your workday, consider using a personal information manager (PIM), or simply *information manager*. Information managers are designed to help you organize and manage random pieces of information (see Figure 7-1 on page 126).

If you carry a personal organizer notebook or day planner, you are using the paper equivalent of an information manager. A day planner is a combination calendar, scheduler, appointment book, address book, expense tracker, to-do list, and general notebook. I use a Day-Timer planner (**http://www.daytimer.com**); many of my associates use Day-Runner planners (**http://www.dayrunner.com**) and some use the Franklin Planner (**http://www.franklinquest. com**). These are probably the big three of personal organizers and planners, you will find others at your local office supply store.

If you're having trouble keeping even a paper-based journal, consider using a paper-based planner. Planners come in a variety of formats to fit your particular needs. The two-page-per-week format offered by some companies works very well for tracking

Figure 7-1
Using an information manager
to track gardening activities

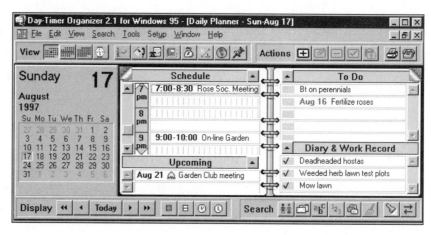

gardening activities. All of the companies offer add-in sheets for a variety of information management needs. I use short-trimmed add-in note sheets if I need to record more detailed information than I have room for on the printed pages, and I use grid sheets for mapping out the garden.

I suggest a paper-based planner because if you already have trouble keeping paper records, a computer-based record-keeping system won't necessarily work any magic. Many of us need to get organized on paper before we can ever be successful using a computer. A paper-based planner will help you develop good record-keeping habits. Then you can use the information manager software from the company that makes your paper-based organizers to make the transition to keeping records on the computer. In fact, the software and the paper-based organizer usually complement each other.

Use the paper-based organizer when you're out roaming the gardens and nurseries. Once you get home, transfer the information in the paper organizer to the information manager. Many information managers will also print schedules, to-do lists, and an address book that you can insert in a paper organizer. (In a later chapter, I'll show you how you can even sidestep paper and go directly to a handheld computer as an electronic organizer.)

Several of my online gardening friends use information managers to track all of their gardening activities, including journal entries. Some information managers have good calendar/schedulers for tracking garden activities, along with a strong notebook section that will even let you keep pictures and sketches of your gardens.

Here's how to use an information manager in your gardening.

Calendar/Scheduling

While the information manager's calendar is designed primarily for scheduling appointments and meetings, you can use it to schedule other activities. If you lead a hectic life, you might use it to make an appointment with yourself to work in the garden. Some of my friends are so organized, they schedule just about every waking hour of their day, including their time in the garden.

The information manager calendar/scheduler lets you schedule recurring entries. For example, if your garden club meets the third Thursday of every month at 12:30 P.M., you can have the scheduler repeat this recurring appointment, complete with a five-day advance notice and an alarm that goes off one hour before the meeting.

Many of the information managers allow you to link the calendar to other types of entries, such as expense records and address book entries. You can also link a notebook entry to several dates. So if you want to keep one main notebook entry for your fertilizer program, you can link back to each date you applied fertilizer previously.

Tasks/To-Do List

A to-do list can be anything from a scrap of paper to an entry in an information manager file. We may need to prioritize the tasks. As we finish each task, we check it off.

All of the major information managers support to-do lists. Many allow you to assign priorities to the various tasks on your lists, and automatically carry unfinished tasks forward to the next day. (So if you do not get the garden weeded today, you will be reminded about it tomorrow.) Depending on the information manager you choose, you might also be able to create repeating tasks, complete with alarms and advance notices.

Address Book

An address book is a valuable addition to any gardener's information system, keeping the addresses of mail-order suppliers, gardening friends and contacts, public gardens, and more just seconds away. If the address book has links to other entries, there is no need to type a phone number or address more than once.

All of the information managers maintain the standard address book fields of name, addresses (work and home), city, state, and zip code, along with one or more phone numbers. Most will also dial a contact's phone number if you have a modem connected to your computer, and some even log the time and duration of your phone calls.

Some information managers contain a more extensive set of fields, including the option to define your own. The more current ones have fields for e-mail and Web addresses. Clicking on an e-mail address brings up your e-mail program with the address entered into the TO field. Clicking on a Web address brings up your Web browser with the Web address entered in the URL Location field.

You do not have to use address books strictly for managing the addresses of people, places, and companies. A friend uses her Day-Timer Organizer's address book to track her plants. She stores the genus in the *Last Name* field, the variety in the *Title* field and the full botanical name in the *Company* field. The address field might contain a description of the plant location in the garden. While this may not be the best way to keep a plant reference, the address book is still much better than a free-form notebook and it's simpler to use than a database.

Phone Logs

A phone log is primarily used to manage customer contacts, so its gardening use is limited. Still, it is a good way to track those phone orders to mail-order garden suppliers and nurseries. Some information managers will even let you set a reminder alarm after a call, so you won't forget when your package of plants is supposed to arrive.

Free-Form Information

The free-form area of your information manager is where you can enter all sorts of notes, comments, and memos about your gardening activities. If you use its links to the calendar, you can also keep your journal here. You can enter the text in any manner you feel appropriate.

To help you organize your notes and memos, the entry area might have a separate title field. Some information managers, like Lotus Organizer, use the first line of the entry as the title; this is then included in a table of contents at the beginning of the notes section, with each note following as a numbered page. Day-Timer displays a sortable list of all note titles; you view a note by opening the list entry.

If the notes area in your information manager is too limiting, you'll find that many of the commercial information managers allow you to attach external files, such as word-processing documents or spreadsheets. To view the document or file, you launch the associated application from the information manager.

Some information managers support rich text formatting, which lets you apply various font styles and paragraph formats to your notes. Some let you paste graphics or objects into your notes, including drawings or scanned photos of your garden, landscape CAD drawings, and spreadsheets with fertilizer calculations.

Object Linking and Embedding (OLE) is the technology that lets you embed an object or file from one application into another, while maintaining links to the first. Using OLE, you can embed a spreadsheet in a word-processing document while retaining the links to the spreadsheet application. While the spreadsheet may look like a picture of the spreadsheet, it is the actual spreadsheet in a special container inside the word processor. When you revise the spreadsheet, it updates the data in the word processor too. You don't need to use OLE specifically to do this—it all happens automatically, behind the scenes.

Where to Find Information Managers

SEE CD-ROM

The screen shot in Figure 7-1 on page 126 is from the trial version of the Day-Timer Organizer 2.1. (A trial version of DTO 2.1 is on the CD-ROM.) You can also obtain an evaluation copy from several sources, including the Day-Timer Web site as shown in Figure 7-2, (**http://www.daytimer.com**). I use the Day-Timer Organizer because it complements my paper Day-Timer planner. The software lets you print out pages that fit into the planner binder. I have also used Lotus Organizer (**http://www.lotus.com/organizer**) because it supports graphics in the notebook (see Figure 7-3).

You'll find several other good information managers, both commercial and shareware, that you can use for tracking gardening activities. The best place to look for them is on the Web. Do a quick search using the keyword "PIM" at CNET's DOWNLOAD.COM Web site (**http://www.download.com**), and you'll find over 100 different ones to try. Look in on CompuServe (GO FileFinder) and America Online (keyword: software), and you'll find a similar number.

Figure 7-2
Visit the Day-Timer Web site for the latest on their organizer software

Figure 7-3
The Lotus Organizer Web site

You can create your own information manager from separate programs, such as a calendar creator, electronic address book, and a journal program. There are many different versions of each of these—check the same sources as above. However, be aware that you likely cannot link entries across the different programs, like you can with an information manager.

You could also use an integrated Works program as an information manager. Many include an address book, to-do list, and a calendar. However, as with individual programs, they lack the ability to link related entries.

You could develop your own information manager using a relational database like Microsoft Access. You might even find an information manager already developed for use with your database management system (try searching online). Although a database gives you extensive flexibility in developing your own information manager, remember that your investment in time will be significant. In the end, it may be less frustrating, time consuming, and expensive to use a commercial or shareware information manager.

8

Gardening References

Gardening references are works we can turn to for authoritative gardening information. Until recently, our major references were gardening books, magazines, and similar printed publications. Computers have brought us new types of reference works, including gardening software, CD-ROMs, online databases, and Web sites.

Gardening references consist of *garden plant references* (electronic versions of plant reference books), *garden encyclopedias, garden guides,* and *garden problem solvers.* They usually contain a large number of graphics, including photographs and some video clips. And because graphics take up a lot of space, most are available only on CD-ROM.

Garden Plant References

Every gardener is bound to have at least one plant reference book on hand. Sometimes it's the old "plant ID textbook" we used in school; often it's a big reference book listing thousands of plants. These references are valuable tools for plant identification and selection.

But all plant reference books have one disadvantage: it's hard to search for a specific plant, particularly if you are trying to find one to fit a certain space. Usually, you end up paging through several references and nursery catalogs in search of a plant to meet your needs. Isn't there some way you can just say "show me all the evergreen trees that have a pyramidal shape and grow no higher than 20 feet?" There is—with a computer.

An electronic plant reference is a specialized database that stores plant information. All let you search the database according to certain criteria, usually based on design or climatic requirements.

Several garden and landscape plant reference databases have been produced over the years. The first ones were strictly text with no graphics; others included data that you could search with a separate database program. Some, like my Landscape & Herbaceous Plant Manager, were custom-developed programs (see Figure 8-1).

SEE CD-ROM

Many were part of landscape-planning (CAD) programs or additions to landscape CAD programs. For example, LandCADD, a professional landscape architecture CAD program, has an extensive plant database used to select plants to incorporate in designs

Figure 8-1
An early DOS-based plant reference
with an Windows-like interface

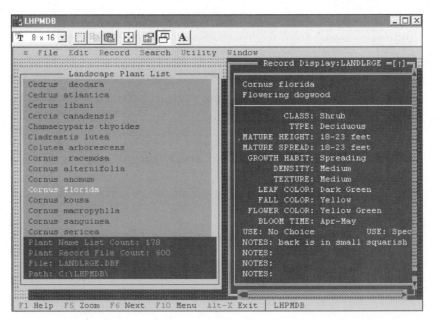

Figure 8-2
Along with extensive plant databases, many professional landscape architecture programs support full 3D capabilities

(see Figure 8-2). The original LandDesigner by GreenThumb Software (now part of Sierra Design, **http://www.sierra.com**) was one of the first home landscape-planning programs with a plant database that you could update.

With the availability of faster processors, better graphic displays, and especially CD-ROM drives, multimedia-based plant references began to appear in the early 1990s. 3D Landscape from Books That Work has a multimedia plant database complete with photographs or color paintings and digitized plant pronunciations (see Figure 8-3 on the following page). The former software company, GreenThumb, was also one of the first to release a stand-alone CD-ROM, complete with over 2,000 color photographs—their Pro Series Plant Database. Table 8-1 on page 136 lists some plant reference CD-ROMs for the serious gardener.

Electronic plant references have their disadvantages. For example, unless you own a notebook computer with a built-in CD-ROM drive, you cannot take them with you. Currently, many won't let you add new plants to their reference file (although this is more of a problem with the CD-ROM-based references). Even though the base genus or species never changes, every spring brings a number

Figure 8-3
Landscape planning programs
such as 3D Landscape include
multimedia plant databases. Notice
the speaker in the upper right for
hearing plant name pronunciations

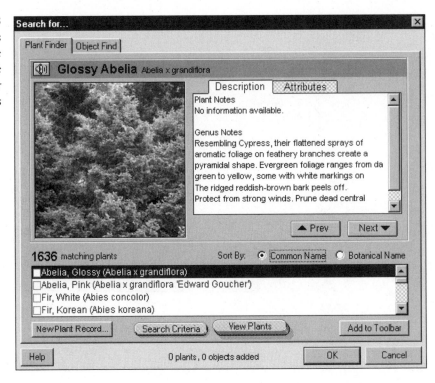

of new plant varieties, and it would be nice to be able to update a plant reference to include them. Fortunately, some companies are starting to put features into their references that allow you to add your own plants or to update the files with new plants from their Web site.

Table 8-1

A sampling of plant reference CD-ROMs available
to professional landscapers and serious gardeners

CD-ROM TITLE	PUBLISHER
Perennials & Annuals	Horticopia
Trees, Shrubs & Groundcovers	Horticopia
Pro Series Plant Database for CD-ROM	GreenThumb
Southern Trees CD-ROM	University of Florida
Canadian Nursery Trades Landscapes	Common Plants of Canadian Association

From *The American Nurseryman Horticultural Books, Videos & Software,* Spring-Summer, 1997 edition catalog. American Nurseryman, 77 W. Washington St., Suite 2100, Chicago, IL 60602-2904, 312/782-5505. This is not a comprehensive list of all plant references on CD-ROM. Listing of these titles does not imply evaluation or endorsement by the author or publisher.

Like information managers, plant references are specialized databases, and you can create your own with a bit of effort. Though many contain numerous images, you don't really need the pictures; in many cases, the plant's description and cultural requirements are enough. Developing your own plant reference system gives you the flexibility to keep the plant information you feel is important for your garden and your area. Many commercial plant references often bring up plants not available in a particular area.

Another advantage to developing your own plant reference is the ability to link your plant reference to other plant information resources you may have developed. With a relational database management system, you can link your plant reference with your garden journal, garden activity records, expense file, and garden inventory. Commercial plant references prevent you from tying the database into your comprehensive plant information management system.

Earlier, I mentioned the problem of carrying a CD-ROM plant reference and a notebook computer into the garden. Your own plant reference can be more portable, though. While you will probably not be able to fit all of it onto a small electronic organizer or handheld computer, especially if you include graphics, you should be able to transfer a fair amount of the text-based information. I'll talk more about using palmtop devices in a later chapter.

Of course, developing your own plant reference takes time. However, if you do have the time—and patience—developing your own is like growing your garden. In the end, you will have a unique body of information to call your own.

Garden Encyclopedias, Garden Guides, and Garden Problem Solvers

Gardening encyclopedias, guides, and problem solvers are similar in content and in the way they present information. They are usually a mix of plant references with articles on a variety of gardening topics. Some titles are a mix of plant reference, encyclopedia, guide, and problem solver.

Figure 8-4
The Garden Encyclopedia uses a familiar tabbed notebook format

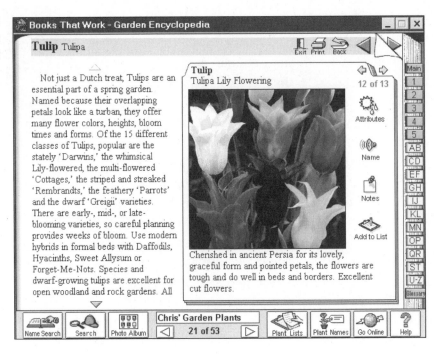

SEE CD-ROM

The garden encyclopedia is arranged alphabetically, like a printed encyclopedia. The Garden Encyclopedia by Books That Work (**http://www.sierra.com**) even uses a book metaphor, displaying a book with index tabs along the side, with which you can jump to various sections (see Figure 8-4).

Where an encyclopedia is an alphabetic collection of gardening articles and topics, a garden guide is more of a "how-to" book on some topic of gardening. With a properly organized collection of information and a well-developed search system, an encyclopedia can be turned into a problem solver. The basic difference between a plant problem reference and a plant problem solver is that in the latter, specific plant problems are identified. With a reference, you ask the questions that describe your specific problem. With a

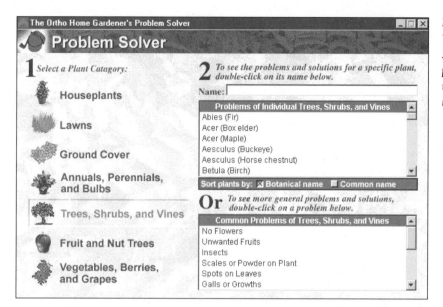

Figure 8-5
The Ortho Home Gardener's Problem Solver walks you through a series of predeveloped queries that strip away unimportant information and display the answer to your problem

problem solver, you work through a series of predeveloped queries that gradually strip away the unimportant information. Then (ideally) the answer to your problem is displayed. The Ortho Home Gardener's Problem Solver from Books That Work is a good example (see Figure 8-5).

As with plant reference CD-ROMs, gardening reference CD-ROMs aren't portable, unless you have a fancy notebook computer. To get around this problem, some publishing companies bundle a CD-ROM version of their reference with their book; you can use the CD-ROM in the house for rapid searches and queries, and take the book with you into the garden (see Table 8-2 on page 140). The Complete Guide to Gardening by Better Homes and Gardens and The Sunset Western Garden by Broderbund and Sunset Publishing are two examples of bundled reference books with CD-ROM versions of the book.

Table 8-2
A sampling of gardening references on CD-ROM

CD-ROM TITLE	COMPANY
Ortho Home Gardener's Problem Solver	Books That Work
Garden Encyclopedia	Books That Work
Complete Guide to Gardening	Better Homes and Gardens
Complete Home Gardener	Expert Software
Vegetable Gardening	Expert Software
Gardeners Companion Deluxe	Lifestyle Software Group
Gardeners Guide	Softkey
Gazebo Gardens: Perennials on CD-ROM	Custom Software Innovations
Sunset Garden Problem Solver	Broderbund Software
Sunset Western Garden	Broderbund Software
Herbalist	Hopkins Technology

This is not a comprehensive list of all gardening references on CD-ROM. Listing of these titles does not imply evaluation or endorsement by the author or publisher. To locate these titles and additional gardening reference CD-ROM titles, check out one of the many online CD-ROM shoppers guide and shops such as the 1st CD-ROM Shopper's Guide (**http://www. cdrom-guide.com**) and The CD-ROM Shop (**http://www.cdromshop.com**).

The Web: The Ultimate Gardening Reference

Like books, gardening reference CD-ROMs are limited in the amount of information they contain, and their information cannot be updated. Usually, we end up getting more books or more CD-ROMs to expand and update our library. CD-ROMs also come with a built-in "hassle factor"—most computer CD-ROM drives are strictly single-play units, so you can search only one CD at a time. With books, we can open two or more, spread them across a table, and refer to several entries at one time. Looking at various sources at the same time often yields more information than looking at one source at a time.

The World Wide Web is changing the way we work with gardening references. The wealth of gardening information on the Web continues to expand every day. Several universities have plant references on their Web sites. The plant dictionary at Ohio State University Horticulture & Crop Science Web Garden site (**http://www.hcs.ohio-state.edu/hcs/Webgarden.html**) is one of

several excellent plant references available from colleges and universities (see Figure 8-6).

Many nurseries are starting to publish their nursery plant stock catalog on the Web. While not true plant references, some of these catalogs contain enough information to permit searching by design criteria. The plant finder at Garden Escape (**http://www.garden. com**) is actually a searchable catalog. You can also buy any displayed plants that match your criteria from one of the nurseries hosted on the Garden Escape Web site.

The countless gardening references on the Web range from articles written and published by home gardeners to extension bulletins from the land grant universities to garden problem solvers at commercial Web sites. A good place to start is at The Garden Gate's Teaching Garden (**http://www.prairienet.org/garden-gate/ teaching.htm**), which contains numerous links to other gardening references on the Web (see Figure 8-7 on page 142).

With all of the resources available on the Web for free, you may ask "Why bother with CD-ROM garden references?" The gardening CD-ROM companies have been asking the same question.

Figure 8-7
Many Web sites such as The Garden
Gate include links to other Web sites
with additional plant databases

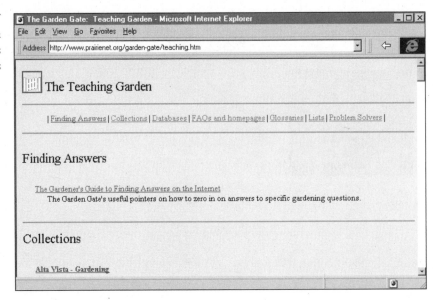

There are some benefits to having a gardening reference CD-ROM. Right now, a CD-ROM can still display multimedia much faster than the fastest Internet connection. Also, many of us don't have a fast Internet connection or a dedicated telephone line. It is much easier to look up something on a gardening CD-ROM than to suffer the wrath of a family member because you tied up the telephone while following strands on the World Wide Web.

Many gardening CD-ROM companies now recognize there are benefits to both CD-ROMs and the World Wide Web. By integrating Web technologies into their CD-ROM software, their CD-ROMs provide a comprehensive foundation of gardening information resources with easy access to updated information at the company's Web site. For example, if you have Internet access, Books That Work's Ortho Home Gardener's Problem Solver and Garden Encyclopedia both provide one-button access to BTW's Gardening.com Web site (**http://www.gardening.com**). At Sierra On-Line's Web site (**http://www.sierra.com**), you can download additional plant images for use in their LandDesigner 4.5 software (see Figure 8-8).

Figure 8-8
Some landscape planner software companies provide additional images and plant
records on their Web sites. Sierra On-Line
provides additional 3D images for loading
into their LandDesigner 3D Version 4.5

As you shop for new gardening CD-ROMs, one of the questions
you may want to ask is "Can I get updates through the Web?" The
ones with Web-based updates will provide you more value.

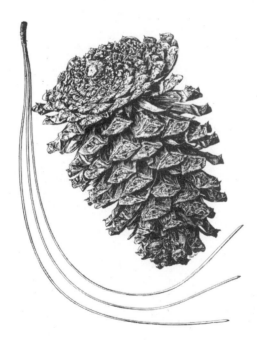

Plan(t) a Computer Garden

When someone mentions garden or landscape planning and design with a computer, you may think of special computer-aided design (CAD) programs. Or you may imagine using the mouse as an electronic pencil, drawing the straightest lines, the curviest curves, and countless tree, shrub, and flower symbols with a few mouse clicks.

Garden planning, and the much broader category of landscape design, is much more than just drawing tree symbols on a piece of electronic paper. Much of the process of planning a garden or landscape does not involve a drawing pencil or CAD program.

While some folks split grass blades over the differences between garden and landscape planning and design, to avoid confusion, I'll use the generally accepted term *landscape design* to cover all aspects. Regardless of the terminology, the process of using a computer is similar. In fact, many of the programs available for home garden design or landscape planning, like LandDesigner 4.5 by Sierra On-Line (**http://www.sierra.com**), have their roots in professional landscape design programs (see Figure 9-1).

Figure 9-1

Some home landscape planners such as LandDesign 4.5 had their beginnings as professional landscape design programs

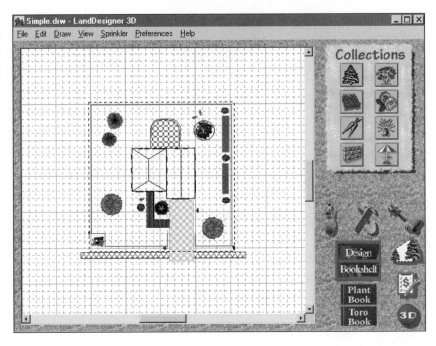

Landscape Design Meets the Computer

For many years, landscape designers didn't have computers to help them visualize their gardens; their only tools were pencils, paper, and various precision-drawing instruments. In fact, many of the better garden designers didn't draw anything on paper. As artists, they were able to envision the entire garden and direct their staff in creating it.

Unfortunately, many of us are not so gifted and need to "get it on paper." It is much easier to show friends or clients a drawing of your proposed garden than it is to describe it, and your computer is an ideal tool for the job. With software capable of displaying designs in three dimensions, we can even view a design from multiple perspectives. Some of the more powerful professional programs allow you to "walk through" a design. Equipped with special glasses, these *virtual reality* programs let you "see" the garden around you. As you turn your head, the view moves as if you were actually looking around the landscape as shown in Figure 9-2.

Figure 9-2
A virtual walkthrough

Visual imaging is a new area of computer design. With visual imaging, you create a digital photographic image using a scanner, digital camera, or video frame grabber. Many of the new home garden and landscape design programs are visual-imaging systems adapted for landscape design. Once your photograph is in the computer, you can add to it a variety of plants from a library of plant photo images, creating a new landscape.

Unlike traditional bitmap painting programs, visual-imaging programs use multilayer concepts found in object-oriented drawing programs. The plant photo images are not merged into the main photo image, but kept as separate objects so that you can move them around to try different ideas. Some landscape visual-imaging systems even include a growth simulator, so you can see how your garden will look next year or ten years from now. This is a good way to make sure that the juniper planted under the picture window won't eventually block your view.

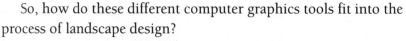

So, how do these different computer graphics tools fit into the process of landscape design?

Landscape and garden design as practiced by professionals is a multistep process, during which you:

1. Determine your needs
2. Analyze the site
3. Develop the area
4. Develop the structure
5. Select plants
6. Place plants
7. Incorporate nonplant features
8. Add the finishing touches
9. Assemble a list of materials
10. Estimate costs

Digital imaging (scanners, digital cameras) and visual-imaging systems are useful tools for the first three steps of the process: determining need, site analysis, and area development. You can also use visual imaging for developing *preliminary* designs for the middle steps of the process: placing plants, incorporating nonplant features, and adding the finishing touches.

Once you are satisfied with the preliminary designs, you can start on the precision designs. In anticipation of later construction and installation of the garden or landscape, you need to create precision drawings for area development, developing structure, placing plants, and incorporating nonplant features.

The plant reference database is the prime tool for plant selection, and the spreadsheet for materials lists and cost estimates. Table 9-1 lists the steps in the design process, together with the best tools for the job.

Visual-imaging systems make it easy to create a preliminary design. With this preliminary image, you can decide if the design is appropriate before taking it to the next step, creating plans for construction and installation.

Table 9-1
The different software tools that fit
best in the steps of the design process

DESIGN PROCESS STEPS	VISUAL IMAGING	CAD	OTHER
Determining your needs	X		X
Site analysis	X		
Area development	X	X	
Developing structure		X	
Selecting plants			X
Placing plants	X	X	
Incorporating nonplant features	X	X	
Adding the finishing touches	X	X	
Assembling a list of materials			X
Estimating costs			X

How to develop a garden with software

To develop a landscape design, you follow a modified version of the design process using the various software tools. The steps are:

1. Do a site analysis with digital photographs.
2. Develop the area and structure using visual imaging and digital photographs.
3. Select plants and materials with database managers.
4. Develop construction and installation plans with CAD or CAD-based landscape design programs.
5. Assemble lists of materials and cost estimates with CAD programs and spreadsheets.

Get Your House into Your Computer

The first step in landscape design with the computer is to get a picture of your house into the computer. You may also want to put other pictures into the computer, such as plants and landscape materials. Digitizing an image—the process of converting a picture into digital form—can be accomplished with a variety of computer devices. Depending on the images you want to digitize, you may need to use two or more methods to get all of your pictures into the computer.

Scanners

Scanners are the major input devices for putting photographs and other graphics into a computer. Scanners work like photocopiers and fax machines, reflecting light off an image and capturing the light with sensors. The sensors pick up the reflected light as a series of dots. The number of dots a scanner can pick up is referred to as its resolution, denoted in *dpi* or *dots-per-inch*. Like video displays, the higher the scanner's resolution, the sharper the image captured into the computer.

When purchasing a scanner, pay attention to its resolution. While some scanners may have an optical resolution of only 600 dpi, many can provide actual resolutions of 1,200 dpi or higher. How is this possible? The scanner assumes that if several dots next to each other are all black, then the space between the dots should also be black. The scanner software then fills in the spaces with additional dots. In ads for scanners, this feature is often listed as *interpolated resolution*. For our garden-planning purposes, however, a personal scanner with an actual resolution of 300 dpi to 600 dpi will be sufficient.

Desktop scanners fit into one of three categories: flatbed, hand-held, and sheet-fed. The scanner you select will depend on the type of material you want to digitize, the amount of scanning you will do, and the cost.

Flatbed scanners

Flatbed scanners operate like photocopiers. You place the image you want to scan on a flat glass plate. During scanning, a light moves under the glass to scan the image.

The resolutions and color depth (number of colors the scanner can record) varies among flatbed scanners, but overall their scans will be better than those of handheld or sheet-fed scanners. Generally, the greater the scanning resolution and color depth, the higher the price of the scanner. Flatbed scanners range from $150 to $1,500 and more. The high-end, higher-priced scanners have higher resolution and color depth and produce much better images, but lower-end scanners should be acceptable for most gardening activities.

The big advantage of flatbed scanners is their ability to scan a large range of materials, from full pages of graphics and photographs to the pages of books and magazines. You can also use a flatbed scanner to scan shallow three-dimensional objects like leaves and pressed flowers.

Flatbed scanners have their disadvantages too. For one, they can be bulky. A typical unit takes up as much space on your desk as a standard desktop computer. Moreover, vertical space is as much a problem as flat desktop space. Because you will need to open the cover on the scanner, you won't be able to tuck it on a shelf under your desk. Their other disadvantage is that many flatbed scanners require a special interface card or a SCSI interface, which is not a standard feature on most PC computers, though some low-end flatbed scanners now connect to a parallel printer port. Though neither of these disadvantages is insurmountable, you may not want the extra hassle or have the extra space.

Handheld scanners

Handheld scanners are also known as half-page scanners, because they can scan widths of only $2\frac{1}{2}$ to 4 inches—about half a standard printed page. To scan a full page requires two passes, one on each side, and you must hope that the handheld scanner's auto-stitching software will correctly assemble the two pieces.

A big problem with the handheld scanner is the scanning mechanism—your hand. Unlike a flatbed, which typically scans in a smooth, direct path, our hands tend to move, twitch, and jerk regardless of how steady we think we are holding the handheld scanner. Images produced with a handheld scanner can be a bit fuzzy or skewed. Manufacturers offer special trays to guide the scanners while scanning, but even with one of these trays, you may have to repeat scanning several times before you're satisfied.

Handheld scanners do have some advantages over other types. One is their ability to scan pages or images from books and other publications that are just too cumbersome for a flatbed scanner or do not fit through a sheet-fed scanner. Also, most handheld scanners connect to the parallel printer port of the computer, which makes them a snap to connect. They're also portable—you can easily connect them to a notebook computer when you're on the road.

Sheet-fed scanners

Sheet-fed scanners have grown in popularity because they offer the resolution and sharpness of a flatbed scanner without taking up much desk space. A few of the half-page models even fit in an empty disk drive bay of your computer.

Sheet-fed scanners work a lot like fax machines. Their primary use is for preparing text documents for faxing or archiving, although several newer ones are being promoted as photo scanners as well. Some are half-page scanners, which makes them perfect for scanning standard 3-by-5-inch and 4-by-6-inch photographs. Others are full-page scanners, which can handle standard sheets of paper and larger graphics or photographs.

Sheet-fed scanners suffer the same problems as fax machines, namely jagged edges in the images. Like a fax machine, the paper being scanned tends to drift as it is pulled through the scanner. Although newer sheet-fed scanners minimize this problem, the clarity of their scanned images will only equal those produced by the low-end flat-bed scanners. There is also no easy way to feed a leaf or pressed flower through a sheet-fed scanner.

The gardening scanner

Of these different types of scanners, which one is best for gardening? Since visual-imaging systems require a scanned photograph of the home or landscape, one of the small-format (half-page) sheet-fed photo scanners may be the best choice. Later, when we want to have scanned images from photographs of plants and gardens, these scanners will continue to serve our information management requirements.

If you plan to scan graphics and photos from printed publications along with standard photographs and drawings, a flatbed scanner will be the ideal choice. You can use a flatbed for a variety of scanning jobs, as long as the items fit on the scanner's glass plate and as long as you have the desktop space for the scanner.

Because they can scan only a small area and because they're hard to use, handheld scanners are not as good a choice as your primary scanner.

Digital cameras

In the recent past, to get a photograph of your landscape into the computer, you took the photo using traditional film, had the film processed, and finally scanned the photo into the computer. Now, with a digital camera, you can bypass the film and create a digital image directly.

A digital camera is like a film camera with a lens, shutter, and various features for controlling exposure. Some digital camera bodies even look like those of film cameras. The major difference between them is that the digital camera replaces the film with a light sensor and memory to store the images. Like a scanner, when light strikes the sensor it creates a digital image. These digital images are then transferred into the computer or stored on removable memory cards.

While photographic film has nearly infinite resolution, the resolution of digital cameras is not even close to that of film, as it is restricted by the optical resolution of the sensor and the memory limitations of the camera. The resolution of the final image is further limited by the resolution of the monitor used to display the image and the printer used to print it.

Still, even with their limited resolution, a personal-use digital camera is fine for capturing images of the home or landscape for use in developing garden designs with visual-imaging software. Most computer monitors display images at the same resolution as a digital camera's picture, and for our purposes we do not need near-photographic quality prints from our printer.

Digital cameras start at about $200; prices for higher resolutions and more features are much higher, but they will undoubtedly continue to drop. Is a digital camera worth the price for photographing the garden as part of the design process and for record-keeping? Yes, if you plan to do garden design with visual-imaging systems on even a semiprofessional level, or if you want to record images as part of a multimedia plant reference. No, if you want high-quality prints of your photographs to paste in a garden journal or to pass around to friends—film cameras with a photo scanner are still a better option. Until the technology improves and the price drops even further, it will be difficult to achieve fine photographs with the digital cameras and color printers within most of our price ranges.

Video frame capture hardware

If you own a video camera or a camcorder, you've got most of what it takes to bring digital images into your computer. All you need is video frame capture hardware, or video frame grabbers, to pull any image you want from a video into your computer.

There are many types of video frame capture hardware, from boards that can capture and digitize full-motion video from any video source (including cameras, camcorders, VCRs, and broadcast signals) to those that capture only individual still frames. For capturing images to manipulate in a visual-imaging system, the simplest video frame capture hardware is all you need. One of the small devices that plug into the parallel printer port on your desktop or notebook computer is an excellent choice for occasional use.

If you have an available slot in your computer, you can install a video capture interface card inside your computer, like an internal modem or sound card. An internal card is generally faster at capturing and storing images than a parallel port device. Most can capture full-motion video and offer extensive video editing capabilities. Although none of the landscape design visual-imaging systems uses full-motion video, capturing a walkaround video segment will make it easier to select different individual views for use in the design software.

If you own a camcorder, video capture hardware is a good alternative to a scanner or digital camera. Parallel port video capture devices and single-frame video capture cards cost less than the low-end flatbed and sheet-fed scanners. Full-motion video capture cards cost about as much as the better flatbed scanners and digital cameras.

Film processing services

For most of my work, I need to take traditional photographic prints and slides, along with digital images. It is still easier for me to carry a tray of plant slides into class instead of a computer and video projector. The slides are much higher resolution than any computer image. However, I need digital images of the plants for the Web and CD-ROMs. I've found that the best way to get all three formats—prints, slides, and digital images—is through a film-processing service.

Several film processors now offer digital-imaging services, which convert negatives, prints, or slides into digital images (see Table 9-2 on the next page). If your local film processor doesn't have this capability, try mail order. When you send in your film, you can get a disk of all your pictures as digital images (for an additional fee) from Seattle Filmworks or York Photo. Seattle Filmworks can even create both slides and digital images from color print film during processing. Both can also return the digital images to you by e-mail, or allow you to download your images from their Web site. It may take up to two weeks to get your prints and images back from one of these processors, but if you aren't in a rush they offer quality results at reasonable prices.

Table 9-2
Some film processors offering digital imaging service

COMPANY	WEB ADDRESS	PHONE
Seattle Filmworks	http://www.filmworks.com	1-800-FILMWORKS
York Photo	http://www.yorkphoto.com	1-304-424-YORK
Kodak	http://www.kodak.com	1-800-235-6325
Fuji Film	http://www.fujifilm.com	1-800-800-3854

The major film manufacturers are also now providing photos on diskette. Anywhere you can find Kodak Premium photofinishing services, you can now have your photos put on disk during processing. In searching through Kodak's Web site, I discovered I can now order this service at the nearby grocery or drug store. Fuji Film offers similar services.

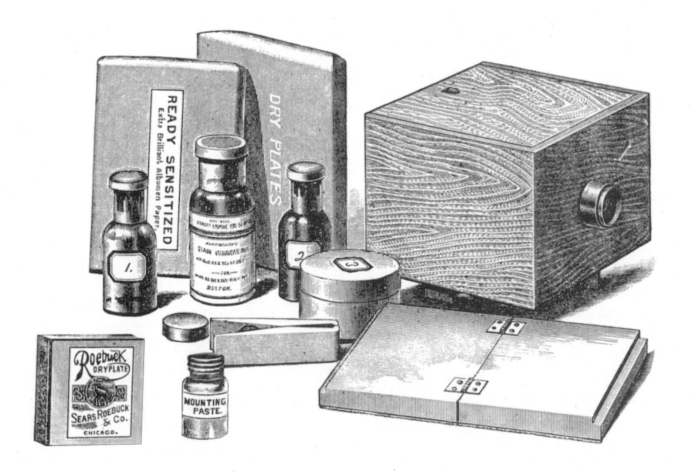

10

Creating Your Electronic Garden

There are many different tools and techniques for creating garden plans on a computer. These tools range from electronic versions of the artist's paintbrushes and palettes to the draftperson's mechanical pencil and triangles. As with any other gardening tool, each tool best fits a particular purpose in planning the garden.

Starting Your Garden with Paint Programs

While not the best tools for creating artistic renditions of your garden, paint programs will do in a pinch. Most paint programs will let you import digital images and paint trees, shrubs, and groundcovers right over them. Though the plants you paint won't be of the same resolution as photographs, these painted images will still give you an idea of how the landscape might look.

All versions of Microsoft Windows include a paint program. The Windows 95 version of Paint can be run with photo images, even though you will have very limited flexibility in modifying the photos. You can also find several different shareware and commercial paint programs. A quick search at CNET's DOWNLOAD.COM (**http://www.download.com**) or ZDNet's Software Library (**http://www.hotfiles.com**) will display several titles.

Image Editing Software Is for the Budding Artist

When you search the Web for programs, you might find paint programs classified under the broader heading of image editing. I prefer to distinguish the two, defining image-editing software as a multi-layer, object-based photo/paint program with a variety of special-effects tools. You can think of image editors as paint programs on massive doses of fertilizer. Would you like your garden design to look like it was done in watercolors? That's possible with some of the advanced image editors, along with other artistic effects such as oil paint, charcoals, pastels, and ink sketching.

Landscape/garden planners such as Planix Photo Landscape or Alpha Complete Landscape Designer are more than just paint programs, and they fit into my definition of image editors. Most commercial programs, like Adobe Photoshop and Corel PHOTO-PAINT 7 Plus, are overkill for most gardeners, although Microsoft Image Composer is a relatively low-cost image-editing program suitable for creating photorealistic garden designs (see Figure 10-1).

Figure 10-1
You can create professional-looking graphics with Image Composer

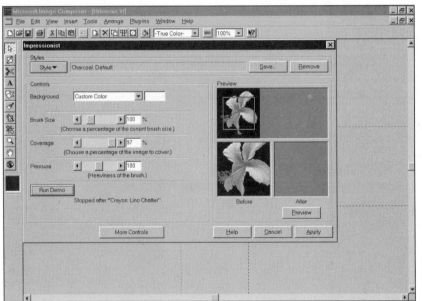

Unfortunately, as of this writing, Image Composer is available only as part of the Microsoft FrontPage Web development software. If we're lucky, Microsoft will release Image Composer as a separate program for those of us who will not be creating Web sites.

Besides the high cost of most professional image-editing programs, an additional downside is their lack of a photographic plant image library. You have to create your own by scanning in pictures from books, catalogs, or photographs, which can be rather time consuming. It's more cost effective to jump right to image-editing software designed for photorealistic landscape and garden planning, all of which cost $50 to $60—much less than professional-level image-editing software.

If you own a scanner, you probably have a basic image-editing program. Many scanners include limited editions of Adobe's Photoshop or Corel's PHOTO-PAINT. While not as heavy duty as the commercial image editors, most of these programs will work for basic visual imaging.

Landscape image designers

Landscape image designers are image-editing programs adapted for use in garden and landscape design. They offer a comprehensive library of plant images, along with a detailed database of plant information. You have not only a clip-art collection of images, but also the ability to search for plants that fit your design criteria. Most of the designers allow you to add your own bitmapped images to your design; some even allow you to add images and information to their plant reference library.

You will find several landscape image designers at computer superstores and in mail-order software catalogs. They range from simple photo paint-type programs to sophisticated image editing-based systems. As with any software, look at the various features to see which program best fits your needs. (Remember DASSSH?) For example, while two of the more popular programs, Planix Photo Landscape and Complete Landscape Designer work similarly, they have significantly different features.

Figure 10-2

A completed design with an

insert of the "before" image

from Planix Photo Landscape

Planix Photo Landscape

Planix Photo Landscape, from Softdesk (a division of Autodesk, one of the largest CAD companies in the world), was one of the first home landscape image designers on the market (see Figure 10-2). It comes with a library of 500 photographic plant images and lets you add your own bitmap images to your designs. You can also grow plants placed in the design to see how they will look several years from now.

Photo Landscape keeps track of all the items you place in your design and creates a list of materials. The night feature is particularly neat—you can place lights around the design and see how it will look after sunset.

Additional details about the Planix Photo Landscape can be found at Softdesk's Drafix Web site, **http://www.drafix.com**. While at their Web site you might explore their Drafix CAD products, which I have found to be among the better general-purpose two-dimensional CAD programs adaptable to garden and landscape design.

Complete Landscape Designer

SEE CD-ROM

Complete Landscape Designer, from Alpha Software, has been getting excellent reviews. Like Planix Photo Landscape, Complete Landscape Designer is an object-based image editor that lets you drop plants or materials into your design and move them around; it too has a plant growth simulator.

Alpha Software is one of the major developers of mid-range database management software, which is evident in Complete Landscape Designer's comprehensive plant reference library, which includes images for just about every plant in the library. You can add your own plant information and images, or download additional objects from their Web site (see Figure 10-3 on page 164).

Find out more about the Complete Landscape Designer at Alpha Software's Web site, **http://www.alphasoftware.com**.

Imagine Your Landscape

Imagine Your Landscape is part of the Imagine Your . . . series by Visual Applications, a developer of visual-imaging programs for the building industry (see Figure 10-4 on page 165). The program includes an extensive library of items and products. There is also a basic drawing program for adding final touches. It includes video tutorials and voice assistance on the CD-ROM.

As landscape design is often considered an extension of other design processes, such as interior design and exterior remodeling, the program integrates well with the other programs in the Imagine Your . . . series. If you are also looking to design or redesign other aspects of the home, this series may be a good choice, because of its common interface across all the programs in the series.

SEE CD-ROM

A demonstration of the program is available on the enclosed CD, with a small set of files with which you can try some plant placement. You can also visit their Web site, at **http://www. showoff.com**, for more information about the product.

No measurements!

One of the advantages of landscape image-design software is that you don't need to take time-consuming measurements of your

Figure 10-3
Garden design with Alpha Software
Complete Landscape Designer. The
first image is a before picture; the
second image is a new design using
visual imaging; the third image is
a projection of the mature landscape

Figure 10-4
The Imagine series from Visual Systems not only lets you create a new landscape but add new siding and a roof to your house

property. You just scan in an image of your yard and start placing plants and other landscape materials. Because the photo already incorporates the true perspective of you standing in the garden, especially if you took the picture, you don't need to make detailed perspective drawings.

However, the lack of precise measurements is also a downside to photorealistic design. Photographs lack the depth you need to determine the distance or spacing of objects in the picture. For example, if you put in a paver walkway, you won't know exactly how wide or long it is. You can get an approximation of its dimensions by referencing the sizes of known objects, such as the side of a building, but you won't know the exact measurements.

You need such precise measurements to determine how much material to purchase or to avoid planting pitfalls. You don't want to be caught short of paver blocks near the end of the installation, on a Sunday morning when all the paver suppliers are closed. And you don't want to plant your live Christmas tree so close to the house that it lifts the eaves on the roof.

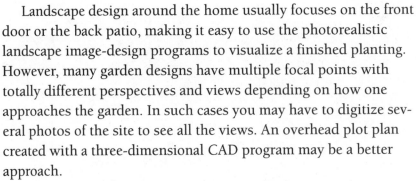

Landscape design around the home usually focuses on the front door or the back patio, making it easy to use the photorealistic landscape image-design programs to visualize a finished planting. However, many garden designs have multiple focal points with totally different perspectives and views depending on how one approaches the garden. In such cases you may have to digitize several photos of the site to see all the views. An overhead plot plan created with a three-dimensional CAD program may be a better approach.

Although a photorealistic landscape/garden-planning program can't produce accurate measurements or show multiple views, it can be a valuable tool to use before developing a detailed precision drawing or CAD rendering. This kind of software allows us to do extensive "what-ifs" before spending time measuring and actually drawing the design.

Drawing the Garden

Now that we've visualized our gardens using landscape image-design software, we'll use our visualizations along with a drawing program to create the precision plans we need to put things in the right place.

Drawing garden and landscape designs to scale on paper is time consuming, but necessary to ensure accuracy. Drawing programs help ease the task if you are willing to continue working "to scale." Any lines, objects, or symbols placed on the drawing can be moved, resized, or edited without affecting other parts of the drawing.

Computer-aided drafting (CAD) programs maintain the real-world dimensions for all objects in the drawing; you don't need to convert actual measurements to scale. If you want a 23-foot-long flower bed, you draw the bed that length.

Computer-aided design programs (also abbreviated as CAD) let you attach information to the objects in your drawing. A tree symbol can contain the information on, for example, *Acer palmatum* (Japanese maple), available from the nursery for $200.

Certain landscape CAD programs even let us create a three-dimensional representation of the design, letting us see the garden from almost any angle (see Figures 10-6 and 10-7). Although not as realistic as the pictures from a landscape image-design program, these three-dimensional views can provide us with additional ways to visualize our garden before even a single shovel of soil is turned over.

Illustration programs

Drawing programs construct images based on algebra and trigonometry as they go, rather than displaying preconstructed bitmapped images. This allows you to create complex graphics that take up less room than the equivalent raster or bitmap images.

Illustration programs differ from CAD programs. CAD has tools for creating precision drawings using real-world dimensions, while illustration programs contain tools for creating complex artwork using Bézier curves (curves created by mathematical formulas involving tangent lines) and other special lines.

Illustration programs work in paper dimensions, usually standard dimensions from $8\frac{1}{2}$-by-11-inch letter size to 11-by-17-inch tabloid size. All of the programs have a standard ruler display in inches, centimeters, or pixels, so you can use illustration programs for garden design if you are willing to work with scale (see Figure 10-5 on page 168).

Although not suited for precision garden design, drawing and illustration programs are fine for quick sketches if you know how to draw with Bézier curves. Treat them the same way you would a quick sketch on a piece of paper, and be sure you can transfer the sketch into a CAD program for more refinement.

General CAD programs

CAD programs use mathematical constructs and data to define an image, and all use real-world dimensions. Many even allow you to change the units of measure to fit a particular task or location. For instance, if you live in the United States but you're designing a garden for a home in Europe, meters are more appropriate than feet.

Figure 10-5
CorelDRAW is a popular
illustration program

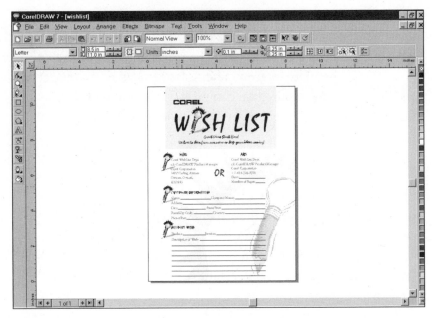

Computer-aided design programs have several features that take into account the overall design process, whereas computer-aided drafting programs focus strictly on precision drawing. All CAD programs support symbols or blocks—complex groups of drawing objects treated as one object. These are kept in libraries for instant placement in a drawing. The process is like using rubber stamps or plastic templates of landscape symbols.

Along with sophisticated drawing features, CAD programs also include several tools for extracting information from the drawing. For example, if you have numerous tree and shrub symbols, you can automatically generate a list of those symbols, complete with a total for each.

All CAD programs support *layers*. Layers are like clear sheets of plastic; while drawing on one layer, *the active layer,* you do not draw over objects on other layers. You can turn layers on or off to see different parts of the design. You can draw the foundation of a house and its property lines on one layer, existing trees and shrubs on a second layer, and new plants on a third layer. Erasing or modifying objects on the new plant layer does not affect the foundation layer or the existing plants layer.

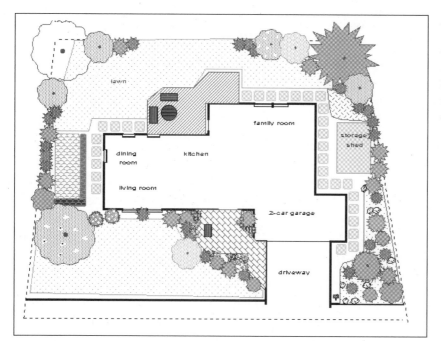

Figure 10-6
Two views of a landscape design drawing with layers. The top image has all layers turned on, except the sprinkler system layer; the second image has all layers turned off, except the foundation layer and the sprinkler system layer

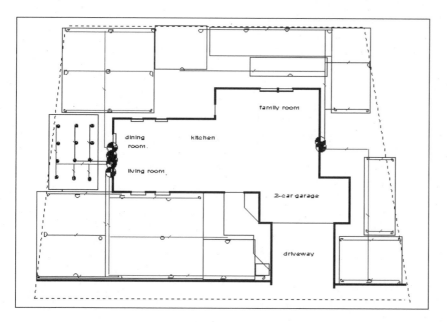

Layers are the key to effective drawing with CAD. You can not only organize and view the different parts of a drawing, but also maintain different drawings in one project file (see Figure 10-6).

You can create sectional, perspective, and detailed construction drawings all within one main drawing file, by keeping the different drawings on separate layers. You can turn off all the layers, and use an overhead bird's-eye view to see a detailed installation drawing on planting and staking a tree.

What about plant reference libraries? General-purpose CAD programs don't come with plant reference databases. However, with the ability of the Microsoft Windows and Macintosh operating systems to run multiple programs at the same time, you can run a separate database while you are using the CAD program. Also, most general-purpose CAD programs include basic landscape symbol libraries, and they let you add more symbols to their existing libraries or create new libraries.

One feature common to general-purpose CAD programs, but lacking in most home landscape design software, is the ability to import or export drawings to other CAD programs and other applications.

If you decide to use a general-purpose CAD program, select one that's geared toward architectural and not mechanical design. CAD programs for architectural design have better tools for working with curves (curved flower beds and water gardens) and parallel lines (walks and paths), along with stronger support for non-graphic information management and reporting.

Several CAD programs, both shareware and commercial, are suitable for landscape design. I prefer to use a general-purpose CAD program rather than a landscape-design-based one. The general-purpose program will have better drawing, editing, and information-gathering tools, and more design flexibility, than the landscape-design-specific CAD program. Like developing your own plant information system with an off-the-shelf relational database manager, tailoring a general-purpose CAD program to do garden and landscape design will take time. But in the end, you will have a system that meets your specific needs. Softdesk's Drafix QuickCAD (**http://www.drafix.com**) and IMSI's TurboCAD series (**http://www.imsisoft.com**) are two good general-purpose CAD programs adaptable to garden or landscape design. (See Figure 10-7.)

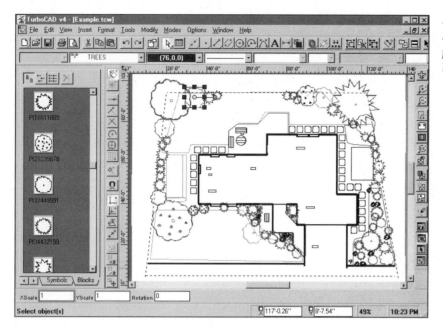

Figure 10-7
Many general purpose CAD
programs can be used for
landscape design

Landscape design and planning programs

CAD programs can be adapted for particular uses, such as landscape design. AutoCAD, the top professional CAD system for
personal computers, has special programming features that extend
its capability. LandCADD, which uses this capability, is a design
program for professional landscape architects that runs in conjunction with AutoCAD. For homeowners and gardeners as well,
a landscape-planning program using a CAD engine at its core is
the ideal design tool.

The two primary features that distinguish a CAD-based
landscape design from a general-purpose CAD program are the
inclusion of extensive landscape symbol libraries and an integrated plant reference database. Most CAD programs for landscape
design also include additional features, such as basic sprinkler
design and a function that lets you create a list of materials for a
design. Many CAD programs for landscape and garden design also
allow you to draw and view your designs in three dimensions,
using one of two methods.

The first method is actually considered "two-and-a-half" dimensions, whereas the other affords full three-dimensional viewing and drawing. With the two-and-a-half dimension method, you develop your design in an overhead plot-plan view, which is a bird's-eye view from straight above your landscape. Once you create the design, the program creates a separate two-dimensional elevation drawing from a different viewing angle, called an elevation view, giving the appearance of three dimensions (see Figure 10-8).

Current three-dimensional CAD programs for landscape design are all true 3D programs. Although you create your design in two dimensions, the program always maintains the information necessary to display it in 3D. When you want to look at a design from a perspective other than the overhead bird's-eye view, the program regenerates the design as it would appear from the new viewing angle.

Creating—or rendering—3D objects in a CAD program takes a fair amount of computing power, which many people using landscape design programs don't have. To maintain all the needed information while keeping the computer requirements low, gardener-level three-dimensional CAD programs do not offer the full editing features found in professional programs. All of the symbols—trees, shrubs, house, fences, and so on—are pre-existing and optimized for the program; you cannot create your own.

Working with three-dimensional landscape design CAD programs is a little different from working with traditional two-dimensional ones. Instead of using full-featured drawing tools that let you invent almost anything, creating a design is like working with doll-house furniture or those peel-and-stick design kits you can find in some home improvement stores. You pick a tree or shrub and drag it to where you want it on the property. You can change the size of the plant symbol and assign specific plant information to the symbols, but that's about it.

Like the landscape image-planning programs, most of the CAD programs for landscape design (including two-dimensional programs) include plant growth simulators, which show the results of growth over a set number of years. Some of the advanced programs

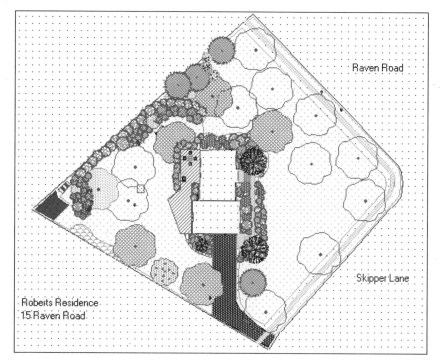

Figure 10-8
A plan view (top) and elevation view (bottom) of a landscape as two separate drawings. The elevation view was created from the plan view by the program

Raven Road

Skipper Lane

Roberts Residence
15 Raven Road

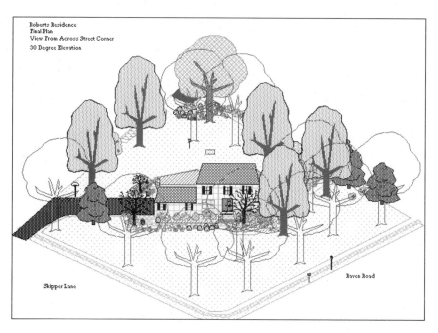

Roberts Residence
Final Plan
View From Across Street Corner
30 Degree Elevation

Skipper Lane

Raven Road

Figure 10-9
2D and 3D viewing in 3D Landscape. Note
the helicopter and camera controls for
viewing the design from a bird's vantage

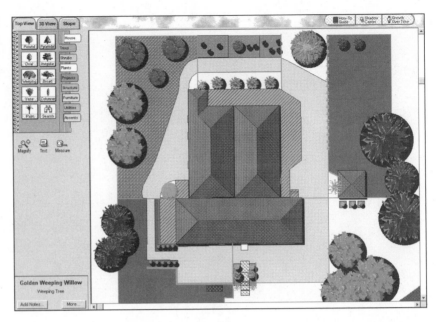

show seasonal changes as well, so that you can see how the plants will look in summer or winter. 3D Landscape by Books That Work even includes a shadow caster so you can pinpoint the unexpected shady areas of your garden (see Figure 10-9).

When viewing a design in 3D, an imaginary camera control usually allows you to change the elevation up and down, or pan left and right. Current three-dimensional landscape design programs use newer technologies from computer game developers to create a 3D view that is nearer to photorealistic images than the older versions, although they are not yet to the level of digitized photo images. Some also include a flyby feature, which lets you move through the design like a bee on the hunt for a fresh flower.

There are several CAD-based programs for landscape design. All of the shareware and freeware programs are two-dimensional CAD programs—usually general-purpose CAD programs with an added symbol library. Among the commercial programs, 3D Landscape, LandDesigner 4.5, and Complete LandDesigner (all from Sierra On-Line) are the most popular for landscape design (see Figure 10-10 on page 176). If you are new to the subject, 3D Landscape has an excellent multimedia tutorial on the landscape design process.

There are some additional low-cost three-dimensional CAD programs, but they have fairly limited features (see Figure 10-11 on page 177). These include Landscape Design 3D by Expert Software (**http://www.expertsoftware.com**) and Pro Landscape 3-D by The Learning Company (**http://www.learningco.com**).

SEE CD-ROM

When selecting a CAD program, particularly a three-dimensional one, beware of the hardware requirements. (Remember to DASSSH.) If you want to use a three-dimensional CAD program for landscape design, you'll need at least a multimedia PC with a fast Pentium processor or a PowerPC Macintosh, and lots of memory.

Figure 10-10
2D and 3D viewing in LandDesigner 4.5.
LandDesigner's 3D view is from the view-
point of one walking around a property

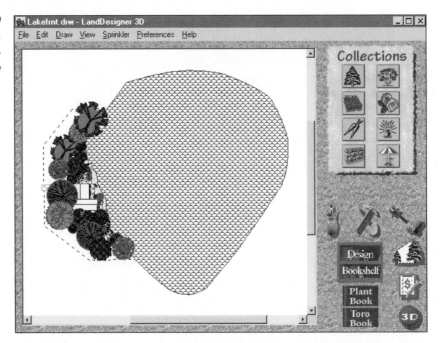

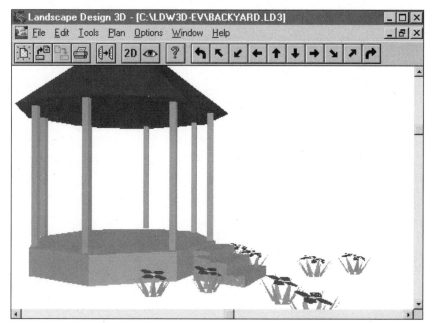

Figure 10-11
For small garden designs with limited
3D requirements, a low cost 3D landscape
design program may be appropriate

11

Garden Design Toolkits

Most landscape-planning programs include a database of anywhere from 500 to 2,000 plants. You will find that all of the garden-design plant databases are organized a little differently from the plant databases in garden encyclopedias. In CAD systems, you search for plants based on design criteria, attributes, or characteristics; you specify height, spread, light requirements, and existing growing conditions (see Figure 11-1).

You do not have to use the plant selector database included with the CAD program; you can easily use any other, including your own. However, one big advantage of using the included one is that it is integrated with the program's drawing system.

In the program's internal database, any symbol with attached plant information is linked to the database record. Several symbols for the same plant can be linked to one database record, making for efficient drawing. When using an external database, instead of one built into the CAD program, you must label each symbol with all textual information, causing your drawings to bloat.

When selecting a CAD program for landscape design, see if the program will allow you to add plants to the database. In simpler, gardener-level programs, this feature is limited. Professional-level programs, however, allow for extensive import and export of data-

Figure 11-1
A search dialog box for finding
plants by design criteria

Find Plants By Attributes

Type	Tree	Sunlight	Any
Shape	Broad	Water Prefs	Any
Deciduous	Deciduous	Flower Color	Any
Usage	Shade Tree	Flower Season	Any
Height	Any	Maintenance	Any

Number of matching Plants: 2

Search...   Cancel   Local Conditions <<   How-To▼

Hardiness Zone — Zone: 5   Zone Map...

Soil pH — ☐ Acid ☐ Neutral ☒ Alkaline

Soil Type — ☐ Clay ☐ Loam ☐ Sand

Soil Attributes — ☐ Organic ☐ Well Drained ☐ Poorly Drained ☐ Moist ☐ Dry

base information. If you work with a particular group of plants, you may not be able to add your favorites to the database unless you have this capability.

If the internal database doesn't work for you, you can develop and maintain your own. Instead of using a CAD program specifically for landscape design, use a general-purpose CAD program with flexible database capabilities. For example, Drafix QuickCAD (**http://www.drafix.com**), along with several other general-purpose CAD programs, has database capabilities that you can use to create your own internal plant database (see Figure 11-2). Some of the more advanced—and expensive—CAD programs even integrate with spreadsheets and database managers, allowing you to link to databases you may already have.

Because gardener-level CAD programs are limited, particularly when it comes to their plant databases, I use a general-purpose two-dimensional CAD program with my own plant information system. While I am sorry to give up 3D, I prefer the flexibility. But remember that I'm fairly skilled at both developing databases and using CAD programs—you may not want to try this at home, especially if you're short on time or patience.

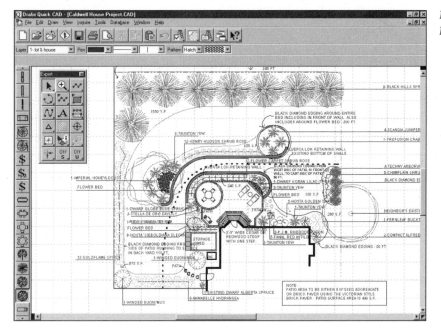

Figure 11-2
Here's a peek at what QuickCAD can do

Create a Garden Design Toolkit

I am often asked which landscape-planning program to buy, a landscape image-design program like Photo Landscape or a CAD program like 3D Landscape? The answer is both types, with a plant database tossed in for good measure.

You can use a 3D CAD program for landscape design, but you need to take all the site measurements and draw the design before you can use the 3D features. A two-dimensional CAD program is acceptable if you are good at visualizing your new design.

Landscape image-design programs let you visualize your new design, but they don't let you pull out accurate measurements to use in installing the landscape. To develop an accurate plan for construction and installation, you need to do some drawing—either on paper or with a CAD program.

Therefore, the best option is to buy both a landscape design visual-imaging program and a CAD program. The two should cost you between $50 and $100—about the same as four quality hostas in two-gallon containers. Sierra On-Line's Complete LandDesigner

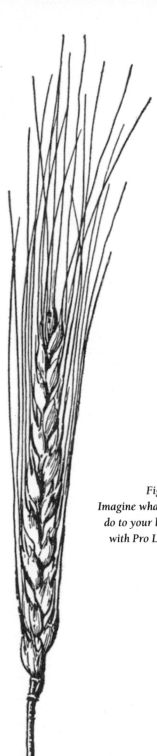

is a combination of 3D Landscape, 3D Deck, Photo LandDesigner, and the Gardening Encyclopedia as one comprehensive solution for about $50.

You can use the landscape image-design program for site analysis, area development, plant selection, and preliminary design. You can see the finished design before pulling out a tape measure, drawing a single measured line, or digging a hole. Once you are satisfied with the "proposed" finished design, you can start doing the traditional steps in the design process—measuring the site, developing the area, drawing plot plans, selecting additional plants, and assembling a list of materials.

If you are serious about garden design or considering design on a semiprofessional basis, consider Autodesk's Pro Landscape (**http://www.prolandscape.com**). Pro Landscape is like Planix Photo Landscape and Drafix QuickCAD together, with a very extensive plant image library and a large, detailed plant reference database (see Figure 11-3). Of course, Pro Landscape costs about $700, but you get an extensive integrated system rather than separate programs.

Figure 11-3
Imagine what you can do to your landscape with Pro Landscape

Manage Your Garden Information with a CAFM System

In business and industry, facility managers need to keep track of an extensive inventory of equipment. They need to know not only what the company owns, but where the equipment is located. To help manage their inventory, many managers turn to CAD programs as the core of a *computer-aided facilities management* (CAFM) system.

CAFM systems use a CAD program to map the locations of all equipment. As equipment is added, moved, or replaced, the facilities manager can adjust the drawings to reflect the changes (see Figure 11-4). Some CAFM systems include extensive database capabilities like the plant databases in CAD programs. The manager can query the database for the location of certain equipment; the objects representing the equipment are highlighted in the drawing.

How does this relate to gardening? In our gardens we manage our plants—adding new plants, moving and removing plants—just like the facilities manager manages equipment. Without a drawing or map of our garden, we can quickly lose track of our plants. How

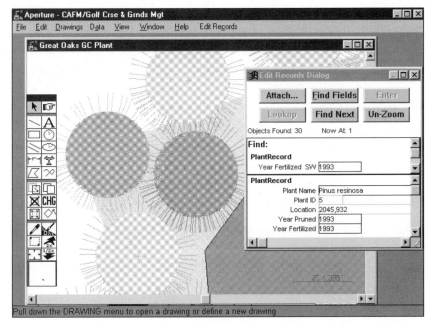

Figure 11-4
By searching the database, plants in a drawing are highlighted that meet the search criteria. The highlighted (darker) tree symbols shown here are two trees that have not been fertilized since 1993

many times have you pulled up a plant in the spring thinking it was a weed, when the plant was actually a valuable perennial?

You can use the same tool you use for designing the garden, a CAD program, to keep a visual record of the garden. Once the garden is installed, you can correct your landscape design drawings to reflect the actual locations of the plants and other materials, changing them to what are known as "as-built" drawings.

You can use a three-dimensional CAD program as the basis for your visual garden information manager. However, three-dimensional views of the existing garden are less important than an accurate two-dimensional overhead plot plan showing the exact locations of every plant and landscape feature. I have found that two-dimensional CAD programs are the best tools for such visual garden information management. In addition, a general-purpose two-dimensional CAD program with a flexible database is better than a landscape design-based CAD system with a plant selector database, because at this point we are more interested in information on location and cultural practices than in design attributes.

Depending on your CAD program and garden information system, you may be able to integrate the two. Many database managers let you insert graphics or images. Thus, you could paste into the location field the zoomed-in portion of the CAD drawing showing the location of plants.

Some general-purpose CAD programs allow you to set up a system like the professional CAFM systems. Depending on the database features, you may be able to search the database for a particular plant and have the CAD program highlight any plant symbols linked to the records in the database.

What Is It? Labeling Plants

Once you have installed your new garden, you may want to label your prize plantings. Using the list of materials from your landscape design and your plant information database or label-making program, you can quickly generate labels.

There is an ongoing debate about whether to label garden plants. Labels are important for visitors when you are absent or when you don't remember a particular plant. Unobtrusive labels also serve as a backup to maps and other records. However, overuse of labels, particularly the large oval plastic label stakes, make the garden look more like a plastic lollipop garden than a plant display.

There are as many ways to label plants in the garden or landscape as there are plants themselves. Labels range from thin wooden or white plastic stakes, to large metal stakes holding cards, to the fancy fired clay labels found in herb gardens. Many botanical gardens and arboreta use engraved two-color plastic laminates or engraved anodized metal plates.

With plastic or wooden stakes, the traditional method has been to write the plant name and other information using indelible felt marker in hopes the ink will stay permanent, at least through a season. To counter the problems of ink markers while avoiding the high cost of engraved plates, some gardeners stick embossed labels to stakes. (Dymo is a common brand of label maker for this purpose.) But it's time consuming to write out the labels or click a label embosser letter by letter, especially considering that the labels will last only a few months—or less if someone walks away with them.

Your computer can help to speed up the label-making process, while at the same time providing a much better-looking label. How you make the labels will depend on the way you'll use them, the amount of information you want to include, and the type of computer printer you are using.

One common method is to use standard adhesive mailing labels. You print the information on the label and apply the adhesive backing to the larger plastic oval label stakes. Most standard 3-by-$^{15}/_{16}$-inch mailing labels can hold up to four lines of information with standard-size printing (about 14 points or just over $^1/_6$ inch), or two lines of large-size printing (about 32 points or $^1/_3$ inch). Larger address labels will let you print much more information, of course.

Another label-making method is to print the information on index cards, which are then placed in special metal cardholder stakes. Index cards let you print a large amount of information using larger fonts, and even leave space for you to include some graphics. Due to the large size of the cards and the holding stakes, this method is best for very large gardens or large plant material, where the card stake is small relative to the plant.

All paper labels deteriorate over time, as rain, wind, and sun take their toll. Eventually, the labels become unreadable and messy. To counter this problem, you can apply a clear adhesive plastic film over the labels, which I have found will allow the labels to last at least a growing season.

Another problem with printing your own labels is the ink. The oil-based inks of older dot-matrix printers hold up well to weather, but the water-based inks of inkjet printers wash out quickly. Laser printer inks also hold up well, although they tend to flake in the heat of the sun. The best way to counter the problem of running, fading, or flaking ink is to print the labels, and then photocopy them and use the photocopies. For extra protection, spray the labels with a clear acrylic paint or cover them with a clear adhesive plastic film.

You can also print labels on plastic. Most nurseries print directly on plastic labels that can go through a pin-feed dot matrix printer. Some newer plastic labels can go through a laser printer without melting. I have seen adhesive label sheets made of Tyvek (the white clothlike material used in indestructible envelopes and house wrapping), which eliminates the problem of paper disintegration. The only difficulty with using plastic labels in your printer is finding small quantities to use in your garden. Usually, the minimum quantity you can purchase is 500 to 1,000 labels, which last me about 10 years.

Printing the labels with your computer is not difficult. Most database managers have templates for printing mailing labels, as do most word processors and all "works" programs (see Figure 11-5). There are also numerous label-printing programs (both shareware and commercial), such as Avery LabelPro (**http://www.avery.com**).

We have seen a number of tools you can use to plan and grow your garden before you ever buy a plant or turn a shovel. Landscape image-design programs let you play "what-if" scenarios

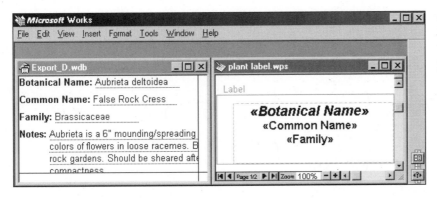

Figure 11-5
Most word processors and database managers in integrated "works" programs can create plant labels

without the expense of ripping out a garden design gone wrong. Landscape design-based CAD programs let you count pavers so you don't come up short while the mortar is drying. And once the garden is actually planted, you can continue to use these tools as part of your garden information system.

Your Computer in the Garden

Sometimes it makes sense to take a computer with you—to take or refer to notes as you check out your garden, to keep track of the watering, or to take notes as you visit other gardens. You can even use a portable computer to keep an eye on the garden without your having to go outside. Imagine watching your home garden grow while you work at your desk!

As gardeners, we are also likely to be weather watchers. However, my rain gauge is always full because I never read it and my evaporimeter is always empty because I forget to check it. How often have you reset the little pointer on those coil-type barometers? And while we are on the topic of weather and water, how about having the computer do the watering?

Let's look at some ways we can use our computer in the garden. Many of these applications are not readily available as "garden products," but rather as adaptations of ideas picked up from other computer users in the green industry. For example, computers control many golf course irrigation systems; a computer can perform the same function in your own backyard.

Carrying the Computer into the Garden

Many computers are small enough that we can take them into the garden. *Notebook computers,* about the size of a standard three-ring binder, match the power and features of desktops in a five- to seven-pound portable package. Some computers, called *subnotebooks,* are smaller still, weighing under five pounds; they may not offer such features of notebooks as a floppy disk or CD-ROM drive. In most cases, subnotebooks complement, but do not replace, desktops.

Handheld computers or *palmtops* fit the basic definition of a computer, at about the size of an overgrown checkbook. They use a stripped-down version of an operating system, like the version of Microsoft Windows known as Windows CE.

New to the scene are *mininotebooks*—shrunken subnotebooks that are about the size of a hardbound novel. Mininotebooks are full-blown notebooks, complete with a small color monitor, the full Windows operating system, and a keyboard just barely large enough for the touch typist.

Electronic organizers, also called digital diaries, have been around for some time. These computer-like devices are the electronic equivalent of a paper-based organizer, or a dedicated version of information manager software. Electronic organizers include an address book, calendar, scheduler with alarms, expense tracker, and memo pad. *Personal digital assistants* (PDAs) are the sophisticated versions of electronic organizers. Some of the more advanced PDAs have small text editors, spreadsheets, and e-mail capability. A few will even recognize handwriting with a special stylus and touch screen.

Generally, the smaller the package, the more limited the system. For instance, the smaller systems have calculator-like keys rather than full function keyboards. But electronic organizers are not necessarily skimpy. My little electronic organizer has 64k of memory for storing memos and addresses (16k more than my first Apple II Plus computer in 1981!). It can hold the equivalent of about 32 pages of typewritten double-spaced text or all 280 plants in my two plant materials courses, complete with botanical names, common names, families, and a few brief notes for each plant. Of course, the more full-featured the system, the more it's going to cost.

Taking it with us

The big advantage of portables is that they let you carry a large amount of information. Today's standard notebook computers can store the equivalent of several gardening references in a package the size of one three-ring binder. With the right references, we have a ready resource for identifying plants. Also, a notebook can store a large number of photographic images on the hard drive or read them from a CD-ROM. Just being able to carry around a readily accessible and easily updated listing of all of our plants is helpful. How many times have you bought a duplicate of a plant, forgetting that you already had one?

With a portable computer, you can update your plant information system on site, rather than making handwritten notes on paper to transfer later into the plant information system.

Can we afford to take it with us?

We work in a dirty environment. Unless you can find some leftover portable military computers that are "hardened" for adverse conditions, most portables are not suitable for outdoor use. One good splash of the sprinkler or a drop in the mud can mean disaster. I'm leery of taking notebook computers outside, even palmtops.

What we need instead is something small and easy to carry, with sufficient capacity to hold a list of the plants in our garden, along with some additional information. It should be safe to operate on a normal garden day, but if damaged it should be cheap enough to replace.

Electronic organizers: The computer for the garden

Although they are not true computers, electronic organizers are the best way to take a computer into the garden. They are small, easy to carry, and can hold a fair amount of information. And if you shop around for the right model, they are fairly low cost. Because they have many of the same functions as information managers, electronic organizers make good complements to the information manager in your desk computer.

When you start looking at electronic organizers to complement your desktop computer, you must keep in mind that not just any digital diary will work. You need to make sure the electronic organizer has a way of connecting to your computer; this connection is commonly called a *PC link*. This linking capability with your desktop computer is the most important feature of the electronic organizer (see Figure 12-1).

With the link, you can back up the information contained in the electronic organizer to your computer. Once in the computer, you can further back up the information onto a removable disk for safer storage. An electronic organizer is a good example of the adage "The data is worth far more than any hardware."

You can enter small chunks of information, such as names and addresses, into the organizer with the keyboard, but it is not designed for entering long lists at one time. With a PC link, you can enter your information on the computer, using the computer's much more comfortable keyboard and easy-to-read display. Once you enter all the information into a file on your computer, you can transfer the data into the electronic organizer in a couple of minutes.

Figure 12-1
A cable links the organizer or handheld computer and the desktop computer

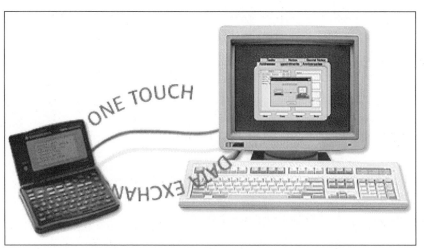

Some transfer programs, such as IntelliLink by Puma Technologies (**http://www.pumatech.com**), support several different information managers, a couple of database formats, and some word-processor formats. IntelliLink will also work with several different electronic organizers, digital diaries, and handheld computers.

Some information manager companies sell transfer software and cables for select models of electronic organizers. And some electronic organizer companies include a docking cradle as a PC link, complete with transfer software and an information manager.

Besides the all-important PC link capability, select an electronic organizer based on the following factors:

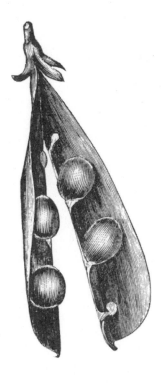

 Usefulness of its features

 Compatibility with your information manager

 Cost

Useful features

When selecting an electronic organizer, choose one with a built-in calculator keypad. In our work as gardeners, we often need to make calculations for such things as fertilizer amounts, seed application rates, and cost of plant materials.

The amount of memory installed in the organizer will dictate the amount of information you can store in it. Most electronic organizers with PC link capability start at 64 kilobytes of memory and go up to 2 megabytes.

Select among organizers based on the type of information you want to keep in it. Because I keep a lot of lists and notes, I prefer an organizer with good memo functions; scheduling and expense tracking are a lower priority. You may find expense tracking more important as you purchase plants and materials for your garden.

Screen size is important too. Many older or lower-priced models have small screens, displaying only 3 to 8 lines with 16 to 26 characters per line. This size is too small for long plant names and detailed notes. Medium-priced organizers that display 10 lines with 40 characters per line or more are much better.

Compatibility with information managers

Will the data from your electronic organizer mesh with your information manager? Will the to-do list in your information manager go into a to-do list on the organizer? Will it end up as a memo entry or an address record? Can you map (cross-link) the various records and fields between the information manager and the organizer?

Cost

Cost is the bottom line. Suitable organizers range from $30 to $300 or more. While even the cheaper ones will link to a PC, the transfer cable and software are usually sold separately and may cost more than the organizer.

Organizers in the $100 range will probably fit your requirements. Depending on their features, cables or docking stations with transfer software add $50 to $100 to the price. Many information manager and electronic organizer companies bundle information manager software, an organizer, transfer software, and cables to provide a complete solution. Often the bundle price is lower than the cost of all the separate items.

Personal digital assistants and handheld computers

You can step up from an electronic organizer to a personal digital assistant (PDA), or a palmtop or *handheld personal computer* (HPC). With more memory and larger displays, these computers are great for handling lots of information. However, these units cost considerably more than electronic organizers, ranging from $300 to $600 and up. (See Table 12-1.)

One of the more popular PDAs is the US Robotics PalmPilot. Unlike the typical calculator-like organizers, the PalmPilot is more like an electronic notepad. Besides the notepad-style display, it lets you "write" notes on the screen or choose icons or menu options with a stylus. Its slim and lightweight design is easy to carry, and it can be hooked to a docking station with automatic synchronization features. Sharp, Casio, IBM, and Apple Computer all have similar models.

Many PDAs have slots for cards containing additional memory or programs. Unlike electronic organizers, most PDAs will accept new software, although the software is usually a version designed specifically for the PDA.

Although they may look similar, the big difference between PDAs and handheld personal computers is the operating system. With the exception of the Psion HPC, all of the current HPCs use Windows CE, a "pocket"-sized version of Microsoft Windows. Windows CE includes pocket versions of Microsoft Word and Excel, along with e-mail and Web browsing software. As with a PDA, you can purchase new software for the HPC.

Table 12-1
A listing of some palmtop computers

ORGANIZERS AND DIGITAL DIARIES

BOSS series	Casio	http://www.casio-usa.com
RGxxx series	Royal	http://royalnet.com
Wizard OZ and YO series	Sharp	http://www.sharp-usa.com
Dictionary organizers	Vtech	http://vtech.com

PERSONAL DIGITAL ASSISTANTS (PDAs)

Newton	Apple	http://www.apple.com
Psion Series 3	Psion	http://www.psion.com
Zaurus series	Sharp	http://www.sharp-usa.com
Mobile Organizer	Sharp	http://www.sharp-usa.com
PalmPilot	US Robotics	http://www.3com.com

HANDHELD PERSONAL COMPUTERS (HPCs)

Cassiopeia	Casio	http://www.casio-usa.com
PC Companion	Compaq	http://www.compaq.com
HP300LX series	Hewlett-Packard	http://www.hp.com
Handheld PC	Hitachi	http://www.hitachi.com
Velo 1	Philips	http://www.philips.com
Psion Series 5	Psion	http://www.psion.com

This is not a comprehensive list of all the different palmtop devices. Listing of these devices does not imply evaluation or endorsement by the author or publisher.

Keeping an Eye on the Garden

You can use a video camera to view your garden on a computer. But why hook the video camera to a computer, when you can just connect the camera to the television? If you just want to look at the garden, the television will do fine.

Smile—your garden is on the computer screen!

On the other hand, when you plug the camera into the computer you can do all sorts of things. You can insert still images into a visual imaging system and use them for design work or include them in your plant information system. You can use full-motion video to create walkarounds of your garden for sending to your friends and relatives.

With a fixed video camera connected to your computer, you can take time-lapse photographs of your garden over the course of a season. To do this, set the computer to capture single video frames at regular intervals—such as one frame per daylight hour over three months. The computer can adjust for seasonal changes in sunrise and sunset. At the end of the season, you will have a time-lapse video of your garden growing and maturing.

Fixed video cameras can also help with security. Software can detect motion through the camera and capture an image, start tap-

ing, or sound an alarm. You can actually see when the rabbits are feasting in your garden, or when the dog decides to dig up your prized petunias.

With the right software and an Internet connection, you can even display real-time images of your garden on the World Wide Web. The Telegarden Project mentioned in the early chapters is a good example of a fixed video camera that displays a garden in real time to anyone on the Web. You can find several Web sites with *Webcams* (cameras used for posting on the Web) showing a view out their window. I recently watched the sun set in Fairbanks, Alaska, from my home in Ohio. A look through the Web search engines with the keywords "garden" and "Webcam" will bring up a few sites with garden Webcams (see Figure 12-2).

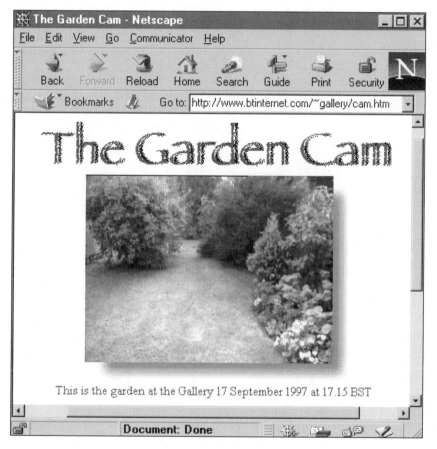

Figure 12-2
A view of a garden in the middle of England from the Midwest United States via the World Wide Web

You can use your video camera for videoconferencing, or face-to-face meetings over a regular telephone line. All you need is a camera attached to the computer and a fast Internet connection. The monthly garden club meeting takes on a whole new perspective when you can not only meet with other members of the club, but also allow them to "visit" your garden with a pan of the camera.

Connecting "eyes" to the computer

There are a couple of different ways to send live video into a computer. One method uses a standard (or analog) video camera and a video frame capture card such as we mentioned in Chapter 9. The other method uses a tethered digital video camera. Each has its advantages and disadvantages.

Analog video cameras

A standard analog video camera delivers video in color or black and white, in several different sizes. For outdoor use, you can use one of the video cameras intended for security systems.

You can place the camera a fair distance away from the monitor or computer input source, using standard video cable. This is a real advantage if your garden is some distance from the computer. Many video cameras used for security purposes are also small enough to be unobtrusive in your garden.

A disadvantage of a standard video camera and its analog output is that the analog signal must be converted into a digital format that the computer can understand. You will need a video capture card or device, depending on what type of images you intend to capture. If you are interested in still images, such as images for posting on the Web or time-lapse images that are updated at regular intervals, a simple "video frame grabber" device or card will suffice. Some of these still-image video capture devices can be programmed to capture images at set intervals, which are then automatically posted on a Web site.

Live action video or video conferencing may require a different type of video capture card, along with software that is capable of handling continuous video input and sending the video back out across a communications line. Usually, you can also use these cards or devices for capturing still images.

You can also get TV tuner cards that plug into an unused connector inside your computer. This hardware creates a small window on your computer monitor that acts as a television screen, so you can watch your current garden while designing your new garden with a CAD program. However, most of the TV tuner cards do not have the capability to capture still images.

Tethered digital video cameras

A tethered digital video camera is simply an imaging sensor in a case attached to a cable, the *tether*, which leads back to a computer. Since the camera is digital, the images it takes are already digital. And because the computer handles the capture, storage, and transfer of images, tethered digital video cameras are relatively inexpensive.

The tethered digital video camera is an excellent choice for a Web camera, which captures a frame at regular intervals, and a good way to keep an eye on your garden in real time. While the display created is not the smoothest, the camera provides acceptable full-motion video, showing us our plantings moving gently in the breeze, or alerting us to forestall damage as the wind picks up. The cameras are also useful in many of the same applications as digital photographic cameras or analog video cameras, such as quick photographs, security, and video conferencing.

For some applications, a tethered digital video camera is a restrictive choice. Most connect through the parallel printer port or standard serial port, and can be extended only about 20 feet away from the computer. Digital video cameras that connect through the newer *Universal Serial Bus* (USB) can go up to 100 feet, with six special hubs connecting each 16-foot segment. Unless your garden is just outside the window of your computer room, the current crop of tethered digital video may not be effective for keeping an eye on it.

Selecting a computer video camera

When selecting a video camera, consider its ability to work with other software. A TV tuner card with a low-cost video camera or a tethered digital video camera is fine if you just want to look at live images from the camera in your garden. However, for video conferencing, make sure that the hardware will work with video-conferencing software.

It's that DASSSH thing again. Decide how you want to use a video camera, select software that will help you achieve these uses, and then get the camera and hardware that will work with the software.

Using a video camera, particularly a digital video camera, to send photographs of your garden to friends via the Internet is likely to be a simpler and more cost-effective method than scanning standard paper-based photographs into the computer. In addition, you can use your video camera to create multimedia videos of your garden. Now you can really "rock your rock garden to rock music."

If you need an analog camera because of distance, check out surveillance video cameras available through home automation systems catalogs. Many of these cameras are encased in weatherproof housing and cost only a little more than most tethered digital video cameras. Trying to weatherproof a video camcorder could cost you four times as much. With the proper coaxial cable, many of the surveillance video cameras can also transmit signals up to a quarter of a mile.

What's the Weather Like?

Many of us take our weather watching as seriously as we do our gardening. We know that while the weather reports may be accurate at the airport, they may not be at our house. Those of us who live near the snow belts of the Great Lakes, for instance, know it could be a matter of a few miles between daily snow cover and open ground.

Keeping our own weather data helps to better plan our gardening activities. Many plants, pests, diseases, and weeds are influenced by the weather. For example, *growing degree-days* (GDDs)—the sum of the degrees above a standard baseline temperature since an arbitrary starting date—is one factor that controls the germination or flowering of many plants and the emergence of many insects. A weather station connected to a computer can calculate the degree-days automatically and alert us when a certain degree-day total is reached, signifying the germination of crabgrass or the emergence of an insect pest.

Similarly, several plant diseases occur at certain combinations of temperature, humidity, and leaf-area wetness. By monitoring these conditions, the computer can trigger an alarm when conditions indicate an imminent disease attack.

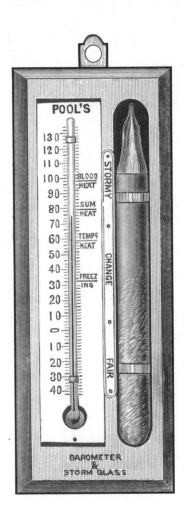

An *Integrated Pest Management* (IPM) program requires such monitoring of the environment. In this way, you can predict the possibility of a disease or insect attack and apply a fungicide or pesticide only when needed.

An understanding of weather and environment helps us to control irrigation as well. Evapotranspiration, the loss of water vapor from the soil and leaves, is usually measured with an evaporimeter—a large open pan of water or similar device. The higher the rate of evapotranspiration, the more we need to water. However, evaporimeters are a hassle to maintain. Instead of an evaporimeter, you can combine a weather station with your computer, and automatically calculate the rate of evapotranspiration. In this way, you can determine how much water a plant is using, and how much you must replace in the soil.

Weather on the Web

The Web is a major source for weather information. Many government and commercial weather organizations, along with university meteorology departments, have Web sites that list current weather conditions and past weather records. (Some of the information is so detailed you need a degree in meteorology to understand it.) My favorite site is The Weather Channel (**http://www.weather. com**), which also has a section on gardening (see Figure 13-1). Intellicast (**http://www.intellicast.com**) is another useful site as shown in Figure 13-2.

Several shareware and freeware programs are available to automate weather information on your computer. Some programs, such as WinWeather, WetSocks, and Weather Vane (available on CD-ROM) can automatically log onto the Internet, download and process weather information, and display current weather conditions on your monitor. For Windows 95 users, WetSocks and Weather Vane can even display the current weather conditions on the taskbar (see Figure 13-3 on page 206). You can dowlnoad various weather programs from CNET's DOWNLOAD.COM

SEE CD-ROM

Figure 13-1
Is it time to turn on the sprinkler or save
on your water bill? The Weather Channel
may have the answer

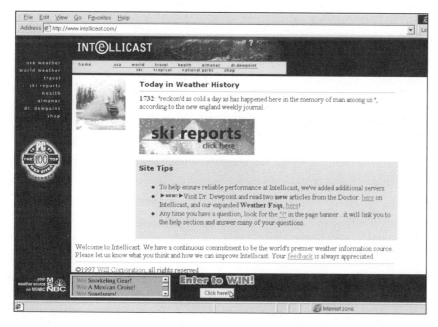

Figure 13-2
Intellicast keeps you posted
with up-to-the-minute forecasts

Figure 13-3
Automatic weather updating from the
Internet. The taskbar icon changes based
on current weather conditions.

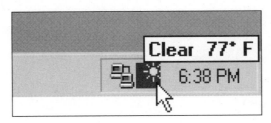

(**http://download.com**) or The Ultimate Collection of Winsock Software (**http://www.tucows.com**).

Still, Web weather, like the weather reports from the local airport, may not match the weather over your garden. For the most accurate information, you may want to set up your own weather station to gather data on local conditions, using the Web weather sites for forecasting.

Setting Up a Weather Station

It's easy to set up a basic weather station in your garden. All you need is a thermometer that registers minimum and maximum temperature, a barometer, and a humidity gauge. You might add an anemometer to measure wind speed, a wind vane for direction, and a rain gauge.

SEE CD-ROM

With this simple setup, you can record daily weather conditions, but you will have to trudge into the garden, write down the data, and enter the data into your garden information management system. (Check out Weather Tracker in Figure 13-4 and on the CD-ROM.) What you need is some way to gather the data from the weather instruments automatically—a tool that will regularly record the data when you forget.

Several electronic weather stations will monitor the weather while you stay comfortably inside. All have weather monitoring devices and sensors placed outside, with the display station inside. Many have digital readouts that display accurate weather conditions. And many will connect to a computer.

Most digital weather stations for the serious hobbyist have a standard computer serial interface that allows you to connect the

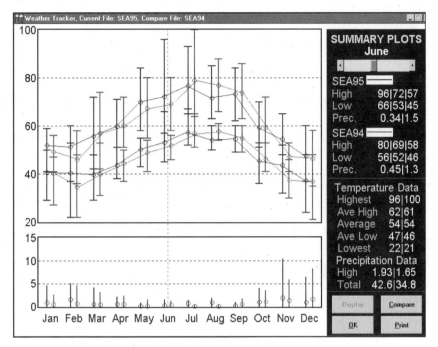

weather station to your computer. Once connected, you can transfer the weather station's data to your computer to chart and forecast the weather.

Most weather stations and software for home and basic industrial use record the basic weather conditions of wind speed and direction, temperature (including minimum and maximum) barometric pressure, and rainfall, and they perform calculations for the wind chill factor. However, if you want to determine the evapotranspiration rate or the growing degree-days, you still need to enter the numbers into a potential evapotranspiration equation or a GDD database. There are some additional weather-related conditions that have an impact on growing plants and managing pest problems, including leaf-area wetness, temperature-humidity hours, solar radiation, and soil temperature. Generally, weather stations with such features for plant growers are research-grade equipment that is well beyond the budget of almost all gardeners.

Figure 13-5
A basic schematic of a weather station
for plant growers and gardeners

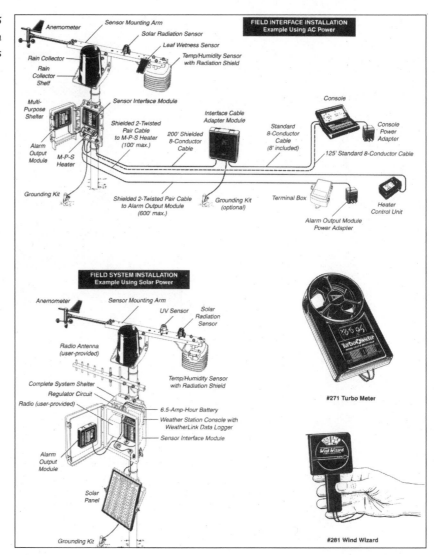

Fortunately, Davis Instruments (**http://www.davisnet.com**) offers a weather station with all the special features that gardeners need (see Figure 13-5). In addition to the standard reports, the GroWeather weather station can calculate evapotranspiration rate and offers an optional soil temperature probe and leaf wetness sensor. The GroWeather software allows you to monitor different crops and pests using growing degree-day calculations, temperature-humidity hours, and leaf-area wetness.

14

Automating Your Garden

Wouldn't it be nice to have a fully automated garden, complete with automatic planting, weed pulling, and flower deadheading? Well, technology isn't quite there yet, but we can use a computer to automate a few gardening activities, like irrigation and outdoor lighting.

Automatic irrigation systems have been around for many years. Along with the standard piping and sprinklers, these systems have several remote-control valves for regulating the flow of water through a section of the system, and a separate controller for opening and closing valves.

Until recently, the controller consisted of an electric clock, timer, and mechanical switches—a sophisticated version of a plug-in lamp timer. However, electromechanical controllers offer limited flexibility in scheduling irrigation running times. By contrast, digital irrigation controllers—simple computers dedicated to controlling irrigation valves—offer more programming flexibility.

Many large commercial irrigation systems, like those found on golf courses, use a standard computer as the central controller. The computer is connected to other controllers scattered around the golf course like satellites. These satellite controllers activate the various sprinkler valves on the course, and the central computer programs the satellite with irrigation schedules. Many of these golf course irrigation systems include a weather station, and a variety of other sensors in the ground and in the pump house, that track the water applied on the golf course. Some systems even have a remote dial-in capability, allowing the golf course superintendent to access the irrigation system from home.

Unfortunately, there is currently no computer-controlled irrigation system for home use. However, some home automation systems will allow us to control irrigation along with outdoor lighting.

Designing and Installing Irrigation Systems

General irrigation-system design and installation are beyond the scope of this book. Several residential sprinkler design books can help you work through the calculations of flow rates, pressure loss, precipitation rates, and pipe sizing needed for an efficient irrigation system.

When you design your own irrigation system, with computer control in mind, be sure to place the valves in a manifold (several valves connected side-by-side) near the house. This will allow for much easier servicing when you decide to connect your irrigation system to your computer.

If you already have an existing automatic irrigation system with electrically controlled valves, you can replace your existing controller with a computer-controlled system. If your system is

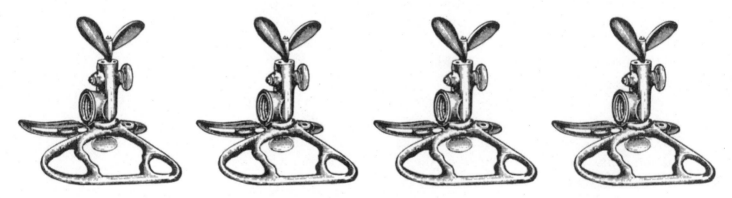

hydraulically controlled, you will need to replace the hydraulic valves with electric valves, unless you can find small electric pilot valves to control the hydraulic valves. (Many large golf course sprinkler systems use a hydraulic valve with a small electric pilot valve to activate their sprinklers.)

Wired Wireless Controls

The late 1970s saw the introduction of a technology called X10 Power Line Carrier, which transmits signals over house wiring. A transmitter plugged into an outlet at one end of the house lets you control lights and other appliances connected to receivers plugged into outlets all around the house, using your existing house wiring. You can also use X10 devices to control your irrigation system.

A simple one-circuit system

You can assemble a simple system to control one irrigation valve, which is enough to control a fairly large drip irrigation layout or a couple of sprinklers in the vegetable garden. Here's a list of what you'll need for this one-circuit X10 system:

Computer with a free serial port
X10 CP290 Computer Interface
X10 Powerhouse Universal Module
X10 control software
110-to-24-volt transformer
24-volt solenoid water valve

The transformer is available from an electrical supply house; the solenoid valve can be found at any plumbing company, irrigation supplier, or home improvement store.

You must use care when working around 110-volt household current. Be sure to include *ground fault interrupter* (GFI) receptacles on the house circuit with the transformer. If you have no experience working with electricity, consider hiring an electrical

Figure 14-1
A simple layout of a single-circuit irrigation system

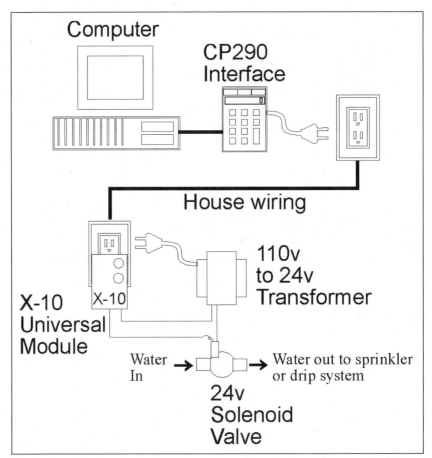

or irrigation contractor—this will be a small job that shouldn't overburden your gardening budget.

For this simple circuit, you just connect the X10 interface to your computer, and plug the X10 universal module into any receptacle in the garage or basement near your water valve. Figure 14-1 gives a simple schematic of the system.

To add on more circuits, add additional X10 universal modules on the low-voltage side of the transformer. You can also buy four-, eight-, or sixteen-relay X10 controllers in one cabinet, instead of using separate modules plugged into a power strip.

Newer X10 devices support two-way communication, so you or the computer will know if a valve is open or closed or a lamp is on

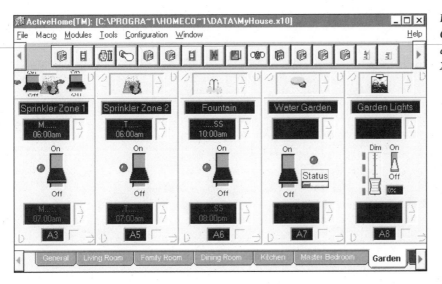

Figure 14-2
Computer interfaces and software
are available for controlling
X10 modules with your computer.

or off. Monitoring the signal at a rain switch can tell the computer when it starts raining and when it should stop watering.

Home automation systems based on X10-compatible technology are available from several sources. I recently noticed ads from the major department stores promoting home automation systems. Many appliance/electronic superstores also sell home automation systems, including the computer interface. See Table 14-1 on page 216 for a listing of resources.

Several manufacturers produce X10-compatible products, including the X10 Ltd. Company (**http://www.x10.com**), which produces the Powerhouse units. Many of these same companies also produce computer interfaces that allow you to control X10-compatible devices with your computer, such as ActiveHome (see Figure 14-2). Some X10 computer interface units can continue to control devices after the computer is shut down or disconnected from the interface.

One advantage that X10-compatible systems offer over all other residential irrigation controllers is wireless remote control, a feature otherwise found only on the most advanced golf course irrigation systems. With a wireless X10-compatible remote control, you can activate your irrigation system from the garden, although your controllers are all in your house. This can be a real advantage if you need to water new plants, but don't want to go into the house to activate the system.

Table 14-1
A few home automation resources for adapting an
irrigation or outdoor lighting system to computer control

MANUFACTURERS AND DISTRIBUTORS

X-10 Powerhouse	http://www.x10.com
Home Automation Systems	http://www.smarthome.com
Worthington Distribution	http://www.worthdist.com

MAGAZINES

HTI Home Toys	http://www.hometoys.com
Popular Home Automation	http://www.pophome.com
Electronic House	http://www.electronichouse.com
Home Automator	http://www.homeautomator.com

Irrigation systems and outdoor-lighting systems are available from a variety of sources. Toro, Rainbird, Nelson, and Hunter all provide residential irrigation-system components (see the White Pages for contact information). Outdoor-lighting systems are available from a variety of suppliers. Start by checking at your local garden center. Many do-it-yourself kits are available if your garden or lawn is small. However, anyone with property of more than $1/3$ acre looking to install a system for the entire property should consider hiring a professional irrigation-system designer

15

Publishing on the World Wide Web

The World Wide Web allows you not only to find information, but also to share it. Many of the more popular gardening Web sites, like Joe & Mindy's Web Garden (**http://www.nhn.ou.edu/~howard/garden.html**) are posted by gardeners for other gardeners to enjoy. But how about putting up your own Web site?

If you have Internet access, you may already have the ability to publish your own Web page. The commercial online services and many other Internet service providers (ISPs) offer you space for a personal Web site.

Developing a Web site can be almost as simple as creating a document in a word processor. All of the latest major word processors let you save files as Web documents for publishing on the World Wide Web, or you can use a stand-alone Web page creation program.

Developing and posting your Web site involves creating your page and then publishing it by uploading it, along with any associated files, to a Web server. The Web server sends out your Web pages to Web browsers connected to the Internet when they request it by visiting your URL.

The Web is a great way to share gardening information with other gardeners around the world. The almost universal availability of viewing Web pages on any computer platform removes the worry of leaving out someone because they have a different computer system. Since most of the commercial online services and many Internet service providers offer members space to establish a Web site or garden home page, I highly recommend taking advantage of the option. A home page is an easy way to show off pictures of your garden to friends, without the hassle of mailing duplicate copies of photographs. So "get tangled in the Web!"

Creating Web Pages

Unlike books, Web publications are dynamic. You can start out with just one or a few pages on your Web site, and then add links to others as you gather and organize more gardening information.

Web pages are written with *HyperText Markup Language* (HTML), which is not some weird spoken language like Klingon, nor is it a programming language. HTML is a set of rules that allow a browser to read, interpret, and display a Web page.

When writing, we capitalize a sentence to mark its beginning and we end the sentence with a period. HTML uses tags. For example, if we want a Web browser to display text in boldface, we preface the text with a tag, <B>, and end the text with another tag, </B>. These tags tell the browser that all text between the <B> and </B> tags should be shown as boldface. Similarly, the pair of tags <P> and </P> tell the browser to begin and end a paragraph.

HTML consists of many different tags used to control the onscreen display of a Web page. Since HTML is made up of keyboard characters in a text file, you could start writing Web pages with any text editor. However, it's a lot easier to write your page using a graphical Web page creation program.

Fortunately, several Web editor programs provide WYSIWIG (What You See Is What You Get) display of Web pages. Using them is like using a word processor. In fact, if your word processor allows you to save your work as HTML, you can quickly convert any garden writings sitting on your computer right now into Web pages.

The best place to learn how to create Web pages is on the World Wide Web itself. Hundreds of sites offer tutorials, courses, tips, and tools for creating Web pages. The Web search guides listed in Table 15-1 will help you find these sites.

Table 15-1
Some Web search guides to use to find
tutorials or instruction on developing Web pages

WEB GUIDES	
Yahoo!	http://www.yahoo.com
Excite	http://www.excite.com
Infoseek	http://www.infoseek.com
Lycos	http://www.lycos.com

Serving Your Web Pages

Creating your Web pages is only the first step. Next, you need a place to put them so they are accessible by anyone with a Web browser. You will need a Web server, the computer system connected to the Internet that holds Web sites and serves up Web pages on request from Web browsers.

If your computer runs either Windows 95 or the Macintosh operating system, you already have the hardware to set up your own garden Web server and connect it to the Internet. The Web server can even run in the background, allowing you to continue doing other things on your computer. However, the hurdle is not the hardware, but the Internet connection. Like a telephone, the hardware is cheap but the connect time can be very expensive. Setting up a Web server with a direct Internet connection is too costly for most individuals and small businesses.

A better way is to rent a piece of an existing Web server. A *Web hosting service* is a company or organization that offers Web server space, often for a fee.

Many colleges and universities allow students and faculty to publish Web sites on their Web servers. If you are taking classes at a nearby school with Web services, see if you can get some free space to publish a small gardening Web site.

If you access the Internet through an ISP, you may already have server space; many ISPs offer Web hosting as part of the monthly charge. A set amount of disk space is available for each user of the ISP. If you keep complex images to a minimum and avoid video or audio clips, you can create a fairly complex gardening Web site without exceeding the allotted space. Most of the commercial online services, including America Online, CompuServe, and Prodigy Internet, also offer Web hosting services to members.

Several Web sites will let you publish Web pages for free, although many offer free hosting only if you allow advertising banners to be displayed on your pages. Some have special Web-based programs that guide you through the setup of your new site (see Figure 15-1). These free services allow you to establish a gardening presence on the Web without having to go through an extensive Web page development process.

Figure 15-1
Several commercial online services let members publish their own Web sites. Some, including CompuServe, provide "wizards" to ease the process of creating a Web page

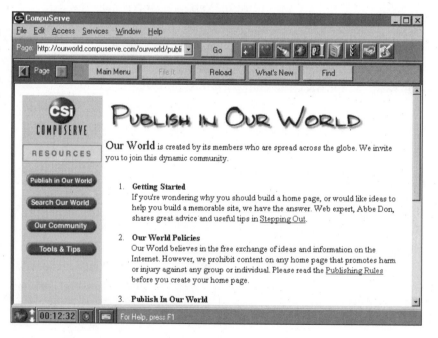

Publishing Your Web Pages

Once you have created your garden Web pages and have found a Web server, you must actually publish your Web site. This requires transferring or uploading the completed pages to the Web server, which is usually located far away. You transfer your pages using FTP software or a program that supports FTP.

FTP (File Transfer Protocol) is a set of rules that governs the transfer of files between computer systems connected to the Internet (see Figure 15-2). You can move just about any computer file between different computer systems and computer networks using FTP.

Most FTP applications for Windows and Macintosh computers have a point-and-click or drag-and-drop interface that makes it easy to transfer files.

Many HTML editors have file transfer capabilities that make it easy to upload your pages to your server. Some include wizards that guide you through the publishing process. These wizards can even keep track of the different pages that make up your Web site, publishing only the pages that are new or changed since your last editing session.

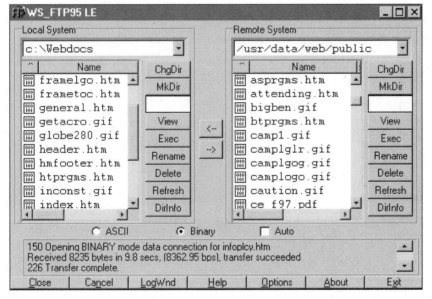

Figure 15-2
FTP programs ease the process of transferring Web page files between your computer and your Web server

Web Development Software

Because graphics play such an important part in Web pages, graphics programs or image editors are as important to developing a good Web site as HTML editors. Like gardening, which you can do with only a spade and a pair of pruners, you can create a simple Web page with just a text editor and an FTP program. As you become more involved in growing your gardening Web site, you will accumulate various programs, just as you collect gardening tools in the toolshed. Fortunately, many of these programs are part of low-cost packages or exist as freeware or shareware, easily downloaded from the Web.

HTML editors

Since all Web pages are text files with HTML tags, you can create a page with any text editor, such as NotePad or WordPad in Microsoft Windows, Edit on DOS computers, and TeachText on the Macintosh. However, typing in HTML tags can be cumbersome, and typos can result in a poorly displayed or broken Web page.

Most simple HTML editors will insert HTML tags at the click of a button. You simply type in the text and file references between the tags. You then load the finished page into a Web browser to see how it will look.

More advanced HTML editors display your Web pages just as you would see them with a Web browser, but without having to load them into a browser (see Figure 15-3). You enter and format text as you would with a basic word processor.

Netscape Communicator 4.0 and Microsoft Internet Explorer 4.0 include basic HTML editors as part of the browser program. Other HTML editors can be downloaded from the Web as freeware or shareware.

Image editors

The graphics that appear in Web pages are typically either *GIF* (Graphics Interchange Format) or *JPEG* (Joint Photographics Experts Group) files. Both GIF and JPEG images can be displayed

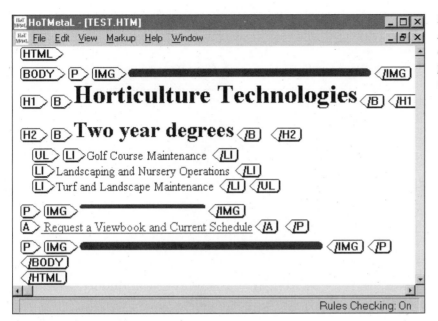

Figure 15-3
An HTML editor that provides a WYSIWYG view of the Web page. The displayed HTML tags can be hidden from view

on a variety of computer platforms, which makes them good formats for the Web.

To create GIF or JPEG files you'll need a suitable paint program or image editor. Most paint programs and image editors available today will save graphics as either GIF or JPEG files. If your paint program does not save in GIF or JPEG format, there are several other paint programs or graphic translation programs available for downloading from the Web to convert your files from one format to another.

Web site viewers

Web pages often link to other Web pages. When a site gets large, with many links to different Web pages, it can be daunting to keep track of them all. Failure to update links can result in broken or dead links, which frustrate the visitor.

Web site viewers display the arrangement of linked pages in a Web site. Depending on the viewer, you can display the Web site as an outline or as an organizational chart (see Figure 15-4 on

Figure 15-4
A Web site viewer displaying all the
Web pages and links in outline view

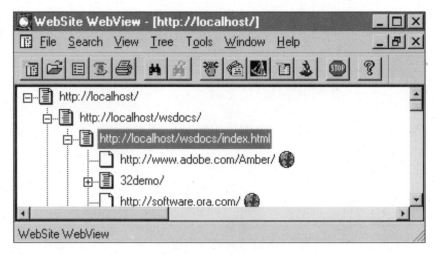

page 226). Some viewers let you move pages around in a Web site, while automatically adjusting the links for you.

There are several different Web site viewers. Some are part of a comprehensive Web development system, such as Microsoft FrontPage 98 or NetObjects Fusion. Others are separate applications like Adobe SiteMill (Macintosh only).

If your Web site is small, consisting only of a few pages with a few links, you will not need any type of Web site viewer. But if your site starts to become extensive and you update it frequently, a Web site viewer that lets you manage your pages and your links will help to avoid a lot of frustration.

Web servers

As your gardening Web site grows, the best way to test it is to publish it on a Web server. However, if your site is located on an ISP or commercial online service, you could incur additional costs in connect charges during your tests. You might also want to decide if you really want people to see your "half-grown" gardening Web site.

Fortunately, you can find software that lets you run your own Web server on your home computer (see Figure 15-5). Many of these can be run without even connecting to a network or the Internet, allowing you to test and modify your garden site until it is "ready for prime time."

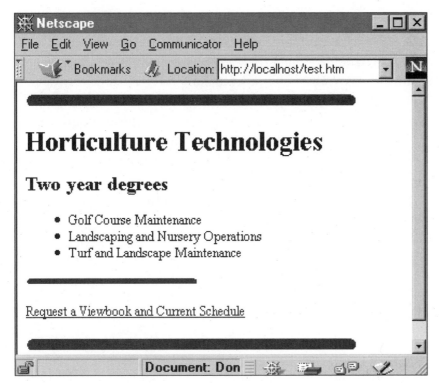

Figure 15-5
This mockup of a Web page in a Web browser comes from a Web server on the same computer. This allows for extensive testing before publishing Web pages on a server connected to the Internet

Several Web development systems, like FrontPage 98, include a small personal Web server for testing purposes. You can also download several freeware and shareware Web servers from the Web.

Besides using it for testing, you can also use a personal Web server on an internal network at work or school for publishing a small Web site. All of these personal Web servers run in the background of Windows 95, Windows NT, or Macintosh computers, while allowing you to do other work.

Other Web tools

There are numerous other tools for developing Web pages and Web sites. Some are designed to help you create complex Web documents that are difficult to format with HTML. Others are used to create scripts and miniprograms to display dynamic Web pages. Most of these tools are best left for advanced garden Web wizards.

Where to Find Web Development Tools

The pioneering spirit of the Web is still very much alive, with a variety of public domain, freeware, and shareware Web development tools available for downloading. Several of the software library Web sites, such as CNET's DOWNLOAD.COM (**http://download.com**) and SHAREWARE.COM (**http://shareware.com**), along with ZDNet's Shareware Library (**http://www.hotfiles.com**), include a number of Web development tools, such as HTML editors and image editors.

A browse through The Ultimate Collection of Winsock Software (TUCOWS) at **http://www.tucows.com** will provide an extensive list of Web development tools, along with Web servers and other Internet tools. TUCOWS is recognized as one of the best resources for Web development tools and Internet software, and each product is rated.

16

Growing Your Own Software

Many of us garden because we do not want to buy plants, flowers, fruits, and vegetables grown by someone else. Many of us also propagate or breed plants (sexual propagation), or grow them from a parent plant (asexual or vegetative propagation), because we want unique plants to fit a special purpose in the garden—plants we can't find in a local nursery or seed catalog. We may propagate plants for the challenge and fun of creating a new plant variety, or to obtain a large number of plants from a hard-to-propagate specimen. For a few of us, propagating plants may be a means of extra income.

Gardeners and landscapers develop software for similar reasons, "propagating" programs to meet their needs. My own Landscape & Herbaceous Plant Manager grew out of my need in the mid-1980s for a low-cost plant database program for students to use in their landscape plant materials courses. Programming, like plant propagation, allows you to create something that is uniquely yours.

SEE CD-ROM

Growing Your Own Garden Computer Programs

Computer programs are lists of instructions for the computer. Like a recipe, a program contains a set of instructions for manipulating ingredients (data) and creating a result (output).

Don't run, walk

If you are thinking of writing garden computer programs, don't try it because you think that programming is easy or that you will save money by writing your own. Programming gurus point out that writing the actual code or instructions for a computer program is the last step in the process. Before that, you'll need to spend a lot of time developing objectives, analyzing the problem, defining variables, and establishing the basic outline of the program.

Developing a garden computer program

Stand-alone computer programs—programs that run completely on their own—are developed using a programming language. Programming languages are collections of English-like statements and instructions that a programmer uses to develop source code. The source code is translated into a computer-usable form by a program called a *compiler* or an *interpreter*. The difference between the two is that a compiler translates the code once, while an interpreter translates the code each time the program runs.

Developing stand-alone garden programs is well beyond the scope of this book. If you do not program regularly, plan on a steep learning curve. If you want to try your hand at developing stand-alone programs for your garden activities, the nearest library or major bookstore will present you with numerous books on the subject. The Web is also an excellent resource for introducing you to programming topics.

Microsoft Visual Basic 5.0 Learning Edition or Professional Edition is a good beginning programming language for developing Windows-based programs (see Figure 16-1). For Macintosh users, Claris HyperCard is a good starting point, although it will not produce full stand-alone applications. The programming languages C and C++, while the professional's languages of choice, require a fair amount of programming expertise and are not for the shade-tree garden programmer.

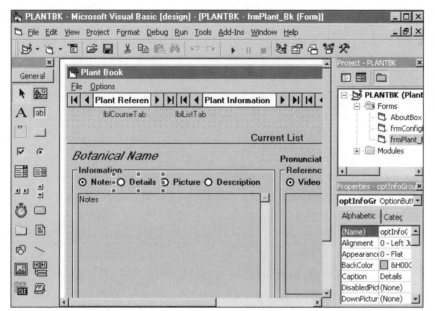

Figure 16-1
Several programming systems have
drag-and-drop components for quick
development of Windows applications.
This screenshot comes from the
author's plant reference program
developed in Visual Basic

Programs in programs in programs

While developing full stand-alone garden programs is beyond
most of our needs, you may at times want to create little miniprograms to automate a routine activity. For example, you might want
a program to italicize the scientific name of a plant as you type it
into a database record. Or you might want to have your program
convert the scientific name of a plant into a coded version, following the rules of the American Nursery and Landscape Association
(ANLA). You can create such miniprograms with *macros* or *scripts*,
which are miniprogramming languages within major software.
Some office productivity programs, such as Lotus SmartSuite and
Microsoft Office, include *application programming languages* that
are very much like a standard programming language but that
operate inside the software.

The ANLA's rules for converting scientific plant names into digital form were established to aid in barcoding nursery stock and to
support computer use in the nursery. These codes are composed of
a seven-character name code and additional digits that specify various nursery stock descriptors, such as size and type of root system

(container, bare root, ball and burlap, and so on). As a short (5- to 7-character) but readable description, the name code is an excellent way to create a key in a relational database management system.

The code works like this: First, all the vowels in the genus, species, and variety names, except for the first letter, are stripped out. Then the first three consonants of the genus are combined with the first two consonants of the species and the first two consonants of the variety/cultivar (if it is a single name) or the first letter of each word (if the variety/cultivar has two or more names). For example, *Pyrus calleryana* 'Cleveland' (Cleveland Callery Pear) converts to PRSCLCL, and *Acer rubrum* 'Autumn Glory' (Autumn Glory Red Maple) converts to ACRRBAG. There are some additional rules for dealing with names that do not have enough consonants such as *Poa pratensis* 'Blacksburg' (Kentucky bluegrass) (POAPRBL).

Though you can create each code manually, it is much easier to have a miniprogram do it for you. The exact rules for converting the botanical name can be found in the publication *Nursery Crops Coding System Manual*, available from the American Nursery and Landscape Association, 1250 I Street NW, Suite 500, Washington DC 20005.

Macros

A macro is a shortcut representing a list of commands, actions, or keystrokes. Macros allow you to automate a series of commands or actions. You run the macro by pressing a key or key combination or clicking a button. For example, let's consider the steps you'd follow to italicize a word or plant name. Normally, you would type the word, highlight it with the mouse, select Italics from the toolbar or from the Format menu, and click the mouse at the end of the word to continue typing. A macro used to italicize a word might look like the example in Table 16-1.

Most major applications that support macros allow you to record your keystrokes or menu selections to create your own macros. I was able to create the italicizing macro in about five seconds using the macro recording capability of Microsoft Word 6.0.

Table 16-1
A simple macro to italicize a word in the
Windows version of Microsoft Word 6.0

MACRO	ACTION DESCRIPTION
WordLeft 1	Move the cursor to the beginning of the word
WordRight 1, 1	Move the cursor to the end of the word and highlight the word
Italic	Italicize the highlighted word
CharRight 1	Move the cursor to the end of the word
Italic	Turn off the italics function

Growing your own software is very much like growing a garden: you start out with a seed of an idea; then you grow the software, pruning and weeding out useless or unproductive parts of a program while chasing out bugs. (Yes, "pruning," "weeding," and "bugs" are also terms used in computer programming.) And once the code has matured, you have a specimen that you are proud to show your friends and neighbors—just like your prize, beetle-free rosebush in the garden.

GROWS ONLY 18 INCHES HIGH.

HENDERSON'S NEW BUSH LIMA BEAN

White Pages Directory

This is a listing in one convenient location, of most of the companies and products mentioned in the book or on the companion CD-ROM. As the listing is a subjective compilation, its entries should not be construed as endorsements of any of the companies' products.

For several of the large corporations, the best place to make initial contact is at the local retailer or the corporation's Web site. A Web site visit or e-mail is also the best way to make contact with most of the smaller companies, particularly the gardening shareware authors.

AAIT Incorporated
58 Kennedy Dr., Unit B
Dartmouth, Nova Scotia, Canada
PH: (902) 435-1676
FX: (902) 462-0005
sales@aait.com
http://www.playfulminds.com,
    http://www.aait.com
Green Thumb Cards software

Abracadata
P.O. Box 2440
Eugene, OR 97402
PH: (800) 451-4871
FX: (503) 683-1925
abracadata@POBoxes.com
http://www.abracadata.com
Home Design software

Adobe Systems Incorporated

345 Park Ave.
San Jose, CA 95110-2704
PH: (408) 536-6000
FX: (408) 537-6000
http://www.adobe.com
Software: Desktop publishing, Web development

Alpha Software

168 Middlesex Turnpike
Burlington, MA 01803-4483
PH: (781) 229-2924
FX: (781) 272-4876
info@alphasoftware.com
http://www.alphasoftware.com
Landscape imaging software

America Online

PH: (800) 827-6364
FX: (800) 827-5551
http://www.aol.com
Commercial Online Service

American Nurseryman Publishing

77 W. Washington St., Ste. 2100
Chicago, IL 60602-2904
PH: (312) 782-5505
FX: (312) 782-3232
Books, software

Apple Computer

1 Infinite Loop
Cupertino, CA 95014-2084
PH: (408) 996-1010
FX: (408) 974-2483
http://www.apple.com
Computer systems

Autodesk Kansas City

10725 Ambassador Dr.
Kansas City, MO 64153
PH: (816) 891-2800
FX: (816) 891-8018
http://www.drafix.com
Software: Planix, Drafix, ProLandscape

Avery Dennison

20955 Pathfinder Rd.
Diamond Bar, CA 91765
PH: (800) 252-8379
FX: (909) 594-4876
productinfo@averydennison.com
http://www.avery.com
Labels

Casio-USA

571 Mount Pleasant Ave.
Dover, NJ 07801
PH: (973) 328-1670
FX: (973)361-3819
gensupport@casio-usa.com
http://www.casio-usa.com
Organizers, digital cameras

Compaq Computer Corporation

P.O. Box 692000
Houston, TX 77269-200
PH: (800) 345-1518
FX: (281) 514-1740
http://www.compaq.com
Computer systems

CompUSA Inc.

14951 No. Dallas Pkwy.
Dallas, TX 75240
PH: (800) COMP USA
FX: (800) 669-8329
customer_service@compusa.com
http://www.compusa.com
Computer products supplier

CompuServe

5000 Arlington Centre Blvd.
Columbus, OH 43220-5439
PH: (614) 457-8600
http://www.compuserve.com
Commercial online service

Corel

1600 Carling Ave.
Ottawa, Ontario K1Z 8R7 Canada
PH: (800) 772-6735
FX: (613) 761-9176
http://www.corel.com
Software: Office productivity, graphics

CyberNiche Software

4271 Carlisle Rd.
Gardners, PA 17324-8930
PH: (717) 486-8308
cniche@pa.net
http://www.cniche.com
Seed Program software

Davis Instruments

3465 Diablo Ave.
Hayward, CA 94545
PH: (800) 678-3669
FX: (510) 670-0589
http://www.davisnet.com
Weather instruments

Day Runner Inc.

2750 W. Moore Ave.
Fullerton, CA 92833
PH: (714) 680-3500
FX: (714) 680-0535
cic@dayrunner.com
http://www.dayrunner.com
Personal organizers

Day-Timers, Inc.

One Day-Timer Plaza
Allentown, PA 18195-1551
PH: (800) 225-5005
FX: (800) 452-7398
dtservice@daytimer.com
http://www.daytimer.com
Information manager software

Dell Computer Corporation

One Dell Way
Round Rock, TX 78682
PH: (800) 915-3355
FX: (800) 317-3355
dcs_on-line_order_support@dell.com
http://www.dell.com
Computer systems

Dept. of Plant Science

Massey University
Palmerston North, New Zealand
T.Stewart@massey.ac.nz
http://www.diagnosis.co.nz/
Plant Diagnosis software

Eagle Point Software

4131 Westmark Dr.
Dubuque, IA 52002-2627
PH: (319) 556-8392
FX: (319) 556-5321
sales@eaglepoint.com
http://www.eaglepoint.com
LandCADD

Ed Hume Seeds

P.O. Box 1450
Kent, WA 98035
FX: (206) 859-0694
HumeSeeds@aol.com
http://www.humeseeds.com/
Gardening software

Esselte Americas

71 Clinton Rd.
Garden City, NY 11530
PH: (516) 741-3200
FX: (516) 747-7476
esselte_new_media@esselte.com
http://www.esselte.com/dymo/
Dymo labels

Expert Software, Inc.

800 Douglas Road, Executive Tower
Coral Gables, FL 33134
PH: (305) 567-9990
FX: (305) 443-0786
sales@expertsoftware.com
http://www.expertsoftware.com
Landscape Planning software

Flywheel

P.O. Box 421
Ione, WA 99139
PH: (509) 442-3138
flywheel@coolscreens.com
http://www.coolscreens.com/index.
shtml
Botanica screen saver software

Franklin Covey

2200 W. Parkway Blvd.
Salt Lake City, UT 84119
PH: (801) 975-1776
comments@franklinquest.com
http://www.franklinquest.com
Personal organizers

GardenTech

1730 Goodman Ave.
Redondo Beach, CA 90278
PH: (213) 372-5810
The Root Directory System software

Gateway 2000

P.O. Box 2000, 610 Gateway Dr.
North Sioux City, SD 57049
PH: (800) 846-2000
http://www.gw2k.com
Computer systems

GLORICON DESIGNS

8433 No. Meadow Lake Rd.
New Hope, MN 55428-2730
FX: (612) 574-1901
73321.1794@compuserve.com
Garden Icons software

Handcraftedfonts Company

P.O. Box 14013
Philadelphia, PA 19122-0013
Weather Font software

Hoferichter Design

345 Charles Lutes
Moncton, N.B. E1C 8Z4 Canada
PH: (506) 383-7567
FX: (506) 383-8171
khoferic@nbnet.nb.ca
Herb Power software

Home Automation Systems, Inc.

151 Kalmus Dr., Ste. L4
Costa Mesa, CA 92626
PH: (714) 708-0610
FX: (714) 708-0614
has@smarthome.com
http://www.smarthome.com
Home automation

HotMail

PH: (408) 222-7000
comments@hotmail.com
http://www.hotmail.com
Free Web-based e-mail service

Hunter

1940 Diamond St.
San Marcos, CA 92069-5190
PH: (760) 744-5240
FX: (760) 744-7461
hunter@hunterindustries.com
http://www.hunterirrig.com
Irrigation systems

IBM North America

1133 Westchester Ave.
White Plains, NY 10604
PH: (770) 863-1234
FX: (770) 863-3030
askibm@vnet.ibm.com
http://www.ibm.com
Computer systems, software

Imation Enterprises Corp.

1 Imation Pl.
Oakdale, MN 55128-3414
PH: (888) 466-3456
info@imation.com
http://www.imation.com/
Super Disk drives, digital media

IMSI

1895 Francisco Blvd. East
San Rafael, CA 94901-5506
PH: (415) 257-3000
FX: (415) 257-3565
sales@imsisoft.com
http://www.imsisoft.com
CAD and graphics software

Ingenieurbüro für Softwareentwicklung

Hertzstr. 29
D-76287 Rheinstetten Germany
100725.3632@compuserve.com
http://ourworld.compuserve.com/
    Homepa
Daisy's Garden software

Innovative Thinking Software

P.O. Box 47
Lawson, NSW 2783 Australia
100243.745@compuserve.com
GrowIt series software

Insanely Great Software

126 Calvert Ave. E.
Edison, NJ 08820
PH: (617) 266-1630
FX: (908) 632-1766
igs@igsnet.com, AdamStein@aol.com
http://www.igsnet.com/weather.html
WinWeather software

Iomega Corporation

1821 West Iomega Way
Roy, UT 84067
PH: (801) 778-1000
http://www.iomega.com
Zip drives, digital storage

IrishStar Enterprise

7393 State Rd.
Wadsworth, OH 44281
irishstar@aol.com
PlantMate II software

JSS, Inc.

HC-1 Box 592-1
Center Point, TX 78010
PH: (210) 634-2070
FX: (210) 634-2077
72271.2563@compuserve.com
JSSi Garden software

KIDware

15600 NE 8th, Ste. B1-314
Bellevue, WA 98008
PH: (206) 721-2556
FX: (206) 746-4655
KIDware@msn.com
Weather Tracker 3.0 software

Kurtz-Fernhout Software

2813 Arbor St.
Ames, IA 50014
FX: (515) 292-4311
info@gardenwithinsight.com
http://www.gardenwithinsight.com
*The Garden with Insight garden
simulator software*

Locutus Codeware

P.O. Box 53587
Vancouver, BC V5Z 1K0 Canada
http://www.locutuscodeware.com
WetSock software

LongLastings

P.O. Box 519
Coupeville, WA 98239-0519
Greenhouse Gardening software

Lotus Corporation

55 Cambridge Pkwy.
Cambridge, MA 02142
PH: (800) 343-5414
http://www.lotus.com
Productivity software

Micron Computer

8000 S. Federal Way, P.O. Box 6
Boise, ID 83707-0006
PH: (208) 368-4000
FX: (208) 368-4435
http://www.micron.com
Computer systems

Microsoft Corporation

One Microsoft Way
Redmond, WA 98052-6399
PH: (425) 882-8080
http://www.microsoft.com
Operating system and application software

Microsoft Network

PH: (800) 386-5550
http://www.msn.com
Commercial online service

MicroWarehouse

1720 Oak St.
Lakewood, NJ 08701
PH: (800) 367-7080
FX: (732) 942-2502
service@warehouse.com
http://www.warehouse.com
Computer mail order

Midnight Software Inc.

P. O. Box 77352
Seattle, WA 98177-0352
FX: (206) 361-0796
102562.1411@compuserve.com
http://www.dcad.com
DeltaCAD software

MJ Services

Box 506
Toano, VA 23168
71170.655@compuserve.com
ChemRef software

Netscape

501 E. Middlefield Rd.
Mountain View, CA 94043
PH: (650) 937-2555
FX: (650) 528-4124
info@netscape.com
http://www.netscape.com
Web browser, online services

Nico Mak Computing, Inc.

P.O. Box 919
Bristol, CT 06011
70056.241@compuserve.com
http://www.winzip.com
WinZip software

PC Connection

528 Route 13
Milford, NH 03055
PH: (800) 800-0018
FX: (603) 446-7791
customerservice@pcconnection.com
http://www.pcconnection.com
Computer mail order

PC Zone

707 So. Grady Way
Renton, WA 98055-3233
PH: (800) 408-9663
customerservice@mzi.com
http://www.pczone.com
Computer mail order

Philips Consumer Electronics Company

One Philips Dr., P.O. Box 14810
Knoxville, TN 37914-1810
PH: (800) 531-0039
http://www.philipsmagnavox.com
Internet TV

Plantsoft Services

30 Reveley Crescent
Stirling, ACT 2611 Australia
PH: 61 (02) 6288
FX: 61 (02) 6287
chackett@netinfo.com.au
http://www.ozemail.com.au/
~chackett/
Plantgro software

Prodigy, Inc.

White Plains, NY 10610
PH: (800) 776-3449
http://www.prodigy.com
Commercial online service

PSG-HomeCraft Software

P.O. Box 974
Tualatin, OR 97062
PH: (503) 692-3732
FX: (503) 692-0382
steve@homecraft.com
http://www.homecraft.com
Organize! software

Psion Incorporated

150 Baker Ave.
Concord, MA 01742
PH: (978) 371-0310
FX: (978) 371-9611
usa-info@psion.com
http://www.psioninc.com
PDAs

Puma Technology, Inc.

2550 No. First St., Ste. #500
San Jose, CA 95131
PH: (408) 321-7650
FX: (408) 433-2212
http://www.pumatech.com
Transfer software

Purdue University

1146 ABE Building
W. Lafayette, IN 47907-1146
PH: (765) 494-1173
FX: (765) 494-1356
fbps@ecn.purdue.edu
*Water Efficient Landscape Planner
software*

Quarterdeck Corporation

13160 Mindanao Way
Marina del Rey, CA 90292-9705
PH: (800) 683-6696
FX: (813) 523-2391
info@quarterdeck.com
http://www.quarterdeck.com
Utility software

Rainbird

145 No. Grand Ave.
Glendora, CA 91741
PH: (800) RAIN-BIRD
FX: (626) 963-4287
http://www.rainbird.com
Irrigation

RJ Best Software

P.O. Box 12128
Honolulu, HI 96828
rbest@pixi.com
Scraps software

RocketMail

http://www.rocketmail.com
Web-based e-mail service

Royal Consumer Business Products

765 U.S. Highway 202
Bridgewater, NJ 08807-0945
PH: (908) 526-8200
FX: (908) 704-6572
hotline@royalnet.com
http://royalnet.com
Organizers

Sagebrush Systems, Inc.

P.O. Box 3094
Corrales, NM 87048
PH: (505) 898-6345
sells@sagebrush.com
WinChime software

Seattle Filmworks

1260 16th Ave. West
Seattle, WA 98119
PH: (800) FILMWORK
FX: (206) 286-8533
info@filmworks.com
http://filmworks.com
Film, digital processing

Shannon Software, Ltd.

P.O. Box 6126
Falls Church, VA 22040
PH: (703) 573-0793
shansoft@shannonsoft.com
http://www.shannonsoft.com
The Garden Assistant software

Sharp USA

http://www.sharp-usa.com
Organizers, PDAs, electronics

Sierra Design, Inc.

3380 146th Pl. SE
Bellevue, WA 98102
PH: (800) 757-7707
http://www.sierra.com
Productivy and entertainment software

SoftKey (The Learning Company)

One Athenaeum St.
Cambridge, MA 02142
PH: (800) 227-5609
FX: (617) 494-1219
http://www.softkey.com
Home landscaping software

Sony Electronics

http://www.sel.sony.com
Internet TV terminal, electronic products

Spider Software

P.O. Box 1488
Florence, OR 97439
spider@presys.com
Flora software

Sunrise Software

4821 Clydelle Ave.
San Jose, CA 95124-4209
71045.767@compuserve.com
HortMan—Horticulture Manager software

Syntrillium Software Corporation

P.O. Box 62255
Phoenix, AZ 85082-2255
PH: (602) 941-4327
FX: (602) 941-8170
info@syntrillium.com
http://www.syntrillium.com
Wind Chimes 1.01 software

The Taunton Press, Inc.

63 So. Main St.
Newtown, CT 06470
PH: (800) 243-7252
FX: (203) 426-3434
service@taunton.com
http://www.taunton.com
Fine Gardening magazine and gardening books

The Toro Company Irrigation Division

P.O. Box 489
Riverside, CA 93002
PH: (800) 367-8676
http://www.toro.com
Irrigation products

Toshiba America

1251 Avenue of the Americas
New York, NY 10020
PH: (212) 596-0600
FX: (212) 593-3875
http://www.toshiba.com
Computer systems, electronic products

Unicorn Software Ltd.

P.O. Box 117
Knob Noster, MO 65336
PH: (816) 429-3558
FX: (816) 429-3558
70272.3317@compuserve.com
OMNIDay for Windows 3.00 software

US Robotics/3Com

5400 Bayfront Plaza
Santa Clara, CA 95052
PH: (408) 764-5000
FX: (408) 764-5001
http://www.3com.com/
Palm Pilot PDA, modems

Visual Applications, Inc.

2301 Burlington, Ste. 220
North Kansas City, MO 64116
PH: (888) 374-6963
FX: (816) 472-0941
http://www.showoff.com
Imagine Your Landscape software

VtechSoft, Inc.

5 Corporate Park Dr., Ste. 210
Irvine, CA 92714
PH: (714) 752-6236
FX: (714) 752-8031
http://www.vtech.com
Organizers

Web TV Network

http://www.webtv.net
Internet TV online service

WinGames, Inc.

3905 Sandia
Plano, TX 75023
PH: (972) 612-0839
wingames@wingames.com
http://www.wingames.com
Botz software

Word Place

11 East 200 No., Ste. 201
Orem, UT 84057
PH: (801) 221-7777
FX: (801) 221-7707
info@wordplace.com
http://www.wordplace.com
Yeah Write software

Worthington Distribution

36 Gumbletown Rd.
Paupack, PA 18451
PH: (800) 282-8864
FX: (717) 226-0470
worthdist@aol.com
http://www.worthdist.com
Home automation supplier

X-10 (USA) Inc.

91 Ruckman Rd., Box 420
Closter, NJ 07624
PH: (201) 784-9700
FX: (201) 784-9464
sales@x10.com
http://www.x10.com
Home automation

Zoot Software

170 West Hill Rd.
Lincoln, VT 05443
PH: (802)453-6474
info@zootsoftware.com
http://www.zootsoftware.com
Zoot 3.1 software

Gardener's Internet Yellow Pages

The Internet has forever changed the "landscape" of gardening information. A gardener is no longer limited to the local library, a few gardening magazines, and the monthly garden club meeting for new tips, techniques, ideas, and views on gardening. A vast, dynamic body of information is just a quick phone connection and a few mouse clicks away. The World Wide Web can not only provide us with text, but can also let us see plants and gardens in all their splendor.

There are thousands of sites on the Web devoted to gardening and the much broader related topics of horticulture, agriculture, and botany. A large number of gardening Web sites have been developed by gardeners for gardeners. Like perennials in the garden, many of these sites grow, mature, flower, and sometimes fade away. The following listing is a weeding of the vast field of sites down to a cottage garden set of sites that are either growing or have matured like a large oak tree.

If you cannot find a Web site in the listing that fits your interest, visit one of the Web sites listed under Link Sites. The sole purpose of these "Web sites of gardening Web sites" is to provide convenient links to other Web sites. The Gardening Launch Pad at **http://www.tpoint.net/neighbor/** is an excellent starting point. Several of the sites in all the categories also have collections of links to other Web sites, many within the same category.

Still want to see more? The Web guides and search engines can also provide a listing of gardening Web sites. As you read gardening magazines, keep an eye out for Web addresses. Many gardening product suppliers now recognize the importance of the World Wide Web by including Web addresses along with their phone and fax numbers.

While this listing is a subjective compilation, its entries should not be construed as endorsements of products or ideas promoted by particular Web sites.

BONSAI

BONSAI CLUBS INTERNATIONAL
http://www.bonsai-bci.com/

Bonsai Clubs International is the foremost non-profit global organization of individuals and clubs devoted to bonsai. The site includes several links to suppliers, other bonsai organizations, and member club sites.

BONSAI WEB
http://www.bonsaiweb.com/

This site includes many links to nurseries, suppliers, clubs, and other Web sites. It allows you to add your name to both electronic and postal mailing lists.

THE ONLINE BONSAI ICON COLLECTION
http://www.the-spa.com/john.novo/bonsai.htm

A great collection of icons (small graphic images) of bonsai, this is a good source of images for the bonsai enthusiast to dress up writing, journals, or Web pages.

BOOK PUBLISHERS

STOREY PUBLISHING
http://www.storeybooks.com/

Storey Books is a major publisher of how-to books on country living skills including numerous titles on gardening.

TIMBER PRESS
http://www.timber-press.com/

An extensive publisher and seller of gardening and horticulture books, this Web site includes many European titles not commonly available in U.S. bookstores.

BOTANICAL GARDENS & ARBORETA SITES

THE ARNOLD ARBORETUM OF HARVARD UNIVERSITY
http://arboretum.harvard.edu/

The Arnold Arboretum is a research and educational institution. It manages a collection of hardy trees, shrubs, and vines located on 265 acres in Boston, and associated herbarium and library collections.

ASSOCIATION OF BOTANICAL GARDENS AND ARBORETA MEMBER WEB SITE LISTS
http://www.mobot.org/AABGA/member-list.html

This alphabetical list contains links to many AABGA botanical garden and arboretum institutional member Web sites.

BROOKLYN BOTANIC GARDEN

http://www.bbg.org/

Like all of the Brooklyn Botanic Garden's world-renowned publications, the Web site aims to offer lots of practical—and scientifically impeccable—information.

CHICAGO BOTANIC GARDEN

http://www.chicago-botanic.org/

The Chicago Botanic Garden, with its magnificent gardens on tranquil lagoons, is the third most-visited botanic garden in the United States.

THE DAWES ARBORETUM

http://www.dawesarb.org/

The Dawes Arboretum includes 1,149 acres of plant collections and natural areas that offer unique educational experience in any season.

GARDEN NET'S LIST OF GARDEN ASSOCIATIONS

http://trine.com/GardenNet/GardenAssn/assngui1.htm

GardenNet's Guide to Garden Associations has over one hundred links to associations and societies related to gardening, with some links to broader botanical organizations.

GARDENNET'S GUIDE TO GARDENS OF THE USA

http://trine.com/GardenNet/GardensOnline/guide1.htm

GardenNet's Guide to Gardens of the United States is a list of gardens open to the public in the USA. The Guide includes gardens of all sizes and types in (almost) every state, including gardens located on the grounds of historic buildings, on university campuses, in cemeteries, or associated with nurseries or farms.

HOLDEN ARBORETUM

http://www.holdenarb.org/

Located near Cleveland, Ohio, the Holden Arboretum encompasses over 3,100 acres and is the largest arboretum in the United States.

LONGWOOD GARDENS

http://www.longwoodgardens.org/

The world's premier horticultural display garden, Longwood Gardens, in Kennett Square, Pennsylvania, includes 20 outdoor gardens, 20 indoor gardens in 4 acres of heated greenhouses 11,000 different types of plants, and spectacular fountains. (This is my favorite garden to visit!)

MAXWELL ARBORETUM

http://www.unl.edu/unlbga/tour/maxwell/max_index.html

A small arboretum at the University of Nebraska-Lincoln in Maxwell Arboretum is home to over 420 varieties of native and introduced species of plants.

MISSOURI BOTANICAL GARDEN

http://www.mobot.org/welcome.html

The Missouri Botanical Garden was first opened to the public in 1859 by Henry Shaw. MBG is home to the Climatron, a unique geodesic dome conservatory. It also hosts several other Web sites including the American Association of Botanical Gardens and Arboreta.

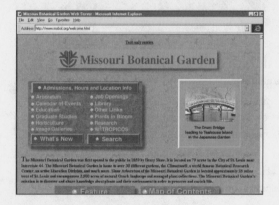

MORRIS ARBORETUM OF THE UNIVERSITY OF PENNSYLVANIA

http://www.upenn.edu/morris/

Morris Arboretum of the University of Pennsylvania includes many of Philadelphia's oldest, rarest, and largest trees, set in a romantic Victorian landscape garden of winding paths, streams, and special garden areas.

THE MORTON ARBORETUM
http://www.mortonarb.org/

The Morton Arboretum in Lisle, Illinois, is a magnificent 1,700-acre botanical garden specializing in the display and study of trees, shrubs, and vines.

THE NATIONAL GARDEN
http://www.nationalgarden.org/

Located in Washington, D.C., the National Garden is the oldest continually operating botanic garden in the United States.

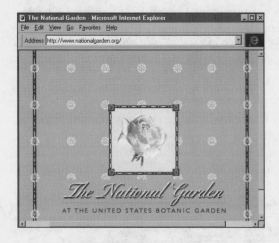

NATIONAL TROPICAL BOTANICAL GARDEN
http://www.ntbg.org/

The National Tropical Botanical Garden in Lawai, Hawaii, is dedicated to the conservation of tropical plant diversity, particularly rare and endangered species.

THE RUTH BANCROFT GARDEN
http://www.ruthbancroftgarden.org/

Preserving an exceptional example of American garden design, the Ruth Bancroft Garden in Walnut Creek, California demonstrates the beauty and excitement possible in a water-conserving landscape.

THE UNITED STATES NATIONAL ARBORETUM—WASHINGTON D.C.
http://www.ars-grin.gov/ars/Beltsville/na/

The mission of the U.S. National Arboretum is to conduct research, provide education, and conserve and display trees, shrubs, flowers, and other plants that enhance the environment.

UNIVERSITY OF CALIFORNIA SANTA CRUZ ARBORETUM
http://www2.ucsc.edu/arboretum/

This site includes information about the arboretum including a calendar of events, a list of University of California Extension courses, and tours of the gardens.

ZILKER BOTANICAL GARDEN
http://www.zilker-garden.org/

Zilker Botanical Garden in Austin, Texas, has taken great care to plan a "feast for the eyes and the senses." The Web site is maintained by Jim Parra, Web administrator of the Gardening Launch Pad, the best gardening links Web site.

BULBS

THE U.S. NETHERLANDS FLOWER BULB INFORMATION CENTER (NFBIC)
http://www.bulb.com/

The NFBIC is a source of news, photographs, video footage, and technical information on flower bulbs and garden trends for print, broadcast and "cyber" journalists. Gardeners and others interested in bulbs are also welcome to visit the site.

COMPOSTING

CORNELL COMPOSTING
http://www.cals.cornell.edu/dept/compost/

Cornell Composting provides access to a variety of educational materials and programs about composting developed at Cornell University.

THE DIGITAL COMPOSTER
http://www.digitalseed.com/composter/

Digital Composter is part of the Digital Seed Web site. While Digital Seed focuses on the needs of Southern California gardeners, the Digital Composter has information of interest to all.

WORMS!
http://www.ciwmb.ca.gov/mrt/wpw/wporgnc/wrmfct.htm

Part of the California Integrated Waste Management Board Web site, Worms! provides information on worm composting, including several classroom activities.

DATABASES (PLANT)

CARNIVOROUS PLANTS DATABASE
http://www.hpl.hp.com/bot/cp_home/

This database includes over 3,000 entries, giving an exhaustive nomenclatural synopsis of all carnivorous plants.

FLOWERBASE
http://www.flowerbase.com/

A database of over 7,000 flowers and plants, this site is searchable by botanical, English, Spanish, Dutch, or French name.

NATIONAL PLANTS DATABASE
http://plants.usda.gov/plants/

The PLANTS Database provides a single source of standardized information about plants. PLANTS provides standardized plant names, symbols, and other plant attribute information.

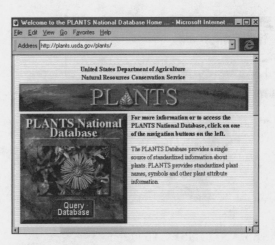

ORNAMENTAL PLANTS
http://www.msue.msu.edu/msue/imp/modop/masterop.html

The Ornamental Plants database, maintained by the Michigan State University Extension, contains information about trees, shrubs, vines, ground covers, perennials, annuals, house plants, insects, diseases, cultural information and other topics. Plants hardy in Zone 6 or colder are the primary focus. This site is text oriented, with little or no graphics, but including a wealth of information. A CD-ROM version is available with an extensive image collection.

PLANTLINK
http://www.plantamerica.com/palink.htm

This is the most comprehensive URL search engine for plant-related Web sites available. Pre-programmed with accurate nomenclature, PlantLink utilizes advanced search capabilities to cross reference several Web search engines.

WEBGARDEN FACTSHEET DATABASE
http://www.hcs.ohio-state.edu/hcs/Webgarden/FactsheetFind.html

Use this site to search the Internet for information related to horticulture and crop science from 50 different colleges and universities across the United States and Canada. Over 13,000 pages of information are frequently updated, in order to provide the most concentrated source of plant-related information available.

DISEASES AND INSECTS

NATIONAL INTEGRATED PEST MANAGEMENT NETWORK
http://www.reeusda.gov/nipmn/

The National Integrated Pest Management Network (NIPMN) is the result of a public–private partnership dedicated to making the latest and most accurate pest management information available on the World Wide Web. The backbone of the National IPM Network consists of Web servers for each of the USDA-defined regions (Southern, Northeastern, North Central, and Western) in the U.S. Within each region, participating institutions are providing state-specific or subject-specific information.

EXTENSION SERVICES

STATE PARTNERS OF THE COOPERATIVE STATE RESEARCH, EDUCATION, AND EXTENSION SERVICE
http://www.reeusda.gov/new/statepartners/usa.htm

This site contains the directory of land-grant universities, which are state partners of the Cooperative State Research, Education, and Extension Service. Also included are links to the Web sites of the schools of forestry, higher education, home economics, and veterinary science, and to state extension services and state stations.

GENERAL GARDENING

CALENDAR OF GARDEN EVENTS
http://www.gardencalendar.com

This calendar lists events that have been submitted via an online form, as well as a sampling from The Garden Tourist, a printed guide to garden tours, garden days, shows, and special events.

FLORIDA PLANTS ONLINE
http://www.floridaplants.com

Florida Plants Online provides a linked directory of research, publications, organizations, agencies, and events concerning the gardens and plants in Florida.

THE FLOWERWEB
http://www.flowerweb.nl

This is an international and multilingual site located in the Netherlands, and listing growers, nurseries, and suppliers of flowers, plants, and trees. Flowerweb also hosts the Flowerbase, a very large database of trees, plants, and flowers.

GARDEN ESCAPE
http://www.garden.com

Garden Escape is a commercial venture with advertising, gardening supplier Web pages, assorted resources, and message boards.

THE GARDEN GATE ON THE PRAIRIENET
http://www.prairienet.org/garden-gate/

The Garden Gate offers gardeners and nature lovers a carefully selected and well-organized collection of links to informative and interesting horticulture sites around the world. This is one of my favorite gardening Web sites.

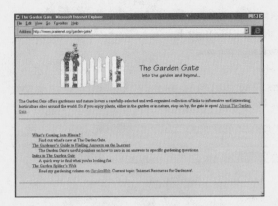

GARDEN GUIDES

http://www.gardenguides.com/

This is a resource for gardeners with guides to flowers, vegetables, and herbs. Most of the guides are geared towards herbs, succession planting, and organic gardening.

GARDEN TOWN MALL

http://www.gardentown.com/

The Web site for this online community for gardeners is organized like a town—with a gazebo, a library, café, and shopping mall.

GARDENING.COM

http://gardening.com

Gardening.Com is the companion Web site to Books That Work, a home and garden software subsidiary of Sierra On-Line. The site's three main features are a plant encyclopedia, a garden site directory, and the revived Ortho Problem Solver.

GARDENING.COM GARDEN SITE DIRECTORY

http://gardening.com/Directory/Default.htm

This is Gardening.com's database of hundreds of garden-related Web sites. Most of the listed sites include reviews by the Gardening.com staff.

GARDENNET

http://trine.com/GardenNet/

GardenNet is a gateway to gardening sites on the Internet. Among the site's useful resources is an online catalog request service. This is one of my favorite gardening Web sites.

THE GARDENWEB

http://www.gardenweb.com/

GardenWeb is a comprehensive site with extensive forums, a calendar of events, contests, glossaries, and links to other sites, including GardenWeb Europe and GardenWeb Australia. This is one of my favorite gardening Web sites.

THE GROW ZONE

http://www.plants.org/

The online professional horticultural resource, the Grow Zone has links to many nurseries, suppliers, and nursery associations. They are also the Web hosting service for the Web site of the American Nursery and Landscape Association (formerly American Nurseryman's Association.)

GROWIT.COM

http://www.growit.com/

This is a site for the nursery industry, with links to wholesale growers, nursery suppliers, and servers, primarily in the south central United States.

THE HORTICULTURAL WEB

http://www.horticulture.com/

The Horticultural Web is a dynamic community where horticulturists can stay informed, conduct business, conduct research, stay abreast of government programs, participate in community activities and communicate with fellow horticulturists.

HORTWORLD

http://www.hortworld.com

This is a commercial horticulture Web site maintained by Betrock Information Services, with links to many different suppliers, services, associations, institutions, and botanical gardens.

ICANGARDEN—CANADIAN INTERNET GARDENING RESOURCE

http://www.ICanGarden.com/

ICanGarden is the top gardening Web site for Canadian gardeners. The site is also useful to U.S. gardeners in the northern border states.

JOE & MINDY'S WEB GARDEN

http://www.nhn.ou.edu/~howard/garden.html

The site is an eclectic mix of gardening topics and links for gardeners by gardeners. It is one of the author's top ten garden Web sites.

NATIONAL GARDENING ASSOCIATION

http://www2.garden.org/nga/

The largest nonprofit gardening organization in the United States, National Gardening Association (NGA) is best known for its high-quality publication, National Gardening Magazine, its innovative science education programs, and its garden-related research.

PACIFIC NORTHWEST GARDENING

http://www.nwgardening.com/

With a mild climate west of the Cascade Mountains, gardening in the maritime Pacific Northwest is different from gardening in any other part of the country. This site offers information on gardening in this unique climate.

SUITE 101 GARDENS

http://www.suite101.com/userfiles/79/gardening.html

Suite 101 is a comprehensive Web guide with numerous sections managed by contributing editors who write articles, discuss gardening, and suggest great links to the Internet. Suite 101 Gardening is a gardening e-zine (electronic magazine).

VIRTUAL GARDEN
http://www.pathfinder.com/vg/

The Virtual Garden is a part of Pathfinder.com, an extensive Web site maintained by the media giant Time-Warner. Many of the resources found in the Virtual Garden are online versions of Time-Warner's extensive gardening book and magazine collection.

WEBGARDEN
http://www.hcs.ohio-state.edu/hcs/webgarden.html

WebGarden provides a growing collection of resources for beginning and professional gardeners, students, teachers, professional agronomists, and horticulturists. This is one of the author's top ten gardening Web sites.

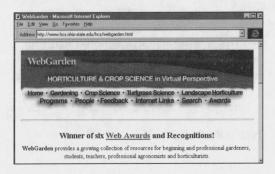

HERBS

HENRIETTE'S HERBAL HOMEPAGE
http://sunsite.unc.edu/herbmed/

Henriette's Herbal Homepage provides all types of information for herbalists.

HERBAL HALL
http://www.herb.com/

This is a good resource for gardeners interested in the medicinal use of herbs.

WHOLE HERB
http://www.wholeherb.com

This is a Web site devoted to the growing and use of herbs. It is maintained by Storey Communications, a major publisher of books for the home and garden.

HYDROPONICS

THE HYDROPONIC SOCIETY OF AMERICA
http://www.intercom.net/user/aquaedu/hsa/index.html

The Hydroponic Society of America (HSA) is the premiere hydroponic organization in the United States. Its members include researchers, educators, hobbyists, and commercial growers using the latest growing methods to produce the best flowers, vegetables, and herbs.

IMAGE COLLECTIONS

FLORA OF EUROPE— A PHOTOGRAPHIC HERBARIUM
http://utopia.knoware.nl/users/aart/

This "Flora on line" is an amateur photo-herbarium, containing almost 700 pictures of flowers, mostly from southern Europe.

FLORIDATA
http://www.streetside.com/plants/floridata/

Floridata is an online photo reference of plants, covering categories such as trees, shrubs, vines, cactus, water plants, and annuals.

FLOWERY BACKGROUNDS ARCHIVE
http://www.cascade.net/flowers/index.html

This is a collection of graphic images for use in Web page backgrounds. The images can also be used in other graphic programs.

GARDEN ART GALLERY
http://garden-art.com/

Garden Art Gallery is a juried art exhibition being developed by artists for artists. Its goal is to enable artists to communicate with one another and exhibit and share their work with the worldwide community on the Internet.

A PRAIRIE GALLERY

http://www.netins.net/showcase/bluestem/gallery.htm

This site includes pictures of prairie plants and related scenes from Heyne Custom Seed Services, a producer/supplier of prairie wildflowers.

SMITHSONIAN CATALOG OF BOTANICAL ILLUSTRATIONS

http://www.nmnh.si.edu/botart/

The Department of Botany of the Smithsonian Institution's National Museum of Natural History has created a database of botanical illustrations. The Web site offers 500 images in the three families that have been completed: Bromeliaceae, Cactaceae, and Melastomataceae.

WILDFLOWERS IN BLOOM

http://aggie-horticulture.tamu.edu/wildseed/

A pictorial resource of wildflower information, this site is a cooperative project between WILDSEED FARMS, the Texas Agricultural Extension Service, and the Texas Horticulture Program.

KIDS ONLY

BUG CLUB'S HOME PAGE

http://www.ex.ac.uk/bugclub/

The Bug Club is a club for young people and the "young at heart" who find insects and other creepy crawlies interesting and even fascinating.

KIDS IN THE GARDEN

http://www.augusthome.com/kid.htm

Here are some simple ideas to make gardening fun for children from the publishers of Garden Gate magazine.

KINDERGARDEN

http://aggie-horticulture.tamu.edu/Kinder/index.html

This site gives an introduction to the many ways children can interact with plants and the outdoors.

MBGNET

http://www.mobot.org/MBGnet/

MBGNet is a place where kids can communicate with and learn from other kids, and where they can investigate the habitats that make Earth such an interesting and diverse place.

LAWN AND GRASSES

ASK EARL, THE YARD-CARE ANSWER GUY

http://www.yardcare.com/

"What's your yard-care problem? Ask Earl, The Yard-Care Answer Guy." A question/answer and yard-care topic site courtesy of the Toro Company.

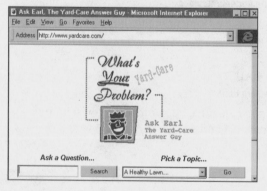

LAWN INSTITUTE

http://www.lawninstitute.com/

The Lawn Institute is a respected authority for monitoring, reporting, and interpreting the latest advances in turfgrass research, landscape horticulture, and agronomic science.

LINK SITES

AGRISURF!

http://www.agrisurf.com

A Web guide to agricultural Web sites, including those related to home gardening.

ENVIRONMENTAL ORGANIZATION WEBDIRECTORY

http://www.webdirectory.com/

This amazing Environmental Organization WebDirectory is the result of a group of hard-working people dedicated to helping others keep in touch and informed on the World Wide Web. While largely environmental, you'll also find links to gardening sites.

THE GARDENING LAUNCH PAD

http://www.tpoint.net/neighbor/

The Gardening Launch Pad is the starting point for all electronic gardening needs, with over 2,000 links in 61 categories.

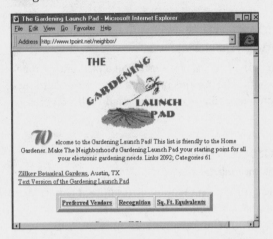

INTERNET DIRECTORY FOR BOTANY: GARDENING

http://www.ou.edu/cas/botany-micro/idb/bothort.html

This is an index of Web sites in the Internet Directory for Botany: Gardening category. The IDB is a multi-Web site index to botanical information available on the Internet, with thousands of links.

THE INTERNET GARDEN

http://www.internetgarden.co.uk/

The Internet Garden is an online gardening directory, emphasizing links to Web sites in the U.K. and other European countries.

MAGAZINES

FINE GARDENING ONLINE

http://www.taunton.com/fg/index.htm

This is the Web site of *Fine Gardening* magazine, one of my favorites.

GARDEN GATE MAGAZINE ONLINE

http://www.augusthome.com/gardeng.htm

Garden Gate magazine is a popular gardening magazine with no advertising.

GROWER'S ALMANAC
http://www.jcsolutions.com/jcsgrower/

Grower's Almanac is an online magazine for northern-climate gardeners by JCSolutions WebDesign of Omena, Michigan

THE GROWING EDGE
http://www.growingedge.com

The Growing EDGE is an international bi-monthly magazine designed for serious hobbyist indoor and outdoor home gardeners and professional small-scale commercial growers.

TRADITIONAL GARDENING MAGAZINE
http://traditionalgardening.com/

This is an online select edition of *Traditional Gardening: A Journal of Practical Information on Creating and Restoring Classic Gardens.*

PESTICIDES

EXTOXNET
http://ace.orst.edu/info/extoxnet/

EXTOXNET is a source of objective, science-based information about pesticides, written for the nonexpert.

MATERIAL SAFETY DATA SHEET "INFO-SOURCE" HOTLIST
http://www.halcyon.com/ttrieve/msdshome.html

This is a list of links to various MSDS Web sites and archives.

MATERIAL SAFETY DATA SHEET SEARCHES
http://research.nwfsc.noaa.gov/msds.html

This site helps you search for publicly accessible MSDS information.

PONDS

INTERNATIONAL WATERLILY SOCIETY
http://h2olily.rain.com/

This site gives information on membership in the society and general information on water lilies.

SOCIETIES

AMERICAN ASSOCIATION OF AMATEUR ARBORISTS
http://www.arborworks.org/

The American Association of Amateur Arborists is a loose association of individuals and groups interested in learning more about trees and other woody plants.

AMERICAN ASSOCIATION OF BOTANICAL GARDENS AND ARBORETA
http://www.mobot.org/AABGA/

The American Association of Botanical Gardens and Arboreta is the professional association for public gardens in North America.

AMERICAN BAMBOO SOCIETY
http://www.bamboo.org/abs/

The American Bamboo Society Web site includes links to additional information about bamboo.

AMERICAN BONSAI SOCIETY
http://www.absbonsai.org/

Founded in 1967, the American Bonsai Society, Inc. is the pioneering national bonsai organization.

THE AMERICAN DAHLIA SOCIETY
http://www.dahlia.com/guide/index.html

The is the official Web site of the American Dahlia Society.

AMERICAN FERN SOCIETY
http://www.visuallink.net/fern/index.html

The American Fern Society is over 100 years old. With over 900 members worldwide, it is one of the largest fern clubs in the world.

THE AMERICAN HEMEROCALLIS SOCIETY
http://www.daylilies.org/daylilies.html

The American Hemerocallis Society is a nonprofit organziation organized exclusively for educational and scientific purposes, and especially to promote, encourage, and foster the development and improvement of the genus *Hemerocallis.*

AMERICAN HORTICULTURAL SOCIETY

http://members.aol.com/gardenahs/

The American Horticultural Society, founded in 1922, is an educational, non-profit organization that recognizes and promotes excellence in American horticulture.

AMERICAN HOSTA SOCIETY

http://www.hosta.org

The American Hosta Society is a nonprofit organization organized exclusively for educational and scientific purposes, and especially to promote, encourage, and foster the development and improvement of the genus *Hosta*.

AMERICAN IRIS SOCIETY

http://www.isomedia.com/homes/AIS/

The American Iris Society is a nonprofit institution dedicated to promoting the culture and improvement of the iris.

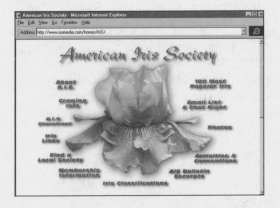

THE AMERICAN ROSE SOCIETY

http://www.ars.org/

The American Rose Society is dedicated to the enjoyment, enhancement, and promotion of the rose.

AMERICAN SOCIETY FOR HORTICULTURAL SCIENCE

http://www.ashs.org/

The American Society for Horticultural Science was established in 1903 for the promotion of the science of horticulture. With 5,000 members from all 50 states and more than 100 countries, ASHS is the world's largest and most-respected professional society for individuals who practice horticultural science.

BROMELIAD SOCIETY INTERNATIONAL

http://bsi.org

The purposes of the BSI are to promote and maintain public and scientific interest in the research, development, preservation, and distribution of bromeliads, both natural and hybrid, throughout the world.

THE CACTUS AND SUCCULENT SOCIETY OF AMERICA, INC.

http://www.hpl.hp.com/bot/cssa

The Cactus and Succulent Society of America was founded in 1929 and has grown to become an international organization with about 100 affiliates.

THE INTERNATIONAL PALM SOCIETY

http://www.palms.org/

The IPS was formed in 1956 as "The Palm Society," to serve as a focus for the .study, culture, and preservation of palms around the world. Its name was changed to the International Palm Society in the early 1980s to reflect a growing international membership. IPS members now number almost 3,000 from over 85 countries.

NATIONAL ARBORIST ASSOCIATION

http://www.natlarb.com/

The NAA is a trade association of commercial tree care firms. The Association develops safety and educational programs, standards of tree care practice, and management information for arboriculture firms around the world.

NORTH AMERICAN LILY SOCIETY

http://www.lilies.org/

The NALS was organized in Boston in 1946 as an outgrowth of the Lily Committee of the American Horticultural Society. It now has members in almost every state and province of North America, many countries of Europe, Asia, Africa, and South America, as well as in Australia and New Zealand.

NORTH AMERICAN ROCK GARDEN SOCIETY

http://www.nargs.org/

The NARGS is for gardening enthusiasts interested in alpine, saxatile, and low-growing perennials.

PERENNIAL PLANT ASSOCIATION

http://garden.cas.psu.edu/garden/ppa.html

The Perennial Plant Association is dedicated to improving the perennial plant industry by providing education to enhance the production, promotion, and utilization of perennial plants.

SPECIFIC PLANTS

THE AFRICAN VIOLET SOCIETY OF AMERICA ON LINE

http://avsa.org/

AVSA On Line is produced by the African Violet Society of America, Inc. It provides information concerning the culture, showing, propagation, grooming, and buying of African Violets.

ALL-AMERICA ROSE SELECTIONS WEB SITE

http://www.rose.org/

All-America Rose Selections is a non-profit association of rose growers dedicated to garden rose research and promotion.

CULTIVATIONS' DAYLILY CORNER

http://www.rjnet.com/daylily/

This is a commercial site on daylilies, with links to software, catalogs, forums, growers, and other daylily information.

DAYLILIES GROWING ALONG THE INFORMATION HIGHWAY

http://www.daylilies.com/daylilies/index1.html

Daylilies Growing Along the Information Highway is maintained by a supporter of Friends of the Daylilies—a group of American Hemerocallis Society (AHS) members interested in publicizing the flower and its culture.

THE ORCHID WEBLOPEDIA

http://conbio.bio.uci.edu/orchid/

This is quite possibly the best orchid resource on the Web.

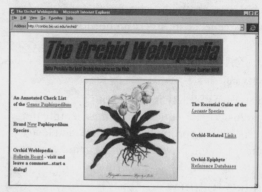

THE ROSARIAN

http://www.rosarian.com/

The Rosarian is a site devoted to roses and the gardeners who cultivate them.

YESTERDAY'S ROSE!

http://www.halcyon.com/cirsium/rosegal/welcome.htm

This site is dedicated to old and old-fashioned garden roses. It includes illustrations and descriptions of over 100 rose varieties, including details of scent, flowering, growth, and culture.

TREES

PLANTAMNESTY

http://www.plantamnesty.org/

PlantAmnesty's mission is to end mal-pruning and improper landscape management practices, and to promote awareness and respect for plants as an integral part of urban ecology.

THE WORLD OF TREES

http://www.domtar.com/tree/

This is an excellant educational site on trees developed by Domtar, a Canadian forestry products, pulp, and paper corporation.

USENET NEWSGROUPS

AGRICULTURE NEWS GROUP
news:sci.agriculture

BONSAI NEWS GROUP
news:rec.arts.bonsai

GARDEN IMAGES NEWS GROUP
news:alt.binaries.pictures.gardens

GARDEN ROSES NEWS GROUP
news:rec.gardens.roses

THE GARDENING NEWS GROUP
news:rec.gardens

GENERAL HORTICULTURE RESEARCH
news:hort.general

HERBAL NEWS GROUP
news:alt.folklore.herbs

ORCHIDS NEWS GROUP
news:rec.gardens.orchids

PONDS NEWS GROUP
news:rec.ponds

SUSTAINABLE AGRICULTURE NEWS GROUP
news:alt.sustainable.agriculture

WEATHER

INTERACTIVE WEATHER INFORMATION NETWORK
http://iwin.nws.noaa.gov/iwin/graphicsversion/main.html

This is an interactive Web site, part of the National Weather Service's Weather Information Network.

METROPOLITAN QUICK-LOOKS FOR THE U.S. AND CANADA
http://grads.iges.org/pix/quicklook.html

Quick-Looks at current weather and forecasts for selected metropolitan areas are compiled from the following sources on the Internet: the Center for Ocean-Land-Atmosphere Studies (COLA) and the National Weather Service/Interactive Weather Information Network.

THE WEATHER CHANNEL
http://www.weather.com

This is the Weather Channel's Web site, one of the best television media Web sites for weather information. During the growing season, they devote several Web pages to weather-related gardening information.

WILDFLOWERS

NATIONAL WILDFLOWER RESEARCH CENTER
http://www.wildflower.org/

The purpose of the National Wildflower Research Center is to educate people about the environmental necessity, economic value, and natural beauty of native plants.

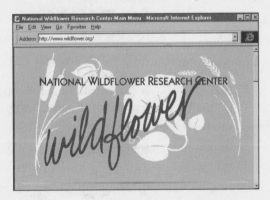

"About the CD-ROM" Table of Contents

About the CD-ROM

T he CD-ROM contains "The Gardener's Computer Companion Software Collection," an extensive compilation of shareware and freeware gardening software. This appendix describes each product on the CD as well as each product's placement within a category. Use it to preview the CD's offerings and to select among the products you wish to install. The line beginning "Installs to:" gives you the product's default installation directory on your hard disk. Pricing for products reflects the price as known to us at press time and is subject to change; please contact the software publishers to confirm their most current pricing.

In general, products marked as DOS products will run under both Windows 3.1 and Windows 95 but we cannot guarantee the operation of any program.

Should you encounter problems running any of the software contained on the CD-ROM, please contact the software publisher directly; contact information is included with each listing.

If you enjoy this CD-ROM and would like to order a copy for a friend, you can! Please send $19.95 for each copy of the CD to:

NO STARCH PRESS
GCC CD-ROM Offer
401 China Basin St., Ste. 108
San Francisco, CA 94107-2192

> **SPECIAL BONUS!**
> Sierra Complete LandDesigner demo—including a demo version of 3D Landscape 3.0!

We'll pay shipping within the United States. All payments must be by check or money order; Visa and Mastercard accepted for phone orders. California residents please add 8.5% sales tax. No C.O.D.s. International orders add $6.95 U.S. for shipping via Air Mail. If you have any questions, please call us at (800) 420-7240 or e-mail (info@nostarch.com).

CHEMICAL REFERENCES

CHEMREF 1.0

A simple reference database of common chemicals used in pesticides and herbicides. Shareware: $15.00. Requires Windows 3.1 or higher.

Installs to: C:\CHEMREF

> Mary Jo Warsinsky
> MJ Services
> Box 506
> Toano, VA 23168
> E-Mail: 71170.655@compuserve.com

CHEMREF 3.0

A reference database of chemicals used in pesticides and herbicides. ChemRef 3.0 has a better interface and more features than ChemRef 1.0. Shareware: $20.00. Requires Windows 3.1 or higher.

Installs to: C:\CHEMREF

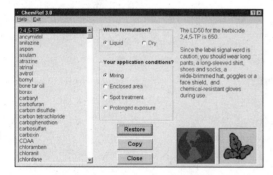

> Mary Jo Warsinsky
> MJ Services
> Box 506
> Toano, VA 23168
> E-Mail: 71170.655@compuserve.com

NOTE: *If you have not installed any other program that uses the Visual Basic 4.0 runtime, you will also need to run VB4RUN32.EXE in the vbRunTme folder.*

COMPUTER-AIDED DESIGN

DELTACAD

DeltaCAD is a two-dimensional computer-aided design program that can be used for landscape design. Shareware: $19.95 to $49.95. Requires Windows 3.1 or higher.

Installs to: C:\DELTACAD

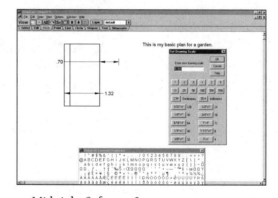

> Midnight Software Inc.
> P. O. Box 77352
> Seattle, WA 98177-0352
> FAX: (206) 361-0796
> E-Mail: 102562.1411@compuserve.com
> Web: http://www.dcad.com

PAGEDRAW

A Postscript-based drawing program for making quick sketches on a standard-size sheet of paper. Printer must support Postscript. Freeware. Requires Windows 3.1 or higher.

Installs to: C:\GCC_WARE\PAGEDRAW

Rajeev Karunakaran
E-Mail: rajeev@netcom.com

NOTE: *In addition to having a Postscript printer, you need Adobe Type Manager from Adobe Systems in order to enter text in a drawing. However, the program can be used without Adobe Type Manager if you do not need to enter text. See the file ATM.WRI for further information on using Adobe Type Manager.*

GAMES

BOTZ

Botz is an arcade game in which you guide your robot around a garden shooting wandering robots with paintballs. Shareware: $10.00. Requires Windows 95 or higher.

Installs to: C:\WINGAMES.INC\BOTZ

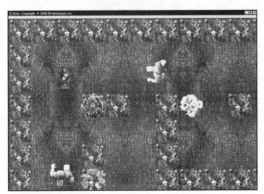

WinGames, Inc.
3905 Sandia
Plano, TX 75023
Phone: (972) 612-0839
E-Mail: wingames@wingames.com
Web: http://www.wingames.com

DAISY'S GARDEN

An action and strategy game, the object of which is to pick all the flowers and fruit while avoiding grubs and gophers. Daisy's Garden 2 Version 1.02e has several additional features. Shareware: $15.00. Requires Windows 3.1 or higher.

Installs to: C:\DAISYG2

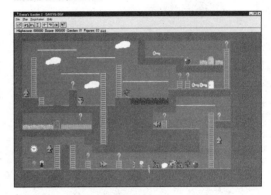

Dipl. Ing. Frank Burkart
Ingenieurbüro für Softwareentwicklung
Hertzstr. 29
D-76287 Rheinstetten Germany
E-Mail: 100725.3632@compuserve.com
Web: http://ourworld.compuserve.com/Homepages

GREEN THUMB CARDS (16 BIT)
GREEN THUMB CARDS (32 BIT)

A strategy card game to grow plants while dealing with typical garden problems and pests. Can be played over the Internet. Shareware: $24.95. Real paper card deck for $9.95. Requires Windows 3.1 or higher.

Installs to: C:\PROGRAM FILES\GTC; Windows 95 shortcut: Playful Minds

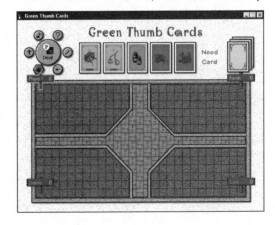

Playful Minds
AAIT Incorporated
58 Kennedy Dr., Unit B
Dartmouth, N.S., Canada
Phone: (902) 435-1676
FAX: (902) 462-0005
E-Mail: sales@aait.com
Web: http://www.playfulminds.com

GARDEN CALCULATORS

HOME LANDSCAPE MAINTENANCE

A simple calculator for determining irrigation scheduling times based on location, irrigation output, soil type, plant type, slope, and rooting depth. Shareware: $10.00. Requires Windows 3.1 or higher.

Installs to: C:\GCC_WARE\LNDMAINT

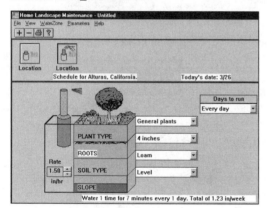

Hal Sturrock
1822 Corte Pulsera
Oceanside, CA 92056
Phone: (619) 630-8068

WATER EFFICIENT LANDSCAPE PLANNER

This program from Purdue University helps to develop water-efficient landscapes. Written with Knowledge Pro expert software with a basic hypertext system. Shareware: $15.00. DOS program.

Installs to: C:\GCC_WARE\WTRLNDPL

Farm Building Plan Service
Purdue University
1146 ABE Building
W. Lafayette, IN 47907-1146
Phone: (765) 494-1173
FAX: (765) 494-1356
E-Mail: fbps@ecn.purdue.edu

GARDEN PLANNERS

ABRACADATA SPROUT!

Sprout is a popular vegetable garden-planning program. Evaluation version (cannot save or print). Retail: $29.95. DOS program.

Installs to: C:\SPROUT

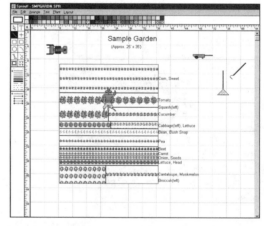

Abracadata
P.O. Box 2440
Eugene, OR 97402
Phone: (800) 451-4871
FAX: (503) 683-1925
E-Mail: abracadata@POBoxes.com
Web: http://www.abracadata.com

THE GARDEN ASSISTANT

The original vegetable-garden planning program, updated to work with hard disk drives and Windows. Shareware: $5.00 to $15.00. DOS program.

Installs to: C:\PROGRAMS\TGA

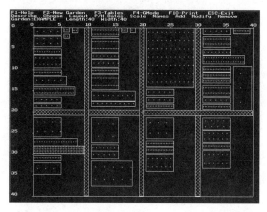

Shannon Software, Ltd.
P.O. Box 6126
Falls Church, VA 22040
Phone: (703) 573-0793
E-Mail: shansoft@shannonsoft.com
Web: http://www.shannonsoft.com

JSSI GARDEN

Help with designing a vegetable garden. Shareware: $20.00. Requires Windows 3.1 or higher.

Installs to: C:\GCC_WARE\JSSIGRDN

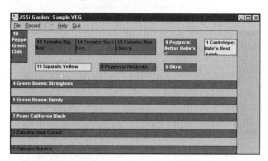

Steve Schiavo
JSS, Inc.
HC-1 Box 592-1
Center Point, TX 78010
Phone: (210) 634-2070
FAX: (210) 634-2077
E-Mail: 72271.2563@compuserve.com

INFORMATION MANAGERS

DAYTIMER ORGANIZER 2.1 TRIAL VERSION

A trial version of the Daytimer Organizer 2.1 information-management software. Trialware, limited to 60 days of use. Retail: $50.00 for Daytimer Organizer 98. Requires Windows 3.1 or higher.

Installs to: C:\DTO21 (Win 3.1); C:\PROGRAM FILES\DAY-TIMER ORGANIZER 2.1 (Win 95)

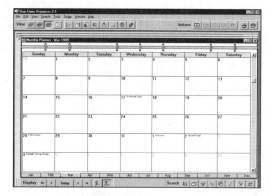

Day-Timers, Inc.
One Day-Timer Plaza
Allentown, PA 18195-1551
Phone: (800) 225-5005
FAX: (800) 452-7398
E-Mail: dtservice@daytimer.com
Web: http://www.daytimer.com

NOTEBOOK

A notebook-style journal program. Includes a calendar with a built-in garden calculator for setting harvest date based on the number of days from planting date. Requires Windows 3.1 or higher. Shareware.

Installs to: C:\PROGRAM FILES\NOTEBOOK

Longreach Scientific Resources
Box 549
Orr's Island, ME 04066
E-Mail: ian@lincoln.midcoast.com
Web: http://lincoln.midcoast.com/~ian/notebook.htm

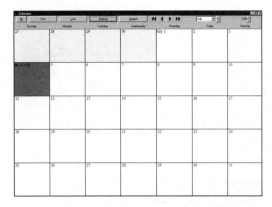

ZOOT 3.1

An information manager for creating reference sets and libraries of information. Can be used for a variety of garden information gathering and organizing activities. Shareware: $79. Requires Windows 3.1 or higher.

Installs to: C:\ZOOT\ZOOTLIBS

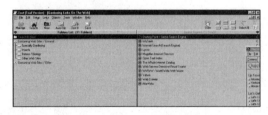

Tom Davis
Zoot Software
170 West Hill Rd.
Lincoln, VT 05443
Phone: (802) 453-6474
E-Mail: info@zootsoftware.com
Web: http://www.zootsoftware.com

JOURNALS

LOKI DIARY

A diary program that can be used to keep a garden journal. The Windows 95 version includes a calendar. Shareware: $15.00 (check), $20.00 (credit card). Requires Windows 3.1 or higher.

Installs to: C:\LOKI16 (Win 3.1); C:\PROGRAM FILES\LOKI32 (Win 95)

Ross A. Goldberg
7201 Wood Hollow Dr. #373
Austin, TX 78731
E-Mail: lokidog@onr.com
Web: http://www.lokidog.com

OMNIDAY FOR WINDOWS 3.00

A computer diary program that can be used to keep a garden journal. Shareware: $29.95. Requires Windows 3.1 or higher.

Installs to: C:\GCC_WARE\ODAYJRNL

Unicorn Software Ltd
P.O. Box 117
Knob Noster, MO 65336
Phone: (816) 429-3558
FAX: (816) 429-3558
E-Mail: 70272.3317@compuserve.com

SCRAPS

This diary program can also store images. Contains a runtime version of Filemaker Pro. Shareware: $19.95. Requires Windows 3.1 or higher.

Installs to: C:\GCC_WARE\Scraps

Installation

1. Read the Installation instructions in the README.WRI file, found in the Scraps folder on the CD.

2. Run INSTALL.EXE in the Disk1 folder inside the Scraps folder on the CD.

3. If you already have Quicktime installed on your system, select the option to install Filemaker Pro without Quicktime.

4. Copy the SCRAPS.FM file to the Fmpro folder on your hard disk drive.

5. Run the Filemaker Pro User program from the Windows 3.1 Program Manager or Windows 95 Start Menu.

R.J. Best
RJ Best Software
P.O. Box 12128
Honolulu, HI 96828
E-Mail: rbest@pixi.com

LANDSCAPE DESIGN

ABRACADATA DESIGN YOUR OWN HOME: LANDSCAPE

An evaluation version of Abracadata's landscape-planning software (cannot save or print). Retail: $29.95 (DOS) $39.95 (Windows). Versions are available for Macintosh and Apple. DOS program.

Installs to: C:\LANDSCAP

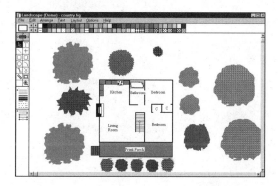

Abracadata
P.O. Box 2440
Eugene, OR 97402
Phone: (800) 451-4871
FAX: (503) 683-1925
E-Mail: abracadata@POBoxes.com
Web: http://www.abracadata.com

EXPERT LANDSCAPE DESIGN 3D

An evaluation version of Expert Landscape Design 3D version 1.0 for Windows (cannot save or print). Retail: $14.95. Requires Windows 3.1 or higher.

Installs to: C:\GCC_WARE\LAND3DDM

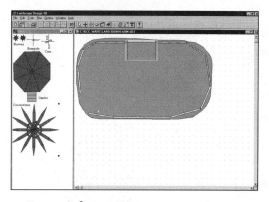

Expert Software, Inc.
800 Douglas Rd., Executive Tower
Coral Gables, FL 33134-3160
Phone: (305) 567-9990
FAX: (305) 443-0786
Web: http://www.expertsoftware.com

LANDSCAPE PLANNER

IMAGINE YOUR LANDSCAPE

A demonstration of Imagine Your Landscape, a visual imaging system. Demoware. Retail: $50.00. Requires Windows 3.1 or higher.

Installs to: C:\SEEIT4

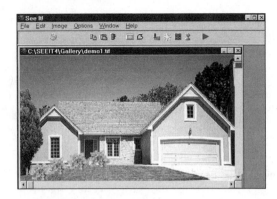

Visual Applications, Inc.
2301 Burlington, Ste. 220
North Kansas City, MO 64116
Phone: (888) 374-6963
FAX: (816) 472-0941
Web: http://www.showoff.com

LITERATURE

SELECTED GARDEN-RELATED STORIES

EText (Electronic Text) editions of three garden-related stories: "A Child's Garden of Verses," "Secret Garden," and "The Troll Garden and Selected Stories." Part of Project Gutenberg to put popular classics in digital format. Freeware: Donations accepted.

Installs to: C:\GCC_WARE\E_BOOKS

Project Gutenberg
P. O. Box 2782
Champaign, IL 61825
Web: http://promo.net/pg

PLANT DATABASES

HOMEGROWN V2.0

This database program for tracking garden seeds calculates when to sow, transplant, and harvest based on planting dates, dates to germination, and days to maturity. Freeware. DOS program.

Installs to: C:\GCC_WARE\HOMEGRDN

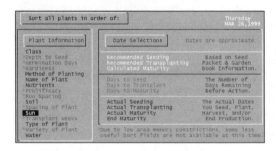

Dale Smith
Phone: (706) 866-2956
FAX: (706) 866-2956
E-Mail: 71023.2644@compuserve.com

HORTMAN—HORTICULTURE MANAGER, VERSIONS 1.2 AND 2.1

A management tool developed for the horticultural profession. Shareware: $45.00. DOS program.

Installs to: C:\GCC_WARE\HRTMGR12 (version 1.2); C:\GCC_WARE\ HRTMGR21 (version 2.1)

Sunrise Software
4821 Clydelle Ave.
San Jose, CA 95124-4209
E-Mail: 71045.767@compuserve.com

LANDSCAPE & HERBACEOUS PLANT MANAGER V1.6

The author's (Bob Boufford's) plant database—a DOS program with a Windows-like interface. Freeware. The large database files are for owners of *The Gardener's Computer Companion* only. DOS program.

Installs to: C:\GCC_WARE\LHPMDB

Bob Boufford
E-Mail: BouffordR@compuserve.com

NOTE: *HERBLRGE.DBF and LANDLRGE.DBF are for owners of The Gardener's Computer Companion only, and should not be passed on to others.*

ORCHID CATALOGING PROGRAM

This DOS database program tracks orchid information. Shareware: $20.00. DOS program.

Installs to: C:\GCC_WARE\ORCHCAT

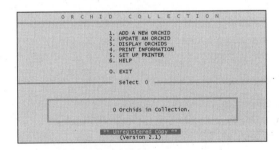

Larry Desiano
113 Townsend Dr.
Middletown, NJ 07748
Phone: (908) 615-0447

NOTE: *May perform poorly under Windows.*

ORGANIZE!

A series of cataloging/home inventory programs. Windows versions may be adjusted for plant cataloging. Shareware: $39.95 (DOS) $59.95 (Windows). DOS program.

Installs to: C:\GCC_WARE\OrgYrGrd

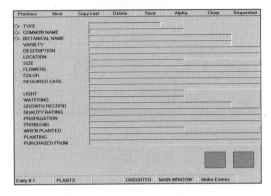

PSG-HomeCraft Software
P.O. Box 974
Tualatin, OR 97062
Phone: (503) 692-3732
FAX: (503) 692-0382
E-Mail: steve@homecraft.com
Web: http://www.homecraft.com

PLANT CATALOGING PROGRAM

This DOS database program for tracking plant information is very similar to the Orchid Cataloging program. Shareware: $20.00. DOS program.

Installs to: C:\GCC_WARE\PLANTCAT

Larry Desiano
113 Townsend Dr.
Middletown, NJ 07748
Phone: (908) 615-0447

NOTE: *May perform poorly under Windows.*

SEED PROGRAM

A database program for tracking garden seeds. Calculates when to sow, transplant, and harvest based on planting dates, days to germination, and days to maturity. Shareware: $25. DOS program.

Installs to: C:\SEEDS

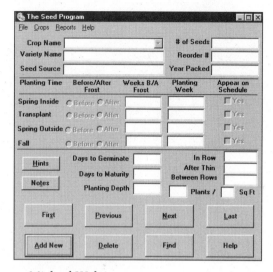

Michael Wolter
CyberNiche Software
4271 Carlisle Rd.
Gardners, PA 17324-8930
Phone: (717) 486-8308
E-Mail: cniche@pa.net
Web: http://www.cniche.com

WINDOW GARDEN

Pick a zone in the U.S. map, and this vegetable gardening reference displays a list of vegetables that can grow in that zone. It includes a companion planting guide. Shareware: $20. Requires Windows 3.1 or higher.

Installs to: C:\GCC_WARE\WINDGRDN

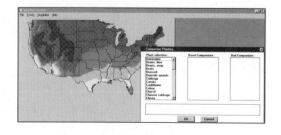

Wesley Garrard
2114 Shady Lane Dr.
Jackson, MS 39204
E-Mail: 74653.347@compuserve.com

WINGARDEN

This garden database and scheduler for starting and planting seeds includes journal features. Shareware: $15.00. Requires Windows 3.1 or higher.

Installs to: C:\GCC_WARE\WINGRDEN

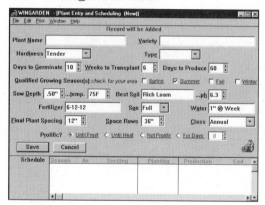

Dale M. Smith
1418 Evelyn Dr.
Rossville, GA 30741
E-Mail: 71023.2644@compuserve.com

PLANT REFERENCE

BONSAI DISCOVERY 2.0

A bonsai reference and database for maintaining records on a bonsai collection. Includes a calendar that can be linked to the database. Shareware: $20.00. Requires Windows 3.1 or higher.

Installs to: C:\BONSAI2

Bill Pennington
P.O. Box 3812
Sarasota, FL 34230
E-Mail: Bonsaikid@aol.com, HJXJ41A@prodigy.com

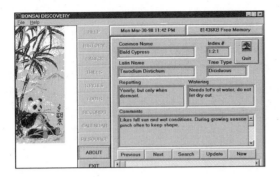

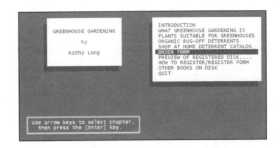

COMMON PLANT NAMES

A text file of common and scientific plant names, gleaned from a seed catalog. The text file is formatted to allow for importing into a database program. Freeware.

Installs to: C:\GCC_WARE\PLNTNMES

Installation

Open the file in any word processor. The names can be imported into any database or spreadsheet. See your specific database or spreadsheet program for details on importing "tab-delimited" files.

GARDEN COMPANION

An electronic reference on various aspects of gardening. Shareware: $20.00. DOS program.

Installs to: C:\GCC_WARE\GRDNCMPN

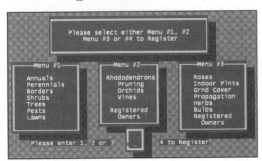

Bill Hammond
5714 N. I St.
San Bernadino, CA 92407

GREENHOUSE GARDENING

A "book on disk" about greenhouse gardening. Shareware: $14.95. DOS program.

Installs to: C:\GCC_WARE\GRNHSE

Kathy Long
LongLastings
P.O. Box 519
Coupeville, WA 98239-0519

GROW'EM 4.0

A reference program on propagating plants from seeds, cuttings, layering, and so on. Shareware: $22.95. DOS program.

Installs to: C:\GCC_WARE\GROWEM4

Paul Postuma
16 Fullyer Dr.
Quispamsis NB E2G 1Y7, Canada
Phone: (506) 849-7087
E-Mail: ppostuma@nbnet.nb.ca

GROWIT 2.2

One in a series of plant databases from Australia. DOS program.

Installs to: C:\GCC_WARE\GROWIT

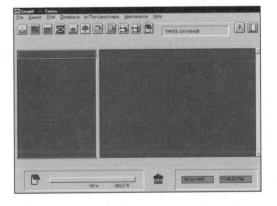

Brian Rondell
Innovative Thinking Software
P.O. Box 47
Lawson, NSW, 2783, Australia
E-Mail: 100243.745@compuserve.com

HERB POWER

This herb database includes information on growing practices and medicinal or culinary uses of herbs. Shareware: $20.00 US. DOS program.

Installs to: C:\HERB

Klaus Hoferichter
Hoferichter Design
345 Charles Lutes
Moncton, N.B. E1C 8Z4, Canada
Phone: (506) 383-7567
FAX: (506) 383-8171
E-Mail: khoferic@nbnet.nb.ca

MOONBOOK GARDENING

This calendar program shows the best time to work in the garden based on phases of the moon. Shareware: $29.95. Requires Windows 3.1 or higher.

Installs to: C:\GCC_WARE\MOONBOOK

Jeff Hume
Ed Hume Seeds
P.O. Box 1450
Kent, WA 98035
FAX: (206) 859-0694
E-Mail: JeffH46718@aol.com

PLANTMATE II

This houseplant reference includes photographs of plants and basic plant information. Shareware: $29.95. Requires Windows 3.1 or higher.

Installs to: C:\GCC_WARE\PLNTMATE

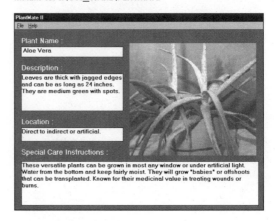

Deborah J. Rakoci
IrishStar Enterprise
7393 State Rd.
Wadsworth, OH 44281
E-Mail: irishstar@aol.com, FVDD14A@prodigy.com

SUCCESS FROM SEEDS

A combination reference and seed catalog from Ed Hume Seeds. Requires Windows 3.1 or higher.

Installs to: C:\GCC_WARE\SUCCESS

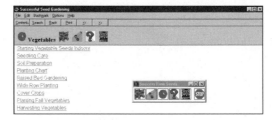

Jeff Hume
Ed Hume Seeds Inc.
P.O. Box 1450
Kent, WA 98035
E-Mail: JeffH46718@aol.com

V-BASE (AFRICAN VIOLET DATABASE)

A series of data files in dBase III and comma-delimited format with information on African Violets. Shareware: $7.00.

Installs to: C:\GCC_WARE\VIOLETDB

Installation

Import the comma-delimited file (*.ltd) or dBase file (*.dbf) into a database manager or spreadsheet for viewing.

Mike Schoenberger
920 Leland Ave.
Lima, OH 45805

WHICH PLANT

This database of plants allows for searching by name, descriptions, or name and descriptions. Shareware: $30.00.

Installs to: C:\GCC_WARE\WhchPlnt

Robert Bolt
2 Chichester Close
Burnley Lancashire B10 4BL, England
E-Mail: 101750.2650@compuserve.com

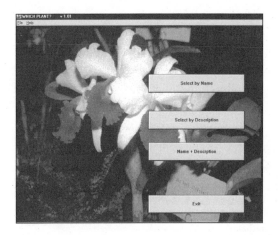

SIMULATIONS

GARDEN WITH INSIGHT

A garden simulation program. You select the plants to grow and various conditions then see the results. A good educational program and simulation. Source code available for programmers. Freeware. Requires Windows 3.1 or higher.

Installs to: C:\GWI100 (Win 3.1 and Win 95)

Paul Fernhout & Cynthia Kurtz
Kurtz-Fernhout Software
2813 Arbor St.
Ames, IA 50014
FAX: (515) 292-4311
E-Mail: info@gardenwithinsight.com
Web: http://www.gardenwithinsight.com

PLANTGRO

A plant growth predictor based on various conditions. Shareware: Version 2, $25 to $100 AUS. Contact author for current pricing on Version 2.1 and above. DOS program.

Installs to: C:\GCC_WARE\PLANTGRO

Dr. Clive Hackett
Plantsoft Services
30 Reveley Crescent
Stirling ACT 2611, Australia
Phone: 61 (02) 6288 8370
FAX: 61 (02) 6287 1301
E-Mail: chackett@netinfo.com.au
Web: http://www.ozemail.com.au/~chackett

SPREADSHEET SOFTWARE

VISTACALC 2.5

A shareware spreadsheet with Excel-like features that can be used for many gardening calculations. Shareware: $19.95. Requires Windows 3.1 or higher.

Installs to: C:\GCC_WARE\VSTACALC

Brandon Fridley
P.O. Box 6174
Vancouver, WA 98668
E-Mail: 74012.1635@compuserve.com
Web: http://ourworld.compuserve.com/homepages

UTILITIES

BOTANICA SCREEN SAVERS, VERSION 1.1

Botanica is a screen saver for Windows 3.1 and Windows 95. It uses mathematical formulas to draw flower and tree-like images on your screen. Shareware. $18.00. Requires Windows 3.1 or higher.

Installs to: C:\GCC_WARE\BOTANICA

Flywheel
P.O. Box 421
Ione, WA 99139
Phone: (509) 442-3138
E-Mail: flywheel@coolscreens.com
Web: http://www.coolscreens.com/index.shtm

GARDEN ICONS

A set of garden-related icons for use with Windows 3.1 Program Manager programs or Windows 95 shortcuts. For intermediate to advanced Windows users. Requires Windows 3.1 or higher.

Installs to: C:\GCC_WARE\GRDNICNS

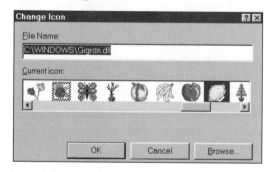

Gloria Lund
Gloricon Designs
8433 N Meadow Lake Rd.
New Hope, MN 55428-2730
FAX: (612) 574-1901
E-Mail: 73321.1794@compuserve.com

VISUAL BASIC RUNTIME MODULES

The Visual Basic Runtime modules required by some programs.

Microsoft Corporation
One Microsoft Way
Redmond, WA 98052-6399
Web: http://www.microsoft.com/vb

NOTE: *The VB 4.0 runtime is for Windows 95 only and will not work with Windows 3.1.*

WINCHIME

Plays wind chimes on your computer. Shareware: $14.95. Requires Windows 3.1 or higher with a sound card.

Installs to: C:\WINCHIME (Win 3.1); C:\PROGRAM FILES\WINCHIME (Win 95)

Sagebrush Systems, Inc
P.O. Box 3094
Corrales, NM 87048
Phone: (505) 898-6345
E-Mail: sells@sagebrush.com

WIND CHIMES 1.01

Plays wind chimes on your computer. You can select 127 different instruments, along with several scales. Shareware: $20.00. Requires Windows 95 or higher with a sound card.

Installs to: C:\CHIMES

Syntrillium Software Corporation
P.O. Box 62255
Phoenix, AZ 85082-2255
Phone: (602) 941-4327
FAX: (602) 941-8170
E-Mail: info@syntrillium.com
Web: http://www.syntrillium.com

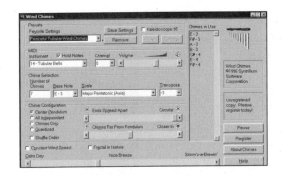

WINZIP

This popular compression/decompression utility for Windows 3.1 (16-bit) and Windows 95 (32-bit) will be useful when downloading compressed files from online services and the Internet. Shareware: $29. Requires Windows 3.1 or higher.

Installs to: C:\PROGRAMS\WINZIP (Win 3.1); C:\PROGRAM FILES\WINZIP (Win 95)

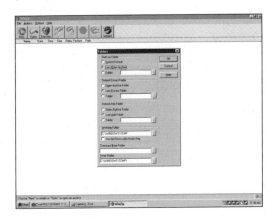

Nico Mak Computing, Inc.
P.O. Box 919
Bristol, CT 06011
E-Mail: 70056.241@compuserve.com
Web: http://www.winzip.com

WEATHER APPLICATIONS

WEATHER TRACKER 3.0S

This program lets you follow trends in the weather by recording daily high and low temperatures and measured precipitation over a calendar year. Shareware: $14.95. Requires Windows 3.1 or higher.

Installs to: C:\WEATHER

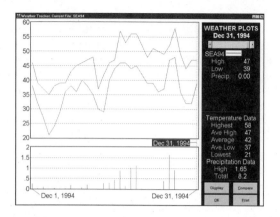

KIDware
15600 NE 8th, Ste. B1-314
Bellevue, WA 98008
Phone: (206) 721-2556
FAX: (206) 746-4655
E-Mail: KIDware@msn.com

WEATHER VANE

This utility sits within the Windows 95 tray and periodically retrieves local weather conditions and forecasts from the Internet. It requires Windows 95 with an Internet Connection. Freeware. Requires Windows 95 or higher.

Installs to: C:\PROGRAM FILES\WEATHER VANE

Mark A. Hallerman
E-Mail: mhallerman@sprynet.com
Web: http://home.sprynet.com/sprynet/mhallerman

WETSOCK

WetSock shows current weather conditions and forecasts as an icon on the taskbar. It requires Windows 95 with a direct Internet connection or a Windows dial-up. Shareware: $12 personal, $25 corporate. Requires Windows 95 or higher.

Installs to: C:\PROGRAM FILES\LOCUTUS\WETSOCK

Locutus Codeware
P.O. Box 53587
Vancouver, BC V5Z 1K0, Canada
Web: http://www.locutuscodeware.com

WINWEATHER

This excellent program shows hourly user-selected weather reports, forecasts, current maps, and much more. Requires Windows 3.1 or Windows 95 with an Internet Connection. 30-day Trial version. Shareware: $19.95. Requires Windows 3.1 or higher.

Installs to: C:\WEATH16 (Win 3.1); C:\PROGRAM FILES\WINWEATHER 3.0 (Win 95)

Adam Stein
Insanely Great Software
126 Calvert Ave. E.
Edison, NJ 08820
Phone: (617) 266-1630
FAX: (908) 632-1766
E-Mail: igs@igsnet.com, AdamStein@aol.com
Web: http://www.igsnet.com/weather.html

WORD PROCESSOR

YEAH WRITE

This simple-to-use word processor is an alternative to production word processors. It can be used for a variety of activities, including keeping a garden journal. Shareware: $19.00. Requires Windows 3.1 or higher.

Installs to: C:\YW (both versions)

Word Place
11 East 200 North, Ste. 201
Orem, UT 84057
Phone: (801) 221-7777
FAX: (801) 221-7707
E-Mail: info@wordplace.com
Web: http://www.wordplace.com

Installing Adobe Acrobat Reader and the PDF File

The free Adobe Acrobat Reader software allows you to view, navigate, and print PDF files. *PDF* (Portable Document Format) files are electronic versions of the actual book pages. They look exactly like the printed book but can be opened and read on your monitor. They offer a few side benefits: We've made all of the Web links live, so when you click on any blue link, your Web browser should open and transport you to that Web site; and when you click on a green link, you'll move to related areas within the book. You can even search the entire book (CTRL + F) for terms or phrases that interest you!

Be sure to install the correct version of Acrobat Reader from the CD-ROM for your system, and read the Help file for more information about viewing PDF files. To get to the Help file, pull down the **Help** menu and choose **Reader Online Guide**. (You can read this PDF file directly from the CD-ROM and, given its large size, you probably should.) Once Acrobat Reader is installed on your computer, simply double-click the **GCC_Book.pdf** file in the PDF directory on the CD-ROM to begin reading and playing—or copy the entire file to your hard disk for faster viewing. Enjoy!

INDEX

clock speed, 50, 51
CNET
    DOWNLOAD.COM, **114**, **130**, **159**,
        204, **228**
    Search.com, **92**
    SHAREWARE.COM, **114**, **228**
code, programming source, 232
colors
    printing, 58
    video display, 49
Common Plants of Canadian Association, 136
communications, 5, 13
    software, 8, 24, 37–38, 67–69
Compact Disk-Read Only Memory.
    See CD-ROM
Compaq, 195
compiler (program), 232
Complete Guide to Gardening (Better Homes
    and Gardens), 139
Complete Landscape Designer. *See*
    Alpha Software
composting, **250**–51
CompUSA, 17
CompuServe, 71–73, 78, 101
    to access, 71, 77
    journal programs on, 114
    PIMs on, 130
    Web hosting service on, *222*
computer
    assembled, 20–21
    buying, 10, 11–12, 16–21
        questions to ask, 19–21
    choosing, 60
    cost, 60–61
    custom system, 17, 18
    desktop, 59
        handheld personal (HPC), 194, 195
            (list). *See also* computer, palmtop
    manufactured, 21
    mini-notebooks, 190
    network (NC), 60
    notebook, 59, 190
    palmtop, 59, 190, 195 (list)
    PC, operating systems for, 15
    portable, for the garden, 190–95
    subnotebook, 190
    system
        described, 6–10
        expandable, 14
    utility programs for (list), 41
consultant, 18
controls, irrigation system, 213–14
copyright, and freeware, 26

Corel
    CorelDRAW, *36*, *168*
    HyperTerminal, *70*
    PHOTO-PAINT 7 Plus, 160, 161
    Quattro, 30
    WordPerfect, 27
Cornell Composting, **250**
cost
    ADSL, 66
    antivirus programs, 42
    AOL, 74–75
    CD-R drives, 55
    computer system, 12–13, 60–61
    digital cameras, 154, 199
    electronic organizers, 194
    home pages, 222
    imaging editing programs, 161
    ISP, 82–83
    landscape design programs, 181
    palmtop computers, 194
    printers, 58
    scanners, 150–51
    software, 24
    video hardware, 155
Country Living Gardener, The: Great
    Gardens (garden guide), 138
CPU. *See* processor
Cultivations' Daylily Corner, **260**

D

dahlias, **258**
DASSSH (analysis)
    buying a computer and, 11–12, 16, 27,
        30, 60
    choosing software and, 34, 161, 175
    video cameras and, 200
database
    CAD programs and, 37, 170
    creating, 137, 161, 180
    described, 8
    flat-file, 15, 32, 38, 117, 118–19
    management systems (DBMS), 6, 24,
        30–33, 38, 113, 115, 149
    multilinked data (pseudorelational)
        file, 117
    plant, **251**
    relational, 15, 32, 117, *119*, *120*, 131, 137
    Scraps, 114
    updating, 161
    uses for, 14, 100, 115, 117–23
    See also references
Davis Instruments, 207
Dawes Arboretum, The, **249**

video frame capture, 154–55
Harvard University (Arnold Arboretum), 248
help systems
    for CAD programs, 175
    for creating Web pages, 221
    questions to ask about, 43
Henriette's Herbal Homepage, 255
Herbal Hall, 255
Herbal News Group, 260
herbs, 255, 260
Hewlett-Packard, 195
Hitachi, 195
Holden Arboretum, 249
Home Automation Systems, 216
Home Automator, 216
home page, 87, 89. *See also* World Wide Web
Horticopia, 136
Horticultural Web, The, 254
Horticulture Manager (program), 116–17, *118*
Hortworld, 254
hostas, 258
Hot Bot, 92, 93
Hotmail, 105
HPC (handheld personal computer) (list), 194, 195
HSA (Hydroponic Society of America), 255
HTI Home Toys, 216
HTML. *See* hypertext Markup Language
http:// (hypertext transfer protocol), 88
Hydroponic Society of America (HSA), 255
HyperCard (program). *See* Macintosh, Claris
hypermedia, 86
HyperTerminal (program), *70*
hypertext, 86, 88
    Markup Language (HTML), 220, 223

I

IBM-PC compatible, 50
ICanGarden, *254*
illustrations
    database of, 255
    drawing programs for, *36,* 167, *168*
Illustrator (program), 36
image
    collections of, 255
    digitizing, 149–56
    resolution of, 34
Image Composer (program), *160–61*
image designer, landscape, 161–63
image editing, software for, 160–66, 225
Imagine Your Landscape (program), 163, *164*
imaging
    digital, and landscape design, 148

visual, for gardens, 4, 33, 35, 148, 149, 163, 181, 196
Imation SuperDisk LS-120 drive, 55
IMSI, **170**
    TurboCAD (program), 170, *171*
index in an electronic journal, 112
information
    computer-aided facilities management (CAFM) and, *183*–84
    personal manager (PIM) for, 125–31, *126,* 194
        to create, 131
        to find, 130
Infoseek, 92, 221
input, devices for, 9–10, 55–56, 150
    See also output
insect control, 252
Intel processor, 49–50, 175
Intellicast, **204,** *205*
Intellilink (program), 193
Interactive Weather Information Network, **261**
interface
    scanner, 151
    SCI, 151
    video capture, 154–55
    X10 module, *215*–16
International Palm Society, The, **259**
International Waterlily Society, **258**
Internet
    accessing AOL from, 75
    access to, 80
    CD-ROMs and, 142–43
    connecting with, 82–83
    described, 79–80
    Directory for Botany: Gardening, **257**
    Explorer. *See* Microsoft
    Garden, The, **257**
    News, *102*
    origins of, 80
    Protocol (IP), 81
    service provider (ISP), 68, 75, 82–83
        choosing, 82–83
        e-mail and, 104
        personal Web pages and, 219, 222
    TV, 60
    using, 13, 37, 68–69, 75, 79–83
    utility programs for (list), 41
    virus protection and, 42
    weather programs on, 204–206
    See also World Wide Web
interpreter (program), 232
interrupter, ground fault (GFI), 213
Iomega Zip drive, 54–55

Navigator, 89, *90*, 91
network
    integrated services digital (ISDN), 66
    Web server on, 227
networking
    dial-up, 68
    utility programs for (list), 41
newsgroups
    categories of (list), 102
    gardening, 101–103, **260–61**
NFBIC (U.S. Netherlands Flower Bulb
    Information Center), 250
NGA (National Gardening Association), 254
North American Lily Society, **259**
North American Rock Garden Society, **259**
NotePad (program), 224
NT (program), 227
Nursery Crops Coding System Manual
    (ANLA), 234

O

Object Linking and Embedding (OLE), 129
Office (application), 53, 233
offline readers, 72–73
Ohio State University, gardening Web site at,
    97, **140**–*41*
OLE (Object Linking and Embedding), 129
OMNIDay (program), 113–*14*
Online Bonsai Icon Collection, The, **248**
online service
    choosing, 78–79
    commercial, 70–79, 219
    communications software for, 68
    e-mail and, 104
    and the Internet, 82
    personal Web pages and, 219, 222
    trial membership, 79
    virus protection and, 42
operating system, 23–24
    communications software in, 69
    HPC, 195
    PDA, 195
    processors and, 49–50
    software requirements and, 15–16,
        42–43, 47
    space requirements of, 53
Orchids News Group, **260**
Orchid Weblopedia, The, *260*
organizer, electronic (digital diaries), 190,
    191–94, 195 (list)
Organizer (program), 129, **130**, *131*
Ornamental Plants, **251**

Ortho Home Gardener's Problem Solver (on-
    line), 98, *139*, 142, **253**
output, devices for, 9–10, 56–58
    See also input
OZCIS (offline reader), 72
OZWIN (offline reader), 72

P

Pacific Northwest Gardening, **254**
Paint (program), 34, 159
PalmPilot (US Robotics), 194
palms, **259**
Parra, Jim, 250
PC (computer), 50, 175
PC Connection, 19
PC link, 192
PC Magazine, 40
PC-Write (program), 27
PC Zone, 19
PDA (personal digital assistant), 190, 194–95
Pentium processor, 49–50, 175
Perennial Plant Association, **259**
Perennials & Annuals (CD-ROM), 136
personal organizer, 59
    See also information, personal manager
pesticides, **258**
pests, integrated management system (IPM)
    and, 204, **252**
Philips, **195**
photography
    digital, 33, 35, 147, 149
    time-lapse, 196
Photo Landscape (program), 181
PHOTO-PAINT 7 Plus (program), 160, 161
Photoshop (program), 34, 160, 161
PIM. *See* information, personal manager for
pixel, 34, 36, 57
Planix Photo Landscape (program), 160, 161,
    162, 182
planner, paper-based, 125–26
planning, **99**
    using a computer for, 4, 13–14, 36–37
plans to scale, 35, 166–77
Plantamnesty, **260**
planting zones, 100
PlantLink, **251**
plants
    dictionary of, 140–*41*
    encyclopedia of (online), 98, 110, 133–37
    to find online, 4, 99, 141
    growth simulator, electronic, 147, 163,
        172, 175
    to illustrate, 36

New! COLOR PRINTER IDEA BOOK

Over a Hundred Really Cool and Useful Projects to Make with Any Color Printer!

by KAY HALL

Now that you've got your color printer, why not use it to do more than just print Web pages? Here are all the steps, sources, and secrets needed to use your color printer to complete 101 practical projects for your home or small business. Learn how to make beautiful labels to use on homemade mustards or jams; how to print pictures of your children to turn into T-shirt transfers; how to make a customized clock for your child or grandchild; and even how to make jewelry! The methods and materials discussed include an eclectic mix from craft stores, office superstores, art materials dealers, and little known publications, both print and electronic. All techniques and materials have been tested and used successfully by the author.

KAY HALL has more than seven years as a desktop manufacturer, creating numerous items that have prompted the question, "You can do that with your computer?" She uses these techniques on a daily basis. In addition to her unique hands-on experience, she is a regular contributor to *Computer User*, and has written for *Home Office Computing, Flash, Dynamic Graphics*, and *Computing Today*.

256 pp., 16-page full-color insert, CD-ROM, $29.95
ISBN 1-886411-20-4

THE NEEDLECRAFTER'S COMPUTER COMPANION

Hundreds of Easy Ways to Use Your Computer for Sewing, Quilting, Cross-Stitch, Knitting & More!

by JUDY HEIM

"This is the 'How-do-I-get-started-and-why?' book you've been waiting for. Don't hesitate." — THREADS MAGAZINE

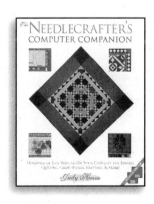

Use your computer to create dazzling needlework designs as innovative as your imagination, or as traditional as the ones in Grandma's hope chest. You'll find opinionated reviews of quilting, cross-stitch, sewing, weaving, and knitting software; how to use your computer to convert family photos into cross-stitch patterns; how to download free craft patterns and get advice from needlework magazines online; where to find craft resources on the Internet and commercial online services (like CompuServe and America Online); how to use computers in your needlecraft business; and much more.

JUDY HEIM, a *PC World* magazine contributing editor, has been an avid sewer for over 30 years. She is also co-author of *The Quilter's Computer Companion*, and author of *I Lost My Baby, My Pickup, and My Guitar on the Information Highway* and *Internet for Cats*, all from No Starch Press.

460 pp., $34.95
Includes two 3.5", high density, IBM-PC disks with trial versions of needlecraft software. Macintosh disk $0.75 additional.
ISBN 1-886411-01-8

New! QUILTER'S COMPUTER COMPANION

Hundreds of Easy Ways to Turn the Cyber Revolution into Your Artistic Revolution

by JUDY HEIM *and* GLORIA HANSEN

This bestselling book shows you how to use your computer to design quilts and the best and cheapest way to do so. And you don't need the latest $4,000 Beyond-Pentium to do it. Design quilt blocks, templates, applique patterns, and stencils; print photos on muslin, organize your fabric stash, and prowl the Internet for art to use in your quilt designs; exchange e-mail with other quilters around the globe; and even put your quilts on display in cyberspace for everyone to see. Authors Judy Heim and Gloria Hansen show you, through hundreds of illustrations and step-by-step instructions, how to use the most popular drawing, painting, and quilt design software to achieve your own artistic vision.

JUDY HEIM, *PC World* magazine columnist and contributing editor, has been an avid sewer for over 30 years. She is the author of three other No Starch Press titles: *The Needlecrafter's Computer Companion, Internet for Cats,* and *I Lost My Baby, My Pickup, and My Guitar on the Information Highway.* She lives in Madison, Wisconsin.

GLORIA HANSEN has been quilting since 1982, and her innovative quilts have won many significant awards throughout the country. Gloria has appeared on cable television (even an MTV ad) and has self-published two successful quilt patterns; she is a frequent contributor to quilting publications, including *Art/Quilt Magazine* and *McCalls Quilting* and her unique fabrics have been featured in *Ladies Circle Patchwork Quilts* and *Miniworks* magazine. Gloria also contributed to the first edition of Judy Heim's *The Needlecrafter's Computer Companion.* She lives in central New Jersey.

352 pp., $29.95
Includes 16 full-color pages and hundreds of illustrations.
ISBN 1-886411-15-8

DR. BOB'S PAINLESS GUIDE TO THE INTERNET

& Amazing Things You Can Do with E-Mail

by BOB "DR. BOB" RANKIN

". . . simple, hassle-free net surfing with a minimum of reading . . ."
— NETGUIDE MAGAZINE

Whether you connect to the Internet through e-mail alone or the latest Netscape beta, *Dr. Bob's Painless Guide to the Internet* will show you how to use every Internet tool—not just the Web. You'll learn how to send and receive e-mail, find the cool and useful Web sites, search for and download the files you want, read newsgroups and subscribe to mailing lists, chat online, and more. Includes a glossary of terms and the "Internet Mini-Yellow Pages," with lots of useful Internet resources for you to enjoy right away.

BOB "DR. BOB" RANKIN is also the author of *The No B.S. Guide to Linux* and *Juno: Free E-Mail and More* (both from No Starch Press). He is well known for his "Accessing The

Internet By E-mail" FAQ (read by hundreds of thousands of people around the world and translated into more than fifteen languages) and is the publisher of the *Internet TourBus* e-zine, an e-mail "tour" of fun and interesting things on the Net.

152 pp., $12.95
ISBN 1-886411-09-3

New! JUNO

Free E-Mail and More

by BOB RANKIN

Bob Rankin, recognized e-mail and Internet expert, shows you how to use Juno—the completely free, advertiser-supported Internet e-mail service—to do more than just send messages. You'll learn e-mail basics like how to Send, Receive, Reply, Forward, and Delete messages, as well as how to work with and manage folders. You'll learn the finer points of Netiquette, Spam, and e-mail privacy, and discover how to use simple e-mail commands with Juno to access almost anything on the Internet, including the World Wide Web, FTP libraries, Usenet newsgroups, and search engines. You'll also pick up some e-mail tricks, such as how to get stock market data, news, weather, and sports information; how to play games by e-mail; how to send free faxes; and much more!

BOB "DR. BOB" RANKIN *(see bio above)*

200 pp., $14.95
ISBN 1-886411-23-9

INTERNET FAMILY FUN

The Parent's Guide to Safe Surfing

by BONNIE BRUNO *with* JOEL COMM

Whether your family just got its first computer or you're a bunch of Internet veterans, *Internet Family Fun* will take you to the best and safest Web sites for your family fast—without a bunch of technical mumbo jumbo. With nearly 250 reviews of fun and informative sites, pre-screened for age appropriateness and family-friendly content, there's something for everyone from preschoolers to parents. Learn how to install and use filtering software; use the Internet for research; find hundreds of games and coloring pages for children; learn about our world through the use of online text, graphics, sound, and video; observe classrooms using the Internet; meet and correspond with families around the world; create your very own home page and more! And, learn how to keep your kids safe online while you're at it.

BONNIE BRUNO is the author of *The Young Reader's Bible* (Standard Publishing, co-authored with Carol Reinsma), *Close to Home* (Chariot Books), and *Mourning: The Prelude to Laughter* (Zondervan Publishers, 1994 Final Nominee for the Gold Medallion Award). She lives in Albany, Oregon.

JOEL COMM is president and CEO of InfoMedia, Inc., a Texas-based Internet content provider. He lives in Plano, Texas.

152 pp., $14.95
ISBN 1-886411-19-0

New! WRITER'S INTERNET SOURCEBOOK

Reviews of hundreds of websites especially for novelists, short story writers, journalists, poets, nonfiction authors, academics, playwrights, and business writers.

by MICHAEL LEVIN

The Internet offers extraordinary opportunities for writers for researching, marketing, and selling their work. The *Writer's Internet Sourcebook* reviews hundreds of websites of interest to writers. find out how to use the Internet to save hundreds of hours of library time; where to find online writing classes, support groups, newsgroups, and mailing lists for writers of fiction, nonfiction, drama, journalism, poetry and academic writing. Descriptions and reviews of online magazines (zines); how to use the Internet to find readers, subscribers, buyers, and online bookstores that can sell your work.

MICHAEL LEVIN, a popular novelist and non-fiction author, is heavily involved in the teaching and business of writing: He teaches in both the UCLA and NYU Writing Programs and he is on the board of the Author's Guild. His novels have been favorably reviewed in the *New York Times Book Review*, the *Los Angeles Times,* and the *Boston Herald.* He lives in the Los Angeles area.

256 pages, $16.95
ISBN 1-886411-11-5

Distributed to the book trade by Publishers Group West

If you can't find No Starch Press titles in your local bookstore, here's how to order directly from us (we accept MasterCard, Visa, and checks or money orders—sorry, no CODs):

Phone:
1 (800) 420-7240 or
(415) 284-9900
Monday through Friday,
8 a.m. to 5 p.m. (PST)

Fax:
(415) 284-9955
24 hours a day,
7 days a week

E-mail:
sales@nostarch.com

Web:
http://www.nostarch.com

Mail:
No Starch Press
401 China Basin St., Ste. 108
San Francisco, CA 94107-2192
USA

License Agreement for *The Gardener's Computer Companion Software Collection*

Read this agreement before opening this package. By opening this package, you agree to be bound by the terms and conditions of this agreement.

This CD-ROM (the "CD") contains programs and associated documentation and other materials and is distributed with the book entitled *The Gardener's Computer Companion* to purchasers of the book for their own personal use only. Such programs, documentation and other materials and their compilation (collectively, the "Collection") are licensed to you subject to terms and conditions of this Agreement by No Starch Press, having a place of business at 401 China Basin St., Ste. 108, San Francisco, CA 94107-2192 ("Licensor"). In addition to being governed by the terms and conditions of this Agreement, your rights to use the programs and other materials included on the CD may also be governed by separate agreements distributed with those programs and materials on the CD (the "other Agreements"). In the event of any inconsistency between this Agreement and any of the Other Agreements, those Agreements shall govern insofar as those programs and materials are concerned. By using the Collection, in whole or in part, you agree to be bound by the terms and conditions of this Agreement. Licensor owns the copyright to the Collection, except insofar as it contains materials that are proprietary to third party suppliers. All rights in the Collection except those expressly granted to you in this Agreement are reserved to Licensor and such suppliers as their respective interests may appear.

1. **Limited License.** Licensor grants you a limited, nonexclusive, nontransferable license to use the Collection on a single dedicated computer (excluding network servers). This Agreement and your rights hereunder shall automatically terminate if you fail to comply with any provision of this Agreement or the Other Agreements. Upon such termination, you agree to destroy the CD and all copies of the CD, whether lawful or not, that are in your possession or under your control. Licensor and its suppliers retain all rights not expressly granted herein as their respective interests may appear.

2. **Additional Restrictions.** (A) You shall not (and shall not permit other persons or entities to) directly or indirectly, by electronic or other means, reproduce (except for archival purposes as permitted by law), publish, distribute, rent, lease, sell, sublicense, assign, or otherwise transfer the Collection or any part thereof or this Agreement. Any attempt to do so shall be void and of no effect. (B) You shall not (and shall not permit other persons or entities to) reverse-engineer, decompile, disassemble, merge, modify, create derivative works of, or translate the Collection or use the Collection or any part thereof for any commercial purpose. (C) You shall not (and shall not permit others persons or entities to) remove or obscure Licensor's or its suppliers' or Licensor's copyright, trademark, or other proprietary notices or legends from any portion of the Collection or any related materials. (D) You agree and certify that the Collection will not be exported outside the United States except as authorized and as permitted by the laws and regulations of the United States. If the Collection has been rightfully obtained outside of the United States, you agree that you will not reexport the Collection, except as permitted by the laws and regula-

License Agreement (contd.)

tions of the United States and the laws and regulations of the jurisdiction in which you obtained the Collection.

3. **Disclaimer of Warranty.** (A) The Collection and the CD are provided "as is" without warranty of any kind, either express or implied, including, without limitation, any warranty of merchantability and fitness for a particular purpose, the entire risk as to the results and performance of the CD and the software and other materials that is part of the Collection is assumed by you, and Licensor and its suppliers and distributors shall have no responsibility for defects in the CD or the accuracy or application of or errors or omissions in the Collection and do not warrant that the functions contained in the Collection will meet your requirements, or that the operation of the CD or the Collection will be uninterrupted or error-free, or that any defects in the CD or the Collection will be corrected. In no event shall Licensor or its suppliers or distributors be liable for any direct, indirect, special, incidental, or consequential damages arising out of the use of or inability to use the Collection or the CD, even if Licensor or its suppliers or distributors have been advised of the likelihood of such damages occurring. Licensor and its suppliers and distributors shall not be liable for any loss, damages, or costs arising out of, but not limited to, lost profits or revenue; loss of use of the Collection or the CD; loss of data or equipment; cost of recovering software, data, or materials in the Collection; the cost of substitute software, data, or materials in the Collection; claims by third parties; or other similar costs. (B) In no event shall Licensor or its suppliers' or distributors' total liability to you for all damages, losses, and causes of action (whether in contract, tort or otherwise) exceed the amount paid by you for the Collection. (C) Some states do not allow exclusion or limitation of implied warranties or limitation of liability for incidental or consequential damages, so the above limitations or exclusions may not apply to you.

4. **U.S. Government Restricted Rights.** The Collection is licensed subject to RESTRICTED RIGHTS. Use, duplication, or disclosure by the U.S. Government or any person or entity acting on its behalf is subject to restrictions as set forth in subdivision (c)(1)(ii) of the Rights in Technical Data and Computer Software Clause at DFARS (48 CFR 252.227-7013) for DOD contracts, in paragraphs (c)(1) and (2) of the Commercial Computer Software Restricted Rights clause in the FAR (48 CFR 52.227 - 19) for civilian agencies, or, in the case of NASA, in clause 18-52.227-86(d) of the NASA Supplement to the FAR, or in other comparable agency clauses. The contractor/ manufacturer is No Starch Press, 401 China Basin St., Ste. 108, San Francisco, CA 94107-2192.

5. **General Provisions.** Nothing in this Agreement constitutes a waiver of Licensor's, or its suppliers' or Licensors' rights under U.S. copyright laws or any other federal, state, local, or foreign law. You are responsible for installation, management, and operation of the Collection. This Agreement shall be construed, interpreted, and governed under California law. Copyright © 1998 No Starch Press. All rights reserved. Reproduction in whole or in part without permission is prohibited.